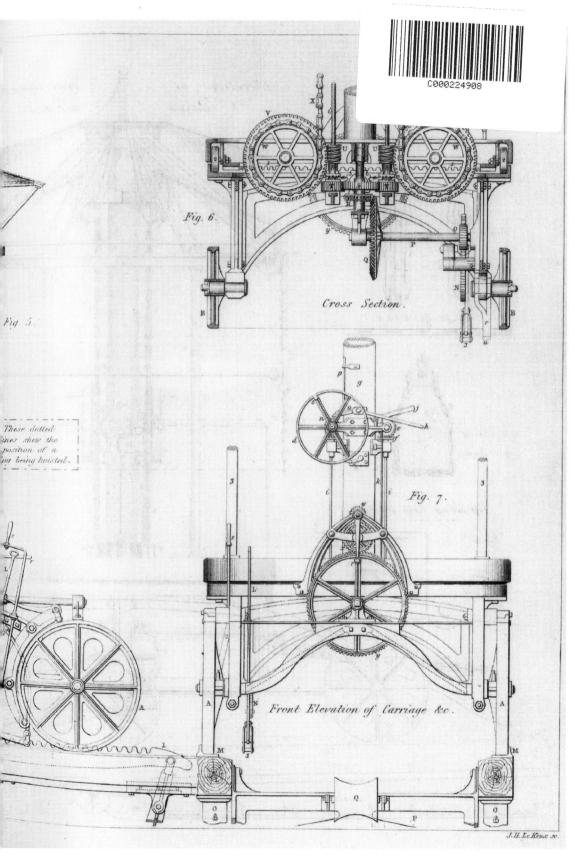

The Chatham Wood Mill's Chinese Enchanter's Car. (The drawing has been bound into an 1843 book, causing the image to be somewhat distorted.)

MARC ISAMBARD
BRUNEL

MARC ISAMBARD
BRUNEL

PAUL CLEMENTS

Phillimore

First published 1970
by Longmans Green and Co. Ltd

This 2006 edition published by
PHILLIMORE & CO. LTD
Shopwyke Manor Barn, Chichester, West Sussex, England
www.phillimore.co.uk

ISBN 1-86077-400-8
ISBN 13 978-1-86077-400-3

Printed and bound in Great Britain by
THE CROMWELL PRESS
Trowbridge, Wiltshire

'England,' said he, 'is a very small place, although thickly inhabited. It is altogether about the third part of the size of the city of Rome. The people are a sort of Christians, though not exactly so. Their priests and even their bishops marry, which is incomprehensible, and most ridiculous. The whole place is divided into two equal parts by an arm of the sea, under which there is a great tunnel, so that it is all like one piece of dry land ...'

An hospitable father introduces his brethren to Edward Lear
(*Journal of a Landscape Painter in Southern Calabria*)

CONTENTS

LIST OF ILLUSTRATIONS

Acknowledgements

The author wishes to thank the following people for their help in obtaining the illustrations used and for permission to reproduce them on the following pages: Brunel Museum, 135, 137; The Guildhall Library, 95, 97, 151, 240, rear endpaper; Miss Anne Hall (Brunel's great-great-great granddaughter), 3; Dr and Mrs H.E. Hurst, 15, 59, 79 and 92 from their collection; Institution of Civil Engineers, 129, 190; Mr Max Millar for the drawing of The Shield (213); The National Maritime Museum, 23 (bottom); The National Portrait Gallery, London, front cover, 207; Lady Noble, 9, 131 and 165 from her private collection; Oxford University Press, 205; Royal Engineers Museum and Library, front endpaper; Science Museum, London, 20, 22, 23 (top), 32 and 34 (22, 23, 32 and 34 are Crown Copyright Reserved); Science Museum/ Science & Society Picture Library, 191; Southwark Public Libraries, 115, 122, 161, 163, 238, and 96 from A *Memoir of the Thames Tunnel* by Henry Law, John Weale, 1845. The photograph on page 83 was taken by the author.

ACKNOWLEDGEMENTS AND
NOTES ON SOURCES

———◆•✦•◆———

General works of reference apart, the material for Part I of this biography
has been gathered from retrospective diary entries and from two books: *The
Brunels—Father and Son* by Lady Celia Brunel Noble (Cobden Sanderson,
1938) and a *Memoir of the Life of Sir Marc Isambard Brunel* by Richard Beamish
(Longman, Green, Longman and Roberts, 1862). Lady Noble's book is
delightful, and Beamish is informative, although he seems a little ponderous
now. I also visited Hacqueville, where the farmer and his wife welcomed
me most hospitably and showed me Marc's little room. In preparing this
new edition, I have referred to *The History of Chatham Dockyard* by James
Crawshaw, *London's Lost Route to the Sea* by P.A.L. Vine, *The Napoleonic Wars* by
Gunther Rothenberg, *Wellington* by Christopher Hibbert, *Nelson* by Arthur
Bryant, and *Napoleon* by Vincent Cronin.

Whilst writing the remainder of the story I continued to consult Lady
Noble and Beamish, but as the work progressed it became possible to rely
increasingly on original material. During Part II, I studied all Brunel's patent
specifications, and these are the key to his career. There is a letter book at
the National Maritime Museum, which illuminates his endeavours whilst at
Portsea, and a sketch book showing some of the block machines; these and
K.R. Gilbert's lucid booklet *The Portsmouth Blockmaking Machinery* (H.M.S.O.,
1956) revealed the importance of this historic plant. I also inspected the
models at the National Maritime Museum, the machines preserved in the
Science Museum and those still in use at the dockyard, where Mr. F.J. Ball
proved a mine of information, and directed my steps to Britain Street, Portsea,
now somewhat brutally redeveloped.

At Chatham Dockyard Mr L.D. Boulter and his colleagues showed me
what was left of the woodmill, and I learned much from the booklets on
the dockyard's history which Mr Boulter has prepared for the Management
Training Centre. He also suggested a visit to the Ministry of Public Building
and Works, and this was a happy inspiration, for Mr R. McG. Airlie at the
Chatham Area Office found a number of Brunel's drawings for the woodmill

which we both examined with great pleasure. I am most grateful to Mr Boulter and to Mr Airlie.

Mr P.A. Penfold at the Public Record Office produced several original drawings for the Woolwich Arsenal woodmill, and I was greatly helped on printing matters by Mr W.R.A. Easthope, Editor of *The Times* Archives, and by Mr J. Mosley of the St Bride Institute Printing Library, who also kindly checked some pages of the typescript. Mr A.P. Coppleston, Editor of the *Totnes Times*, enlightened me regarding the Totnes bridge. Monsieur A. Schèrer, le Directeur des Services d'Archives de la Réunion, was helpful regarding the Bourbon bridges; and Mr S. Bohan and Mr Charles A. Kelly—Cork City's Librarian and Architect respectively—told me the history of their charming little Jail Bridge.

Mr Ian McNeil corrected my references to Bramah; Miss Naomi Evetts, of the City of Liverpool Libraries Department, undertook research into the history of Brunel's swing bridge and embarkation pier; and Mr P.D. Pocklington, City Librarian of Chester, lent me a volume of the *Journal* of the Chester Archaeological Society containing an article by J.W. Clarke on 'The Building of the Grosvenor Bridge'. I am grateful to them, and also to Mr R.D. Leakey, for providing a glimpse of the early, unsuspected, history of the circular saw. This first came to my notice when I chanced upon his letter to *Yachting Monthly*, and I am indebted to the Editor for permission to reproduce part of it.

There is no shortage of original material covering the tunnel, and I have based my account on Brunel's weekly reports to the Court of Directors, which are preserved in the Institution of Civil Engineers' Library. His contemporary diaries, and the day-to-day reports of Richard Beamish and Thomas Page describing their labours under the northern half of the Thames, which are also in this library, illuminate Brunel's other work and also the anxieties of the engineers and the tribulations of the men during their long agony.

At Humshaugh, Sir Humphrey and Lady Noble made me comfortable in the room which they have made into a private Brunel museum, and I spent a number of happy days reading slightly earlier diaries and Journals of Transactions of Marc and Isambard Brunel. Other diaries of both father and son are preserved in Bristol University Library, and I am indebted to Mr J. Lightbown for placing them, and a quiet room, at my disposal.

Marc and Isambard were harnessed to the same plough during the first half of the tunnel's construction, and it is impossible to write of them except as a team. I have drawn freely on L.T.C. Rolt's *Isambard Kingdom Brunel* (Longmans, 1957), and can only hope that this book is a worthy prelude to his vivid and absorbing biography.

Other sources not acknowledged in the text include *A Memoir of Suspension Bridges* by Charles Stewart Drewry (Longman, 1882); *The Life of*

Isambard Kingdom Brunel, Civil Engineer by Marc's grandson, Isambard Brunel (Longmans, Green, 1870); *The Life of Richard Trevithick* by Francis Trevithick (1872); *A Memoir of the Thames Tunnel* by Henry Law (1857), valuable because it contains drawings of the second shield, *The Tunnel* by David Lampe (Harrap, 1963), and Minutes of Proceedings of the Institution of Civil Engineers.

Mr Percy Clare and his assistants at the Central Library, Bermondsey, gave me facilities to study their collection of 'Tunnel' broadsheets, prints, press cuttings and the two Acts of Parliament. Mr E. Atkinson at the British Railways Board's Historical Records Department was similarly helpful, as was Mr Godfrey Thompson of the Guildhall Library, where there are many interesting press cuttings, booklets and curiosities.

I wish to thank Dr and Mrs H.E. Hurst for showing me their collection of Brunel drawings and mementoes, also the Rev. C.B. Timms of the Church of St Andrew, Holborn, and the authorities at Portsmouth Cathedral for their help in the course of my fruitless search for evidence of the baptism of Brunel's children. Mr A.W.H. Pearsall, Custodian of Manuscripts at the National Maritime Museum, Mr H.C. Richardson, Librarian of the Institution of Civil Engineers, and Miss Betty Greenhill, Assistant Reference Librarian at Brighton Library, all gave me unstinted help, for which I am most grateful.

There are others whose freely given assistance is all the more appreciated because it lay outside the path or duty. Mr K.R. Gilbert checked the chapters dealing the block machines, Mr A.C. Edrich, Civil Engineer to London Transport, conducted me through the Tunnel in the small hours of the morning. My father and Dr F.W. Wartenberg read the book in draft form and offered invaluable advice, as did Sir Humphrey Noble, in addition to all his other kindnesses, and Mr L.T.C. Rolt, who also lent me a volume of Newcomen Society transactions, containing a paper by Professor A. W. Skempton, which shed much light on Roman cement.

I should like to thank John Chambers at the Royal Dockyard Library at Chatham; Charlotte Hughes at the Royal Engineers' Library at Brompton Barracks, Chatham; Robert Hulse at the Brunel Museum at Rotherhithe; John Wood and Paul Vine of the Wey and Arun Canal Trust for their freely given help; Dr Richard Whatmore of Sussex University for illuminating 19th-century Europe, and both Susi Khan and Christel Blackman for making my scrawl intelligible.

Finally I want to thank Howard and Beryl Leathes for the use of their house, Mrs Eleanor Nixon for her encouragement and diligent research, especially through microfilm copies of *The Times*, and Jimmy Chesterman for reading the proofs.

P.C.

Author's note

In 1800, France, with approximately 26,000,000 inhabitants, was the most populous European country (Russia with 18,000,000 more being partly in Asia) while Britain and the Habsburg Empire (Austria-Hungary) each had about 8,000,000 fewer.

The Habsburg Empire, which included Holland, was bigger than France in area and formed Europe's strategic hub because it bordered Poland in the north-east, the Ottoman empire in the south-east, Switzerland and German-speaking principalities in the west and Prussia in the north west. Vienna was its capital and, for simplicity's sake, I have referred to it as Austria.

FOREWORD

To be born the son of a famous father is a handicap which few succeed in overcoming. Isambard Brunel is one of the rare exceptions which prove this rule, for his engineering exploits won him a reputation and a popular fame that almost erased the name of Marc Brunel from popular memory. Yet Charles Macfarlane, who knew both men, wrote of them: 'I had liked the son, but at our very first meeting I could not help feeling that his father far excelled him in originality, unworldliness, genius and taste ...'

I think the reason why Marc takes second place lies in that one word 'unworldliness'. He was far more equable in temperament than his son. His 'indifference to mere lucre', as Macfarlane put it, and his touching faith in the innate goodness of his fellow men were saintly attributes scarcely calculated to ensure material success in the brash commercial world in which he moved. Like many an engineer before and after him, Marc Brunel sorely needed a true and sympathetic partner whose guiding hand would lead him through the commercial jungle but, unlike James Watt, he never found his Matthew Boulton.

The Brunel crest of a spur and the family motto 'En Avant' were singularly appropriate in Isambard's case, for it was the spur of pride and ambition that drove him relentlessly to fame. So it could be said with some truth that the son succeeded because of his faults whereas the father failed because of his virtues. Yet both equally deserve to be recognised by posterity as engineers of singular genius.

To call a man a genius is to make a large claim, but I think it is fairly substantiated by this book, the first to assess Marc Brunel's total engineering achievement and therefore the first biography which could be described as definitive. As a new writer, Paul Clements is to be congratulated both on the energy and enthusiasm with which he has tackled a formidable job of research and on the skill and lucidity with which he has presented its fruits.

In researching for my biography of Isambard it was inevitable that I should learn quite a lot about his father, so it is a sincere tribute to Paul Clements to say that, having read his biography, I now have a much deeper understanding of Marc Brunel both as an engineer and as a man. As an engineer he is popularly remembered for only one work, the Thames Tunnel—a fact which conveys the misleading impression of limited range. This the book corrects by revealing that, in fact, Marc Brunel was an engineer of extraordinary versatility, the equal, if not the superior in this respect, of his son. Certainly he excelled Isambard as a mechanical engineer.

As a man, the qualities which emerge most clearly from this book are Marc's courage, his unwavering determination and his inexhaustible patience. They enabled him to meet with fortitude a series of misfortunes and difficulties such as would have driven most men to despair. 'Courage!', he would say, 'A man who can do something and keep a warm, sanguine heart will never starve.' His life story exemplifies the truth of these words.

                                                                    L. T. C. ROLT

INTRODUCTION TO THE 2006 EDITION

Revisiting this biography, which I wrote more than 35 years ago, has been a curious experience. Whereas the fields I ploughed by the village where we lived have yielded crops of houses, my view, through older eyes, of Marc Brunel's life has changed very little; but I hope I may have acquired a better understanding of some of the events which shaped it.

In 1792, after serving for six years in the Caribbean as an officer cadet in the French navy, Marc returned to a France to which he felt he no longer belonged. He fell in love, but had to flee to newly independent America where he became Chief Engineer of New York. This, however, was not the challenge he sought and on 13 March 1799, some three weeks before his 30th birthday, he landed in England.

Within a month he had filed the first of his 16 patent applications. Then, on 1 November, he married his brave sweetheart Sophia Kingdom* and lived happily with her until the end of his life.

It was an astounding life. Nine of his patents bore fruit. He begat mass production. He transformed the sawing of wood and the handling of timber in naval dockyards. He designed and built steam engines and bridges. He shod the British army at Waterloo. He and Sophia were imprisoned for debt. He invented the tunnelling shield and build the first tunnel under the Thames which, unlike later tunnels, was conceived with twin carriageways. It is the oldest tunnel in London's Underground and, just a stone's throw from Rotherhithe station, there is a fascinating museum commemorating his work. It is inside the original engine house flanking the shaft from which the tunnel was driven.

Marc Brunel was a courageous, confident, engineer/artist, whose block-making machinery a visitor thought 'so perfect [it] appears to act with the happy certainty of instinct and the foresight of reason combined'. He was also an accomplished musician who needed very little sleep.

During his 50 years in England, he lived 'as if there were no rogues in this nether world'; but was supported by Sophia, by Isambard, his better-known son, and by the Duke of Wellington, his foul-weather friend. Four

---

* Whom he always called Sophie.

xvii

sovereigns reigned in the course of Marc's sojourn here and there were 17 changes of Prime Minister, although four of them—Pitt the Younger, the Duke of Wellington, Viscount Melbourne and Sir Robert Peel—served on two occasions. In France there were fewer but more dramatic changes and throughout Europe there were wars and battles which altered the continent's political map. These events affected those who played parts in the drama of Marc Brunel's life and I have added text outlining some of the major changes to the scenery clothing the stage on which these actors played.

With the blessing of his Directoire—but unaware of the Royal Navy's return to the Mediterranean—Napoleon invaded Egypt, taking Alexandria at the beginning of July 1798 and Cairo on the 22nd. Nine days later, however, Nelson fell upon the French fleet lying in the Nile delta at Aboukir bay and destroyed it. This action, fought more than seven months before Brunel set foot in England, did not end Napoleon's Egyptian adventure; but instead of posing a threat to British interests in India, as he had intended, his Egyptian army was thereafter in danger of being cut off from France.

Only one of Napoleon's subsequent campaigns depended on sea-borne supplies, but he continued to threaten England and expensive measures to protect vulnerable stretches of coast were put in hand to thwart him. The mouths of navigable rivers in Sussex were fortified, low-lying shores east of Newhaven were shielded with Martello towers and the great naval bases of Chatham and Portsmouth were connected by an inland waterway, wider than the earliest canals, to guarantee that essential supplies would never again be interrupted by unfavourable winds or unwelcome marauders in the English Channel.

The northern section of this new route linked the river Wey Navigation south of Guildford to the river Arun Navigation north of Pulborough. The middle section joined the Arun at Ford to Chichester harbour near Birdham, and the western section connected Chichester harbour with Portsmouth naval base by way of the Thorney channel, the Langstone channel and a short canal cut into Portsea island. This remarkable waterway (currently being resurrected by the Wey and Arun Canal Trust) was completed in 1823 after a decade's hard labour. It was used to transport gold bullion from Portsmouth to London and cargoes of gunpowder from a factory near Guildford to Woolwich and Chatham.

But not for long. Paddle steamers, with engines owing much to Marc Brunel's triangle frame design, soon provided cheaper and swifter transport between London, Chatham and Portsmouth; and by 1870 almost all the remaining inland cargoes had been lost to new railways.

The end of the waterway's short life coincided with the fall of Paris during the Franco-Prussian war and with hindsight it seems ironic that, even before the canal navvies began their task, a young French-born man—then living and working in Portsea—had almost certainly made their toil unnecessary.

But neither he, the British government nor Napoleon could have known.

PART I

PROMISE

With hues of genius on his cheek,
In finest tones the youth could speak..
— While he was yet a boy ...

W. WORDSWORTH
Ruth: or the Influences of Nature

I

BOYHOOD

———◆•••◆———

Halfway between Paris and Rouen on the northern road lies Gisors, in a hollow of the rolling plain. The town's cathedral, château-fort and late 18th-century houses of grey-white stone mingle agreeably with timbered buildings, whose upper storeys jut out across narrow side streets punctuated by little bridges and long-disused wharfs which mark the course of the River Epté and another stream.

Westwards 13 kilometres is Etrepagny, a substantial village, whence a by-road leads south across hedgeless fields, bringing the traveller after five more kilometres to a church, a farm or two and a handful of houses of stone, flint and mellow brick, with pantiled roofs and shuttered windows. This is the hamlet of Hacqueville. It is an unpretentious place. The church has been enlarged, yet has a weather-beaten look. Some of the cottages boast small, rather ragged orchards, but land fragmentation and rural squalor have not come this way.

The farms are substantial, and in summer the red-brown plain is heavy with wheat, barley, beet and potatoes. There are occasional pastures where fat cattle graze, and planted woodlands interrupt the horizon and speak of great estates and field sports.

One spacious farm stands a stone's throw from the church; although half rebuilt with russet brick in the 19th century, a wing of oak and plaster still endures, and through this ancient frontage a carriage gateway leads, below a little garret, to the courtyard behind.

In 1490 Jean Brunel was born in this farm and became its first recorded tenant. For three centuries the property remained in the tenure of the Brunels, 'cultivateurs d'Hacqueville', the eldest son of each generation succeeding his father as farmer, while younger brothers entered the Church—the disposition of a 'living' was one of the family's perquisites—or became lawyers.

For a span of ten generations the relationship between the Brunels and their landlords, the noble Le Coulteux family, endured. The landlord claimed his rent, and occasionally visited the property to commandeer a fine horse or such household chattels as his tenant had no time to hide, while for their part the Brunels tilled the farm diligently, and when harvests were good saved a

La Ferme Brunel from within the courtyard. The door to the left of the gateway leads into Brunel's room.

little to tide over lean times and gradually to extend the family's influence in the locality, gaining control of the local posting arrangements when the farm became the stopping-place for stage coaches.

The even tenor of this life was to end when the Jacobins claimed the landlords, for aiding the Royal flight to Varrennes, as peremptorily as formerly the nobles had claimed their rent; but twenty years before the cataclysm there was a happy event at La Ferme Brunel.

On 25 April 1769, Maria Victoire Lefebre, wife of Jean Charles Brunel, bore her third child and second son. The parents' rejoicings were undimmed by thoughts of the future. Their first son would tend the farm; the Church would welcome the younger. But the babe, whom they christened Marc Isambard, was to be the herald of a new age.

When he was seven, the boy's mother died, and his father introduced him to a classical education to which he proved exceedingly resistant, preferring a visit to the village wheelwright to hours spent studying the campaigns of Caesar. Jean Charles punished his son sternly, often shutting him alone in a gloomy room hung with portraits of his forebears, whose canvas faces gazed down at him disapprovingly. One cheerless abbé had a particularly piercing stare, and one day, unable any longer to endure the unblinking reproach, the boy dragged a heavy table across the room and cut out the canvas eyes with his penknife.

Construing indiscipline a greater fault than indifference to the classics, Jean Charles despatched Marc, now eight, to the College of Gisors, where the boys, in military coats with swords on their belts and little cocked hats on their powdered wigs, were schooled as army officers. Here he excelled at drawing and mathematics, but his Latin and Greek were his masters' despair. Holidays were spent sketching the farmhouse and the great Château Gaillard of Richard the Lion Heart, and in minute attendance on his friend the wheelwright when that craftsman shrunk a glowing tyre around the smouldering felloes of a new wagon wheel.

Marc delighted in music. He learned the flute, and after studying the construction of the harpsichord, made a working model of a musical machine which combined the functions and produced the sounds of both instruments; but his dour father was unimpressed when presented with this little masterpiece.

'What do you want to be?', he demanded.

'An engineer,' replied his 11-year-old son, nodding his large head with enthusiasm, 'an engineer.'

Jean Charles could not have known that a decade hence the enraged artisans of Rouen would dismember and smash textile machines imported from England, and he would scarcely have heard of the Scots who, half a century earlier, with equal vigour dealt with a 'new-fangled machine for dighting the corn frae the chaff; thus impiously thwarting the will o' Divine Providence by raising wind by human art instead of soliciting it by prayer, or patiently waiting for whatever dispensation of wind Providence was pleased to send upon the shieling hill'; he was a countryman of Normandy; he understood the seasons, knew his family's place, and respected the power and influence wielded by the Church.

'You will only benefit the world and starve yourself,' he replied, and forthwith transferred the boy to the Seminary of Sainte Nicaise at Rouen. Marc unwillingly exchanged his cheerful coat and cocked hat for sombre vestments and a priest's hat, while the widower Jean Charles brooded on his son's 'perverse and useless gifts'.

In the Seminary's Superior the boy found a friend who recognised his artistic talent and arranged for him to receive special instruction. It seems too that there were facilities for woodworking, for when he was 12 Marc could carve and carpenter with the precision and elegance of a cabinet maker, and one day, to buy a tool newly displayed in a shop window, he pawned his priest's hat and returned to the Seminary bareheaded.

But on fine days it was to the quayside that he hurried when lessons ended. Here were barques and barquentines, schooners and sailing barges and full-rigged ships. The quays were stacked with merchandise and thronged with sailors from strange lands. He sketched the craft and made detailed drawings of their rigging and of the tackles used to hoist their cargoes ashore. He examined windlasses and steering gear, and marvelled at the skill of the shipwrights and sailmakers. This was even better than the wheelwright's yard.

One evening as he roamed the docks his attention was riveted by two enormous cast-iron cylinders.

'What are these?' he asked a friendly waterman.

'Part of a "fire engine" for pumping water.'

'Where from?'

'England.'

'Ah,' said the boy, 'quand je serai grand, j'irai voir ce pays-là.'

The Superior realised that Marc was endowed with exceptional gifts, but equally it was clear, even to the most sanguine, that the divine call to the Church was not in him. Bluntly these conclusions were relayed to Jean Charles. 'The boy must be encouraged,' said the Superior, adding with finality, 'but he is not for the Church.'

'Why,' pondered the father, 'should the unique misfortune of such a son be mine?' Healthy, cheerful, industrious and most single-minded, the lad was regarded with affection by his family and friends. Yet there was nothing in rural Normandy that he could do. The farm he could not have; law and the Church he would not have. Other professions were unsuitable, and a tradesman-son unthinkable. Only one thing was certain; the boy would have to go away.

No sooner had the father arrived at this unsatisfactory conclusion, than Providence, in the shape of Mme Carpentier, smiled on the boy. Mme Carpentier, an elder cousin of Marc, lived in Rouen with her husband, François, who had left the sea to become the American Consul in that city. If the boy could lodge with them, then their friend, M. Dulague, would be his tutor, and the arrangement might enable him to enter the Navy as an officer cadet.

Vincent François Jean Noel Dulague was Professor of Hydrography at Rouen's Royal College. An astronomer and hydrographer of the first rank, and author of the textbooks on navigation used in all French naval schools, he was now in his early fifties. His offer to accept Marc as a pupil would hardly have been forthcoming had he not received favourable reports of the boy—most probably from the Superior of the Seminary. It was a fine opportunity and, to the boy's delight, his father eventually agreed to the arrangement.

On the eve of his first great adventure, Marc, 13 years old or thereabouts, went to bed for the last time in his cool, dim little room. The evening light entering the single window outlined the rafters above his head, and in the shadows between these strong supports the familiar adze-marked oaken floorboards of the loft showed faintly.

Early next morning he waited in the courtyard for the stage coach, and when it eventually arrived, climbed in, with his spare clothes and his precious tools packed in bags beside him. But when the diligence finally rumbled out through the gateway, Jean Charles, unbending to the last, appeared with clenched fists at the garret's open window shouting, 'Va-t-en, mauvais garnement!'

For the next four years Marc lived with his hospitable cousin and her husband, who clearly enjoyed his society. Professor Dulague also was agreeably surprised with his pupil, who took Euclid in his stride and verified the height of Rouen Cathedral with a homemade theodolite after his third trigonometry lesson.

It is difficult to imagine a boy receiving a better mathematical education anywhere in Europe at this time. The Navy, which was being reinvigorated by the Maréchal de Castries, Louis XVI's Minister of Marine, attracted some of the keenest brains in the realm. One such was Dulague, Marc's tutor, another was the mathematician Gaspard Monge, inventor of mechanical drawing—the art of presenting three dimensional objects on a plane surface—and later, during the Revolution, Navy Minister and designer of gun foundries and powder factories.

Certainly everything that Dulague knew, and everything that Monge knew, Marc learned and understood, and when not engrossed in theory, filled his sketchbooks with drawings of Rouen's notable buildings, and his room with ship models whose accuracy revealed every detail of construction.

So greatly did the boy please his professor that Dulague resolved to bring him to the notice of the Maréchal de Castries himself. The opportunity arose in 1785, when Louis XVI and his Minister, having inspected the Fleet at Cherbourg, paused at Rouen, en route for Paris. By means of a 'humble petition'—a device by which it was possible during the *ancien régime* to waylay royalty—Dulague succeeded in presenting his pupil to the Maréchal, who signified his approval by promising to nominate him Volontaire d'Honneur to a new frigate bearing the Minister's name.

It has been claimed that a similar distinction was bestowed on the circumnavigator Louis Antoine de Bougainville, but it is probable that Marc's honour was unique, for de Bougainville, after whom the climbing plant Bougainvillaea is named, was 32 when he entered the service in 1761.

Some months later, while being introduced to his future captain, Marc noticed a Hadley's quadrant on the ship's chart table. Back in Rouen after the interview, he busied himself making a replica of the instrument, and for once Jean Charles unbent and parted with a few crowns, which enabled Marc to make a better quadrant of ebony, which he used throughout his naval career.

In 1786, after a delay resulting from a smallpox epidemic, the 17-year-old cadet joined ship at Rouen, and embarked on a six-year naval career, during which he visited many of France's Caribbean possessions.

He proved an efficient officer who served his king proudly, but, save for a brief mention of a coffee-husking machine, which he designed at Guadaloupe in 1790, we know little of his wanderings or achievements. We know enough of him, however, to be certain that he became familiar with every detail of the warship, be it the timber used by her builders, the distinctive features of her hull, the design of her rigging or the disposition of her armament. The navigation of the ship and the effect on her passage of the varying forces of the wind and the tides were also subjects he studied profoundly. He seems, too, perhaps during visits to American ports, to have acquired a working knowledge of the English tongue.

At last the *Maréchal de Castries* recrossed the Atlantic, reaching Rouen, where she paid off her crew, in January 1792. As he descended the gangplank and set foot again on the familiar quay, Brunel exchanged the ordered comradeship of life afloat, a life regulated by the naval code and the orbit of the moon, for an uncertain future in a land confused by a welter of contradictory decrees.

France had been stripped of wealth, privilege and the notion of chivalry. The Revolution was in its third year.

2
ROYALIST AND SUITOR

L ooking on the new disorder with barely concealed disdain, Marc made his way to the home of his hospitable kinswoman. The Carpentiers welcomed him affectionately and pressed him to move again into his old room and rejoin their household. Their offer was accepted, and for the next 18 months Brunel led an uncharacteristically aimless but nevertheless eventful life in Rouen.

François Carpentier, like most of the inhabitants of Normandy, shared Marc's royalist sympathies, and when the Royal Family was imprisoned following the sack of the Tuileries on 10 August, the men of Rouen formed themselves into a national guard, the better to defend themselves against the sans-culottes.

A diary entry written 40 years later sheds some light on the troubled times:

> August 12th. On this day in 1792 I had a very narrow escape when at Rouen, endeavouring to save the Suisses [Swiss Guards] that had escaped on the 10th from Courbevoir or the Tuileries.
> On entering the gates of the barracks we were surrounded by thousands of the mob, so that we could not have escaped had they closed up on us, but they were intimidated by the sight of a few of the national guard coming down the Cours Dauphin.

The following January Marc and François paid a visit to Paris. The fevered capital was full of rumours concerning the King's trial, and on the evening of the 16th—only four days before sentence of death was pronounced—Marc rashly predicted the coming doom of Robespierre to a crowd gathered in the Café de l'Échelle near the Palais Royale. Only the sympathetic intervention of Louis Taillefer, a future member of the Chamber of Deputies, who created a diversion, enabled Marc and François to escape from the enraged citizens and gain the shelter of a nearby inn. There they hid until nightfall, before returning warily to Rouen. The following day barricades were erected at the capital's boundaries.

A few weeks earlier, on 2 December, a 17-year-old girl named Sophie Kingdom had boarded ship at Portsmouth and sailed for Le Havre. She was

8

Marc Isambard Brunel. A self-portrait in miniature which he painted for Sophia during his sojourn in America.

Sophia Brunel. A portrait in oils by an unknown artist which resembles the miniature of Sophia that Brunel painted whilst in America.

the youngest of 16 children born to Joan Spry, the wife of William Kingdom, a Royal Navy contractor at Plymouth. Unhappily Kingdom had died some years earlier, and it was Sophie's eldest brother, acting as family guardian, who had imprudently sent her to France. She hoped to learn French, and was accompanied by two friends, a M. de Longuemarre and his English wife.

The trio came to Rouen, staying with acquaintances of the de Longue-marres, and here Sophie became ill. Then her erstwhile protectors hastened back to England after a friend, who had played a royalist air on a piano, had been murdered by the mob. Thus, when Marc and François returned home from their Paris jaunt, they found Mme Carpentier sheltering an English waif.

So one ship from the west brought home a high-spirited royalist, another ship from the north arrived with a fair young English girl, and by a series of chances the two half-orphans found shelter beneath the same roof in turbulent Rouen. The slight, dark, high-spirited young Frenchman, who had seen half the world, seemed a prodigy to the girl. The modest maiden, with her serene air and lively intelligence, appeared as a fairy-tale princess to the young man.

'Ah, ...' he murmured to his cousin one evening, as Sophie examined one of his paintings, 'quelle belle main.'

'Oui,' interposed Madame sharply, 'mais elle n'est pas pour toi.'

The Jacobins descended on Rouen to crush the royalist insurrection. The summer nights, lit by flaring torches, echoing to the sounds of pillage, were times of dread for law-abiding citizens, and in the pale light of morning, the city's squares bore grisly witness to the mob's pursuit of Liberté, Egalité, Fraternité.

But danger is the catalyst of love, and as the threat to Marc and the alien Sophie increased, so interest grew to friendship, and quickly to a deeper affection. Seldom was a declaration of love so certain, yet so hopeless; she a prisoner in a strange house; he a royalist fugitive who might endanger her sanctuary.

As the long summer dragged on, the situation grew daily more hazardous, and it became clear that Marc must go. But leaving France was no easy matter. Following the imprisonment of the Royal Family, the trickle of refugees had become a torrent which the revolutionaries sought to staunch at the country's frontiers and ports, consoling themselves, when their prey eluded them, by guillotining wives and children. Fortunately, the resourceful François was able to enlist the help of a colleague, the American vice-consul at Le Havre, and obtained for Marc a passport on the pretext, made plausible by the bread shortage, that he would go to America to buy grain for the Navy. So, early one morning, the young man bade farewell to his good friends and to his beloved Sophie, and left Rouen on horseback.

Halfway along the Cours Deauville, urged too fast perhaps by its impatient rider, the horse stumbled and Marc was thrown to the ground, where he lay concussed. He had hardly regained consciousness when a cabriolet came down the street. The occupant reined his horse and dismounted.

'Where are you going?'

'Home,' replied Marc warily, for he recognised his questioner, 'to Le Havre.'

'You may come with me,' replied the Revolution's Navy Minister, who was travelling there to interview cadets. So Marc climbed into the cabriolet, and Gaspard Monge drove him to Le Havre, whence, on 7 July, aboard the American ship *Liberty*, he sailed for New York.

Twelve days out an incident occurred which revealed the Revolution's long arm and the fugitive's absent mind. A French frigate was sighted with all sails set. Knowing well what was in store, Marc sought his passport, but it was nowhere to be found. Suddenly, he realised that he had lost it when his horse had thrown him. Nothing daunted, he forged a substitute complete with seals and, when the boarding party arrived two hours later, he boldly presented it for inspection before those of the other passengers. It passed scrutiny.

On the evening of 6 September, the *Liberty* anchored off Sandy Hook and the following morning Brunel set foot in New York. But he did not linger, for sheltering in the harbour were remnants of the French squadron which had escaped from the massacre of San Domingo, and the crews were republicans or, as he said, 'banditti', and he had no wish to be shanghaied back.

A French community was taking root in Philadelphia, and thither he moved. The nostalgic atmosphere seemed agreeable, and for a week he whiled away the evenings discoursing with compatriots—including the wily Talleyrand, whom England would not shelter—in the back parlour of a bookshop, where they pondered the latest news from home.

However, Philadelphia offered neither excitement nor an objective to distract his thoughts from Sophie, so Marc resolved to throw in his lot with two fellow émigrés, Pharoux and Desjardins, with whom he had become friendly on the *Liberty*. He travelled to Albany and rejoined his compatriots 'after a long journey in a gig without springs over almost impassable roads'. The pair, evidently not without means, planned to survey a 220,000-acre tract of land lying between the forty-fourth parallel, the course of the Black River and Lake Ontario—with a view to parcelling it out for sale to migrants. Being perfectly qualified for the project, and an agreeable companion to boot, Brunel was welcomed into the partnership and on 18 September the trio, accompanied by three Red Indian guides and suitably equipped with guns, tents and axes, set out from Schenectady in a boat, paddled their way up the Mohawk River, and disappeared into the silent forests.

Later, Marc would recall nostalgically the majesty of the spacious continent and speak of chance encounters—one with a party including Louis-Philippe, the son, some say, of Philippe Egalité, and later King of France. Communications were scanty and the distances considerable; we do not know exactly how long the expedition took or with what success it was attended, but early in 1794 the party returned to Albany and boarded a river boat bound for New York. After sailing some way down the Hudson, the vessel grounded on a sandbank and was detained, providentially it transpired, for two tides.

While Marc was busy surveying the new, sunnier side of the world, Sophie's plight became desperate.

At first she paid for her board by teaching English to girls whose fathers could afford a few crowns for her services, but after the execution of Louis XVI, England joined the alliance against France and in October 1793 the Council of the Revolution enacted a decree ordering the arrest and imprisonment of all English nationals and the confiscation of their papers and possessions.

Late one winter's night armed men beat on the Carpentiers' door, 'Ouvrez, au nom de la Nation!'. They seized Sophie and bore her off.

The Reign of Terror was at its height, and as the poor girl was bundled into a cart and driven into the darkness, away from her protectors and the eagerly awaited letters from America, she must have felt that death was near.

She was taken to the little fortified port of Gravelines, halfway between Calais and Dunkirk. There, since all the prisons were full, she was consigned to a convent where the nuns, themselves prisoners and forced to wear secular clothes, slept on hard boards with the other women and shared their staple diet of bread mixed with straw.

Outside in the courtyard a guillotine was set up and, when room was needed for new arrivals, put to work, accompanied by 'the roaring of the mob, the clanging of the tocsin ... and the rolling of the tambours that marked the fall of each head'.

Good republicans testified that Sophie had taught their daughters, and the Carpentiers pressed unceasingly for her release; but at Gravelines she remained, wondering each morning whether the knife would fall on her neck before nightfall. Spring passed, summer came, but only paper flowers, which the good nuns taught the women to make, decorated the convent, and the only scent was the smell of death. At last, on 24 July, when hope had almost gone, the convent doors were flung open. Robespierre had fallen. The women were free.

Somehow the ragged, emaciated little 19-year-old made her way back to Rouen, where to her relief she found the Carpentiers still in possession of their home. Kindly, they nursed her back to health, and the following year a passport was obtained and she returned to England.

3

AMERICAN CITIZEN

————◦•◦◦•◦————

arc and his two partners prowled the ship waiting for her to float off the sandbank in the peaceful Hudson River. But the vessel was in no hurry and, while she lay stranded, a traveller named Thurman came aboard. He was a wealthy New York merchant, 'un homme sage', Marc later invariably called him.

Sensing a patron the three Frenchmen expounded to Thurman their favourite plan. If the Mohawk were made navigable and a canal cut to link it with Lake Oneida, then a waterway might be opened to Lake Ontario and barges could ply between New York and the Great Lakes. Thurman was impressed by the enthusiasm of the Frenchmen but shrewdly concluded that they would be the immediate beneficiaries of the scheme, since their land would flank the new waterway.

So Brunel and his friends fell back on Plan Two. Why not cut a navigation channel linking the Hudson to Lake Champlain, from which the Richelieu flows northwards, east of Montreal to Sorel? Why not a thoroughfare between New York and the St Lawrence? This interested Thurman and he agreed that they should make a survey.

The trio had found a backer. May saw them on Lake Champlain, and soon after they completed the survey and Thurman approved it. Better still, money was raised and the work was entrusted to them.

At this stage Thurman realised that he had chosen his men wisely. Young Brunel in particular was a marvel of resource, who cleared blocked rivers and by-passed swamps like an instinctive engineer; and between patron and protégé an accord was established which gratified Thurman and wholly restored Marc's self-confidence. He abandoned all notions of a naval career, and returned to his first love; he would be an engineer.

Brunel was not the man to rely on chance encounters, however fruitful. As the navigation neared completion he entered a competition to design a new Capitol building which was intended to reflect the majesty of Congress.

It may seem surprising that a little-known 27-year-old alien could contend for the national shrine, but America was young, and the contestant was no brash backwoodsman. He had sketched with minute detail the châteaux of Normandy, the civic buildings of Rouen, and much of the best Parisian architecture. He had, behind his artist's eye, the brain of a mathematician, which could calculate fit proportions for any buttress and subject visions to cold analysis. Above all, he had a craftsman's innate understanding of materials.

It seems that the design which Brunel submitted may have been inspired by the Palace of Versailles. It combined splendour with light and charming detail. It was the first example of what, a generation and a half later, was called 'the Brunel touch'. The judges pronounced it outstanding, and the intelligentsia of New York and Washington buzzed with delight. Unhappily the cost proved too high, even for Congress, and the plan was passed over. But it was not dead; the New Yorkers thought well of it, and a much-modified version became their new Park Theatre in the Bowery.

Brunel received no fee for this work and no acclaim from posterity, for the theatre was burned to the ground in 1821. But New York had taken him to its heart and in the autumn of 1796, after taking American citizenship, he became the City's Chief Engineer.

Recognition did not tame his high spirits, as the Park Theatre's first-night audience discovered. No sooner had the curtain risen than they were treated to a satiric commentary on New York manners by a hidden voice with a strong French accent issuing from a mobile stage windmill. The city's outraged elders stormed the stage, and the miscreant fled, through a trap door, to his sanctuary, Philadelphia.

It may have been during his stay in this peaceful city that Marc painted the two miniature portraits—one of himself and the other, from memory, of his love—which he sent to Sophie in England with yet another letter telling of his adventures and affection.

New York kept him busy. He designed houses and commercial buildings, and the following year built a cannon foundry which was acclaimed a technical advance—in Europe as well as in America—and reflects to the credit of Brunel's unwitting rescuer Gaspard Monge. Certainly Brunel made use of mechanical drawing and his mentor's ideas on ordnance plants and foundries undoubtedly assisted the young engineer.

His services to New York brought Marc into contact with city elders and members of the American Government. Alexander Hamilton, the illegitimate son of a Scottish Caribbean trader, became a particular friend. Hamilton, an honourable and intelligent man—destined to die from a dueller's bullet—had practised as a lawyer and had been George Washington's aide-de-camp during the War of Independence, when he held the rank of lieutenant-colonel. Although there was no professional bond between Brunel and Hamilton, they were united by temperament and by suspicion of Republican France,

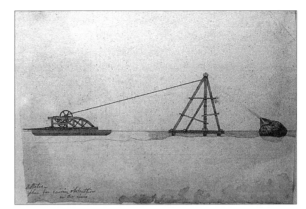

RIGHT *A drawing by Brunel of 'a plan for raising obstructions in rivers'.*

CENTRE *A design by Brunel for a bank in Wall Street.*

BELOW *A tinted drawing by Brunel almost certainly from his design for the United States Capitol building.*

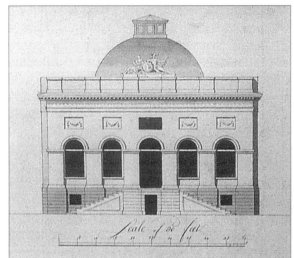

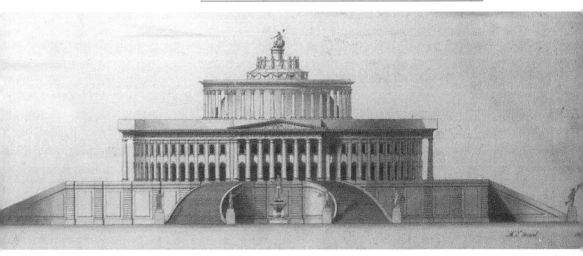

which was waging an undeclared naval war against the United States. As George Washington's First Secretary to the Treasury, Hamilton had repeatedly warned his countrymen against French designs and at this time, although no longer in office, he remained Washington's intimate and would soon be a major-general and second-in-command of the United States Army.

One evening during the first half of 1798 Marc dined at Hamilton's home, and was delighted to meet another émigré, a Monsieur Delabigarre, who had recently arrived from England. The talk turned to ships, from ships to navies, and from navies to battles—and in particular to the British victories at Camperdown and St Vincent, which had excited the admiration of the American public.

Perceiving Brunel's minute understanding of warship design, Delabigarre mentioned the difficulties with which Pitt's government struggled as they expanded the Royal Navy. Ships' blocks were a pressing supply problem, and he described a visit to the Southampton factory of Messrs Fox and Taylor, where they were manufactured. Marc questioned him closely and later, after bidding his host goodnight, returned home in a thoughtful mood.

Delabigarre had said that the Royal Navy required 100,000 blocks a year. There must be a quicker and better mode of manufacture than that used by Fox and Taylor. Mentally he broke a block down into its components—shell, sheave, coak* and pin—and considered the operations involved in making each. The individual processes were quite simple, and yet each was repeated at least three hundred times each working day. Surely this work could be done by machine.

'My first idea for the block machinery,' he wrote later, 'came to me when dining with General Hamilton; the second, when resting in the forest under a tree in which I cut certain initials in the bark. The curve of one of the letters (S) struck me—"This is it," I cried, "my pulley shall have this curve."'

Hamilton encouraged him. He would have encouraged anyone whose efforts promised to check the French, and when Brunel confided his intention of sailing for England as soon as he had completed plans for the defence of The Narrows, he wished his young friend good luck and gave him a letter of introduction to Lord Spencer, Pitt's Navy Minister.

At the close of the year Brunel resigned, and on 7 February 1799 left America for England in the packet *Halifax,* bringing with him Hamilton's letter and 'some small means and many great ideas'.

---

* The then current name for a bush.

PART II

PROFIT AND PENURY

And what is business in the lump? It is
hiring land from landlords and spare
money from capitalists, and employing
the hungry to make enough money out
of them day by day to pay the wages
for their keep and bring in a profit as well.

GEORGE BERNARD SHAW
The Intelligent Woman's Guide to Socialism

4

THE INVENTOR'S LOT

⟡

After a wintry 28-day passage, the *Halifax* put in to Falmouth before proceeding to Plymouth where Brunel disembarked on 13 March. He made his way at once to London, and three days later, after taking rooms in the parish of St Mary Newington, introduced himself at Somerset House to the brother with whom Sophie then lodged.

Marc found the fair and constant Sophie, now 24 years old, as serene and enchanting as in memory. The girl had become a woman, and many a would-be suitor had been sent sadly on his way since her return from France. But Brunel, then nearly 30 and grown quite serious, with his head full of strange and novel schemes, was to her liking, and the couple announced their engagement—although the Kingdoms looked upon the French-American with reserve. He found agreeable lodgings at Canterbury Place in Lambeth and settled himself into the land of the steam engine.

Britain and her allies Austria, Holland and Portugal were at war with France and their land war had gone badly. French armies had overrun Switzerland and much of Northern Italy and had wrested Belgium from the Austrian Empire. Spain had been induced to end the alliance with Britain and had declared war on her. However, the sea war had gone well. The Royal Navy had won control of the Mediterranean and France was being blockaded. The pictures of France that Marc—a royalist sailor—saw was of a country isolated initially by her illegitimate government and subsequently by being driven from the sea.

Within a month he filed his first patent application, which described a 'duplicate Writing and Drawing Machine' or 'Polygraph', as he liked to call it. The busy executive of stage-coach days could take his polygraph with him, folded up inside its carrying box. Arrived at his inn, he would move the water jug aside, and set up the apparatus on the washstand in his room, proceeding then to make not one, but two or three copies of his correspondence or reports, all simultaneously.

Independently suspended quills were ingeniously coupled so that they would write on paper or books in a manner corresponding to the master quill in the writer's hand. By means of a sliding base, the paper could be moved away as each line was completed, and when the master quill was dipped in ink, the slave quills drank likewise from their separate wells.

Portable writing boxes were the vogue but this little aid, trivial perhaps in retrospect, revealed surprising skill. The problem of achieving perfect balance between the quills was overcome with subtlety, and the drawings proclaimed an unusual ability to express ideas on paper and an absolute mastery of the draughtsman's technique.

This was only an overture. The 'great ideas' were blockmaking machines, and for their successful promotion Brunel needed two working models. Drawings were intelligible only to engineers—there were but a handful of these men—and the power to judge and decide lay elsewhere.

During the early summer of 1799 Brunel became acquainted with a fellow-émigré named De Bacquancourt, with whom he discussed his aspirations. De Bacquancourt mentioned a small engineering shop in Wells Street, which runs north from Oxford Street across Mortimer Street, where a Mr Henry Maudslay had his business.

Maudslay had served an eight-year apprenticeship with Joseph Bramah, the distinguished engineer who contributed much to the craft of lock-making, and engineering practice generally, and whom we should salute, for he fathered the fountain pen, the banknote-numbering machine, the beer engine and the first practical water closet.

Another, and perhaps the most notable, of Bramah's achievements was the invention of the hydraulic press, which he patented in 1795. Subsequently Maudslay helped his master develop machines to produce his patent lock, but Bramah, it seems, failed to reward his resourceful pupil adequately, and after a dispute about wages in 1798 Maudslay left him. He put up his sign at 64 Wells Street, engaged a journeyman assistant, and sought engineering commissions from riverside merchants and manufacturers.

Maudslay, a wide-browed stocky man, was destined to become the greatest mechanic of his generation. The screw-cutting lathe, the slide-rest lathe, the planing machine and the micrometer were incubated in his works, and he invented processes for printing calico. He speeded and refined the practice of engineering and was a founder of the machine-tool industry. His modest workshop grew into the famous firm of Maudslay, Sons and Field, and was to be the school in which Richard Roberts, fleeing the militia officers, and Joseph Whitworth, of screw-thread fame, were to learn their trade. Joseph Clement, the builder of Babbage's calculating machine, James Nasmyth, inventor of the steam hammer, and many others served their apprenticeship with this master craftsman.

Maudslay retained the respect of his pupils, and the affection of his staff. 'It was,' said an old workman after his death, 'a pleasure to see him handle a

Henry Maudslay 1771-1831.
A lithograph by H. Grevedon.

tool of any kind, and he was *quite splendid* with an eighteen-inch file.'

In the summer of 1799 Maudslay was twenty-eight. His formal education had been rudimentary, and his world was bounded by Woolwich, his birthplace; its arsenal, in which he had worked with his father; and London, where he had served Bramah. For one whole year he had been his own master. There was a young man to see him? Well, he was not too busy. A strange visitor, with an atrocious accent, who wants models made? Had Mr Brunel any drawings?

Maudslay examined the drawings. They were remarkably precise certainly, but apparently unintelligible; however, as Brunel explained them it dawned upon him that they revealed, as never before, every detail of his visitor's ideas. And as he answered the mechanic's questions, Brunel recognised a craftsman of unusual perception. Encouraged, and confident that his plans were in safe keeping, he took his leave.

Did he guess that the hand he firmly shook would give an iron substance to his 'great ideas'? Perhaps, but how Maudslay's craftsmanship and genius for production would, for more than two decades, accept each challenge from his restless brain, could not have been foretold. At the little house in Wells Street, Brunel had found his Boswell.

Throughout the summer and autumn, Marc was a regular visitor to Maudslay's shop. With painstaking slowness the models, one of a sheave-making machine, the other of a mortising machine, took shape, and in their growing ate into the savings which he had brought from America. He was earning nothing but, confident that the machines would find a ready acceptance, he faced the future cheerfully, rejoicing in Sophie's companionship and planning with her their life together.

Great events had shaken Europe. Enraged by Napoleon's seizure of Malta,[*] Tsar Paul had declared war on France a year previously. Then, during the summer of 1799, Austro-Russian forces evicted the French armies from Italy and Switzerland. Even more significantly, as it transpired, on 23 August Napoleon left his Army of the Orient, slipped across the Mediterranean and made his way to Paris where he was received without enthusiasm. Eventually, after a lengthy power struggle, his gift for leadership and his reputation for bravery brought him victory. The power of the Directoire was curtailed and early in December Napoleon was proclaimed First Consul of France.

Marc and Sophie's long-awaited wedding day arrived on 1 November 1799. They were married at Sophie's parish church of St Andrew, Holborn and lived together happily until parted by death.

They lived in rooms that Marc found in Bedford Street which were only a few minutes walk from Maudslay's workshop. Between visits to Maudslay's, Marc busied himself preparing drawings of four machines, each of which would perform a separate step in the process of block production.

At this period a ship's block with a single pulley or sheave was an assembly of four components. Within the slotted elm *shell* a lignum vitae sheave or *shiver* rotated on an iron *pin* which pierced the shell's unslotted sides. A bearing for this pin was provided in the form of a split bell metal bush or *coak* which was fastened to the centre of the shiver.

Designing machines to make this useful article occupied Brunel throughout 1800, but early the following year Maudslay finished the two models, and Marc's thoughts and draughtsmanship were embodied in a patent application entitled, *A New and Useful Machine[†] for Cutting One or More Mortices, Forming the Sides of and Cutting the Pin-Hole of the Shells of Blocks, and for Turning and Boring the Shivers, and Fitting and Fixing the Coak Therein,* which he filed on 10 February 1801.

It is fascinating to observe the evolution of the inventor's ideas. Between cutting Sophie's initial on a tree in an American forest and the final accomplishment, there was an immense expenditure of thought and labour. The patent specification, which marked the halfway stage between the gleam of an idea and the fruitful functioning of the world's first series of mass-production machines, described three machines for forming shells and one for making shivers.

---

[*] While en route for Egypt.
[†] The 'machine' consisted of four separate 'engines'. In other words, there were four machines.

A horse-powered block-mill of the late 18th century.

A pair of reciprocating chisels would cut two mortises (in the case of a twin-sheaved block) through a rough cuboid piece of elm secured in the travelling clamp of the first machine; then, after passing to the second machine, the embryonic shell would be rotated in the path of a slender reciprocating saw, and in this way a smooth curve would be imparted to its two slotted sides.

The third machine, a modified lathe, would bore the hole for the iron pin and radius the shell's remaining sides and corners; whilst the fourth machine, also multi-purpose, would convert a rough disc of lignum vitae into a finished shiver, complete with grooved rim, turned faces and machined recesses for the two halves of the bell-metal coak.

Of the four machines described, the most original and sophisticated were the mortising machine and the sheave-making machine, and both of these Brunel could demonstrate in model form.

Having filed the specification, Marc and Sophie moved to Gerrard Street, Soho, but they did not stay long in this agreeable locality, moving a month or two later to a house in Queen Square Place, just east of Southampton Row, which was almost certainly the birthplace of their first child, a daughter, who received her mother's name.[*]

Now Brunel was ready to sell his invention, and he gladly accepted an offer of help from a brother-in-law living in Portsmouth, who was an undersecretary to the Navy Board and made frequent visits to the Southampton factory of Messrs Fox and Taylor.

All that Brunel had learned regarding Fox and Taylor augured well for the success of Kingdom's approach, which followed swiftly. Besides being the

---

[*] The exact date of this move, which followed the filing of the patent specification, is indeterminable, and records of baptism do not reveal Sophia's birthday. The most probable times have been indicated.

Navy's principal supplier of blocks, the Taylor family had been responsible for notable developments in the art of blockmaking. Twenty-two years earlier Walter Taylor had been granted a patent for the *Improvement of Coghing or Bushing of Cast Iron or Metal Shivers for Ships' Blocks* and, although the shivers continued to be made of lignum vitae, this patent marked the introduction of the bell-metal coak and the iron pin. A further patent describing improvements to 'made'* blocks followed in 1781.

* Very large blocks whose shells were fabricated from strips of elm and externally bound with iron.

RIGHT *The block-mortising machine.*

BELOW *Maudslay's model of the block-shaping machine.*

Walter Taylor enjoyed the fruits of commercial success and a well-deserved eminence as an innovator—he has even been credited with the invention of the circular saw. He was sixty-seven at this time, and control of the firm had passed to his son Samuel who, on 5 March, replied to Kingdom's initiative.

> I will just describe in a few words how we have made our blocks for upwards of twenty-five years—twenty years to my own knowledge. The tree of timber, from two to five loads' measurement, is drawn by the machine under the saw, where it is cut to its proper length. It is then removed to a round saw, where the piece cut off is completely shaped, and only requiring to be turned under the saw. The one, two, or three, or four mortices are cut by hand, which wholly completes the block, except with a broad chisel cutting out the roughness of the teeth of the saw, and the scores for strapping the rope. Every block we make (except more than four machines can make) is done in this way, and with great truth and exactness. The shivers are wholly done by the engines, very little labour is employed about our works, except the removing of things from one place to another.
>
> My father has spent many hundreds a year to get the best mode, and most accurate, of making the blocks, and he certainly succeeded; and so much so, that I have no hope of anything ever better being discovered, and I am convinced there cannot. At the present time, were we ever so inclined, we could not attempt any alteration. We are, as you know, so much pressed, and especially as the machine your brother-in-law has invented is wholly yet untried. Inventions of this kind are always so different in a model and in actual work.
>
> Believe me, dear Kingdom,
>> Yours in great Truth, Samuel Taylor.

5

BLOCKS FOR THE NAVY

⟡

The tonnage of the navy had increased by more than 60 per cent during the previous decade. The battle of Trafalgar was but four years distant. Nine hundred and twenty-two smartly painted blocks gleamed in the rigging of every new 74-gun ship. Each year Fox and Taylor produced 100,000 of these indispensable adornments, 'with great truth and exactness', and received £24,000 for their pains. They were indeed much pressed.

Supplying the fleet lined pockets far less wholesome than those of Samuel Taylor. Ships put to sea with sails whose weight and whiteness dissolved in the first shower. Rascally victuallers grew fat, while press-ganged sailors starved for want of wholesome rations, and contracts were awarded in return for favours by equally rascally officials who were pleased to call themselves servants of King George III.

The burden of this system of nepotism and graft, just tolerable in peaceful times, was insupportable in crisis, and in 1796 Brigadier-General Sir Samuel Bentham, K.S.G., had been appointed Inspector-General of Naval Works, with the object of by-passing the Navy Board, a department which, wrote Beamish 'seems to have been only calculated to enlarge patronage, decrease responsibility, and multiply the links in the official drag-chain of the naval service'.*

Forty-four years of age in the spring of 1801, Bentham could look back on an eventful career. After some education at Westminster, he had been apprenticed to the Master Shipwright at Woolwich Dockyard at the age of fourteen. A year or two later he went to sea and, after visiting many ports of Northern Europe, landed in May 1780 at St Petersburg, where he entered the service of Catherine the Great at the age of twenty-three.

Bentham travelled the length and breadth of Russia—from the Crimea to the snowy regions of Siberia, and eastwards to the frontier of China— inspecting mines and metal works. In the winter of 1782 he reported to the Empress, and after a further period in her service on engineering works, which included the Fontanka Canal, he was made a Knight of the Russian Order of

---

* *Memoir of the life of Sir Marc Isambard Brunel*

25

St George. He returned to England in 1791, and settled down to study the practice of woodworking with a view to its mechanisation. The fruit of this labour was a patent filed in 1793 which described a number of woodworking machines, including a machine for mortising and a rotary planer.

Following his appointment as Inspector-General three years later, Bentham overhauled the administration of naval dockyards and, brooking no opposition, introduced many technical innovations including inventions of his own. Block supplies were a major preoccupation, and at Portsmouth Dockyard he installed a 12 hp steam engine to power woodworking machinery. Later, in 1802, he despatched his Portsmouth engineering manager, Simon Goodrich, to the works of another block contractor, William Dunsterville of Plymouth, where there were wood-framed saws, both circular and reciprocating, a twin circular saw-cum-morticing machine, and lathes and boring machines which were used for the manufacture of shivers, pins and coaks. Thus, while Samuel Taylor was reflecting complacently on the perfection of his methods, the Inspector-General of Naval Works was seeking more productive and economical machinery.

Following Taylor's rebuff, Brunel sought an interview, on the strength of Hamilton's letter, with Lord Spencer, who had vacated the office of Navy Minister following Pitt's resignation the previous year, and in due course the meeting took place, either at Althorp (the Spencers' family home near Northampton) or, more probably, at Lord Spencer's town house at Wimbledon.

George John, the 2nd Earl Spencer, had been educated at Harrow and Trinity College Cambridge, and was 11 years Marc's senior. He had been Northampton's Member of Parliament since 1780, was a Master of Trinity House, and would again hold office as Home Secretary in Lord Grenville's government of 1806. Although no engineer, he was a sound judge of character, with a cultivated and receptive mind, and the young French-American's erudition and enthusiasm were understood.

Lord Spencer was to be for Brunel in England what Thurman had been in America, and henceforth no door would be closed to the engineer. Through Spencer, Brunel gained the friendship of Faraday, Babbage and other members of the intelligentsia, and became an intimate of the landed ruling class, a stratum of society in which, as a respecter of tradition, he found much to admire. The well-born, for their part, found him socially agreeable; engineers were looked upon with the mixture of wonder and awe which we today bestow on media celebrities, but, unlike many of his contemporaries, whose speech and manners proclaimed their humble birth and scanty education, Brunel was cultured, literate and travelled. As a former royalist French officer, he did not suffer from the class prejudice which might have been an impediment to the younger son of an English yeoman farmer. He deferred, perhaps excessively, to English customs, but he was warm, carefree and considerate. When an ageing hostess complained that her fingers had grown stiff, he invented a machine to shuffle her cards, and another to wind her knitting wool into balls. Neither was patented, but the second had important applications in the textile industry.

Lord Spencer undertook to arrange a meeting with Bentham. Thus he launched Brunel and, until his death 33 years later, remained the engineer's most faithful friend.

The outcome of the subsequent meeting with Bentham was also satisfactory, and it is to the General's credit that he commended another's ideas, and arranged for Brunel to demonstrate his models before the Lords Commissioners of the Admiralty.

Marc wrote later,

> I received an order to be at the Admiralty with my small models, which gave such satisfaction that my proposition was adopted. Accordingly, General B. took me to Portsmouth. Having had occasion then of seeing what had already been done by the steam engine and building ... I made my dispositions accordingly.

On 15 April 1802 Bentham officially recommended the installation of the block machines at Portsmouth Dockyard. His was the decision that counted, and after a fitting interval the Navy Board graciously concurred.

The waiting period proved fruitful; Brunel developed and refined his ideas to a remarkable extent, and this new work was given tangible form by Maudslay, who made a series of working models, for which Brunel drew on his American savings. His boldness was rewarded, and immediately the plant was sanctioned he ordered the first set of production machines for blocks of seven to ten inches in length. These Maudslay made with commendable speed, and by the end of the year Brunel no longer needed to spend his days at Wells Street, so he and Sophie packed their belongings once again and moved to a modest house in Portsea, which was a short walk from the Dockyard.

On Bentham's advice the Navy Board agreed to reward Brunel with a sum equal to the savings resulting from one year's full-scale operation of the new plant. In the meantime he was to receive an allowance of one guinea a day whilst engaged on His Majesty's service, plus an extra ten shillings a day whilst in Portsmouth or when travelling, plus coach fares.

The tide of the European war ebbed and flowed during the two and a half years following Marc and Sophie's marriage. Napoleon revitalised France and her army and, during 1800, repeatedly out-fought and out-gunned the

armies of Austria and Russia. The culmination on 3 December was the battle—
or rout—of Hohenlinden, a few kilometres east of Munich when Austria,
unwilling to suffer further losses, sought and was granted a Christmas Day
armistice. This was the prelude to the harsh Peace of Lunéville, concluded
on 9 February 1801.

The Russians also withdrew from the conflict and in December Tsar
Paul placated Napoleon by concluding a pact—the Northern League of
Armed Neutrality—with Sweden, Denmark and Prussia which bound the
four participants to close their ports to British ships. However, the course
of war—especially a war between coalitions—can be subject to surprising
changes of direction.

On 23 March 1801 Tsar Paul was murdered and his son, Alexander,
succeeded him at the beginning of April. Ten days later, following unsuccessful
negotiations with the Danes, a British fleet nominally under the command
of Admiral Sir Hyde Parker—but in fact commanded by Nelson—attacked
the Danish fleet lying at Copenhagen behind a screen of fixed and floating
batteries.

Early in the afternoon,* when the defending fire faltered, Nelson sent
a message under a flag of truce to the Danish crown prince which began,
'to the brothers of Englishmen, the Danes ...'. Many Norfolk families have
Danish ancestors and Nelson much preferred to fight the French. With a
notable absence of rancour, he then negotiated a satisfactory armistice which
presaged the collapse of the Northern League and curtailed Napoleon's
influence with Russia and the Baltic states.

The French were understandably proud of their military successes during
the first two years of Napoleon's rule; but many thousands of families had
been bereaved and their war-weariness broke surface early in September 1801
when Napoleon's Army of the Orient capitulated in Egypt.

Napoleon needed time. Time to restore morale and time to re-equip his
army.

At the beginning of 1802 he gratified his countrymen by assuming the
title of President of the newly created Italian Republic. At the same time he
began making discreet diplomatic overtures to Britain.

Our government had twice demonstrated Britain's determination and
ability to rule the waves but it had no intention of becoming embroiled in a
war in Europe without allies. The two naval victories had been costly and far
too many warships still flew the flags of France and Spain. Britain also needed
time. Time to re-equip and expand the Royal Navy.

---

* After Nelson had responded to Hyde Parker's 'Cease Action' signal by applying a telescope to
his blind eye.

The war in Europe ended on 27 March 1802 when the Peace of Amiens*
was concluded by the government of Henry Addington, a former speaker of
the House of Commons and William Pitt's successor.

It was a peace of convenience.

* At which Britain agreed to cede Malta to France but it not do so.

6

MASS PRODUCTION

—◆·•◆·•◆—

When Marc took his leave of Sophie at their home in Britain Street, Portsea, he had only to walk past St George's Church in its pleasant square, and onwards half-a-mile along the waterfront road, to reach the naval dockyard. The extra ten shillings a day 'whilst in Portsmouth or when travelling' was, on the face of it, easily earned.

The chosen site in the dockyard, between a pair of substantial two-storey buildings, was roofed over to create a single-storey factory for the block machinery. Beneath the floor of this shop were storage vaults and, at a still lower level, great cisterns into which the nearby dry docks drained by gravity. In one of the taller buildings alongside, Bentham had installed some woodworking machinery and a 12 hp steam engine whose power was transmitted by a vertical shaft in the centre of the ground floor to line shafting to which his belt-driven machines were harnessed. The vertical shaft also served as a capstan, drawing baulks of timber into the shop from the yard outside. Under the roof, above the upper storey, there was a large tank which supplied water to all parts of the manufactory—a prudent precaution in view of the fire risk.

Almost before their foundations were ready, wagons began arriving with Maudslay's machines, and Brunel was fully occupied installing them, extending the line shafting to drive them, training operators in their use and, more important, in their maintenance. He had to work quickly.

The first set of machinery, for which Maudslay was paid by Brunel, who recouped himself from the Navy Board, was producing by the middle of 1803. Installation of a second set, for blocks of four to seven inches long, and of a third set for 10- to 18-inch blocks, was effected in 1804 and 1805 respectively, and for this machinery, costing £12,000, the Navy Board paid Maudslay direct.

That Brunel could not have chosen a better craftsman is confirmed by Maudslay's earlier development of a screw-cutting lathe, and by even the most cursory examination of the block-making machines. As a result of this substantial contract Maudslay moved his shop to a larger house, a few hundred yards away, number 75 Margaret Street.

Throughout the installation period, Simon Goodrich, Bentham's assistant at Portsmouth, functioned as the link between his chief and Brunel. Liaison was further strengthened in 1804 when a perceptive young draughtsman named Joshua Field transferred from the dockyard to Bentham's office, but when the first set of block machines was commissioned a staff problem of another sort arose, and on 7 January 1803, Brunel wrote to Bentham requesting the services of one James Burr: 'On account of his being already so well practised in the working of wood by your machinery of various kinds, I cannot but express my wish that he might be entrusted with the management of my machinery for making Blocks and Blockmakers' wares.' As a result Burr assumed the additional responsibility of day-to-day block production and the department's growing staff of machine operators, whose wages ranged from 15s. to £2 10s. for six 12-hour days, depending upon each individual's burden of responsibility and on whether he was on piece- or time-work rates.

The extent of the revolution which Brunel wrought at Portsmouth may be glimpsed by considering the step-by-step production process.[*] Elm for a block's shell was first clamped in a boring machine, which drilled a small hole for the iron pin through from one face and then, at 90 degrees, one larger hole per sheave which was elongated to a slot by a mortising machine. This machine resembled the first machine described in the patent specification. Its chisels were invisible at their working speed rate of 400 strokes per minute— so that slots they cut grew longer, as if by magic.

After a corner saw had cut off its corners, the slotted shell, along with nine others, was transferred to a shaping machine which imparted predetermined curves to each of its four sides. Finally, a scoring machine cut grooves in the shell's two unslotted sides to accommodate the bight of rope in which the ship-borne block would hang.

Sheave making was also accomplished in five steps by means of separate machines. First a rough cross-cut disc of lignum vitae was made perfectly circular, and simultaneously drilled through its centre by a special rounding saw. Next, an ingenious coaking machine milled three recesses, at 120° intervals, around each side of the disc's central hole to accommodate the perforated ears of each half of the coak—which was then secured by iron pins clenched by a power-driven riveting hammer. After the coak's central hole (which had a spiral grease-retaining groove) had been smoothed and very slightly enlarged by a broaching machine, the shiver was finished in a novel face-turning lathe, which also grooved its rim.

The block's iron pin was machined from a forging which was cylindrical except for a square end section which bit into the shell and prevented the

---

[*] See Appendix B for a more detailed description of the block machines and the process of manufacture.

pin rotating. Each pin was machined by an automatic pin-turning lathe, and burnished by a pin-polishing machine—both machines being of Brunel's design. Finally, after smoothing its mortises and painting, the shell together with its shiver and pin were assembled by hand.

This brief outline of the production cycle does not convey the originality of Brunel's ideas, or the subtlety with which he put them into practice. A random look at the plant affords a better glimpse of these qualities.

The clamps of the boring machine are one example. Besides holding the shell, they impressed marks upon its ends, by which it was located in

A block's components; their manufacture and assembly. Top: shell; centre: sheave; bottom: assembly.

subsequent machines. Nothing like the mortising machine had been known previously, and from it has evolved the slotter for cutting keyways in wheels. This machine also had a cone clutch, enabling the operator to stop the chisels without destroying the flywheel's momentum—the earliest use of a cone clutch yet discovered. The saw and drill of the rounding saw, although driven at different speeds, were mounted on concentric shafts. The coaking machine had an expanding arbor, actuated by a tapered plug, which gripped the sheave's centre hole. This is almost certainly the first practical application of an idea of Leonardo da Vinci. A split nut in the pin-polishing machine, which facilitated rapid resetting, anticipated Whitworth's patent by over thirty years.

The machinery already described formed the heart of the block mill, but in order to feed this plant and to mechanise the production of certain special types of blocks, hitherto supplied by contractors, Brunel designed and installed a number of other machines. One was for making deadeyes (sheaveless blocks), another for boring the large 'made' blocks, and yet another, a reciprocating saw, for reducing the timber from which their shells were fabricated. The blocks used in powder magazines had coakless sheaves, which revolved on lignum vitae pins—to lessen the risk of sparks causing explosions—so a special lathe was installed to turn these pins.

There were reciprocating saws for cross-cutting elm and lignum vitae, circular saws for ripping elm (of which more later) and two other novel and ingenious circular saws. The first of these was a pendulum saw used for cross-cutting short lengths of elm; its blade, which formed the bob of the pendulum, was belt-driven in the manner of a low speed dentist's drill. The other was the lignum vitae saw, whose horizontal blade traversed so as to cut slices from a log of lignum vitae which was held in rotatable clamps.

In all, 45 machines of Brunel's design were installed, and three of these were still in use at Portsmouth 20 years after the end of the Second World War—a working life of more than 150 years.

The installation in government premises of the main part of this plant was largely completed within three years of Bentham's letter of approval. In this brief span, design work was finalised, production effected, installation completed, teething troubles overcome, a single 12 hp steam engine was replaced by one of 30 hp (a second 30 hp engine was on the way) and rates of pay were fixed for the unskilled machine hands.

At Portsmouth the era of mass production dawned, almost unnoticed, and it is thought-provoking to consider the record of this government department which applied the spur of profit-seeking to outflank the threat of war.

Brunel's personal achievement is an even greater cause for wonder. He originated and effected a technological revolution, and the agents of his will

The pendulum saw (above) and the sheave-coaking machine (right).

were simple workmen, unable, for the most part, to read or write. Not more than six firms in the kingdom could have supplied his material needs, yet the machines were installed expeditiously, and he betrayed no irritation when the cautious officials of the Navy Board demanded his pass whenever he entered the dockyard.

The machines required from their attendants neither the exercise of judgement nor the application of skill, but as the plant came into production, a flood of blocks of undreamed-of 'truth and exactness' testified to their inventor's genius. Suddenly, 10 unskilled hands at Portsmouth became as productive as a 110 craftsmen at Southampton. This new technique took a long time to disperse throughout our primitive industry, but its effects were quickly felt. In 1803 Samuel Taylor's contract was renewed on a specifically short-term basis, and on 24 March 1805, seven months before the battle of Trafalgar, he paid a heavy price for doubting 'anything better ever being discovered', for on that day blockmaking by contractors was discontinued.

Of course, the inventor's ideas dispersed eventually. Henry Maudslay knew every detail of the plant, and to his knowledge, derived in the course of manufacture, was added that of the draughtsman, Joshua Field,* who joined his firm in 1805 after a year in Bentham's office. Like Maudslay, Field had learned Mechanical Drawing from Brunel but, in addition, he had been

---

* Joshua Field later became Maudslay's partner, the firm being renamed Maudslay, Sons and Field. It is notable that, following this reorganisation, it was almost invariably the comparatively well-educated Joshua Field who replied to Brunel's letters. Field was a founder-member and early Vice President of the Institution of Civil Engineers, and became a Fellow of the Royal Society in 1836.

privileged to witness the block machinery's installation and its harvest; he was therefore uniquely equipped to assess the development potential of Brunel's ideas. So Henry Maudslay's firm became the repository of the new technology, and Maudslay's later inventions and those of his pupils disseminated this learning throughout the machine tool industry.

Great men rarely lack detractors, and in 1852, two years after Brunel's death, Bentham's widow credited her husband with the invention of the block machines—taking care at the same time to belittle Brunel's role. James Nasmyth was another critic who waited for Marc's demise. He became Maudslay's pupil in 1829, and 25 years later, doubtless from motives of misplaced loyalty, attributed the plant's invention to his 'good old master'.

Simon Goodrich's correspondence affords ample refutation of these claims, but Joshua Field, speaking with unrivalled knowledge of Maudslay, Bentham and Brunel, gave his views much earlier to Richard Beamish:

> The works in progress when Mr Brunel arrived were a new steam engine[*] and some buildings intended for the reception of machinery, which General Bentham had proposed to erect, but had not erected. The General had already introduced saws of various kinds, and machines for tonguing, grooving and rabetting timber; but there was no machinery whatever especially applicable to blockmaking. That was altogether the invention of Mr Brunel. The character of the drawings was different to any we ever had before—the proportion of the parts—the whole thing, in short; and I never once heard, during all the time of my connection with the dockyard, with General Bentham, with Mr Goodrich, and with Mr Maudslay, that anyone ventured to deny Mr Brunel's claim to be the sole inventor of the block machinery.

The plant proved a sound investment. Three early years' production sufficed to recoup its capital cost, and its working life was extraordinarily long. Production in quantity continued until after the Great War. Landing craft which transported men for D-Day were equipped with Brunel blocks, and the remnants of the plant have been used in recent years to make replacement blocks for Nelson's *Victory*.

The Portsmouth block machinery was soon included in the itinerary of distinguished sightseers. Sir Walter Scott in 1816 recorded his impressions of a visit to 'these wonderful sights', but the novelist Maria Edgeworth paid the aptest tribute. 'And now for the Block Machinery,' she wrote in a letter, '... I will only say that the ingenuity and successful performance far surpassed my expectations. Machinery so perfect appears to act with the happy certainty of instinct and the foresight of reason combined.'

[*] From Boulton and Watt; the second was ordered from their rivals, Murray and Wood. (So intense was the rivalry between these firms that Boulton and Watt surreptitiously bought land adjoining Murray and Wood's factory, thus preventing the expansion of their foundry.)

7

THE BUSINESS MAN

AT FIRST, when Marc returned in the evening to his terraced home,[*] two smiling faces greeted him at the door. Before the last set of block machines commenced production, a third had joined them.[†] The new baby, named Emma, inherited her mother's serenity, but was less robust than Sophia, her lively, bright-eyed elder sister, whom Lord Armstrong later called 'Brunel in petticoats'.

The pleasures of parenthood were accompanied by an increasing preoccupation with money. Having paid Maudslay over £1,200 for working models, Marc's 'small means' were sadly depleted; and whilst 100,000 blocks had been made in 1805, the Navy demanded yet higher production to equip the growing fleet. The cost of developing special saws to feed the block machines with enough elm cuboids and lignum vitae discs for continuous production was met, of necessity, from his dwindling funds. The allowance he received took no account of this.

Now Sophie was pregnant again.

Another tantalising aspect of the situation was the basis of the award to be made for his invention—a sum equal to the savings resulting from one year's full-scale operation of the plant. The amount saved would increase as production rose, so, whilst the Navy expanded, the longer he waited the more he would get. Clearly it would be improvident to seek an early settlement; but meanwhile his family grew.

At this time of unceasing activity Brunel again demonstrated his extraordinary originality. There had been a portent in November 1802, before the move to Portsea, in the shape of a patent specification entitled *Trimmings and Borders for Muslins, Lawns and Cambric*. This unillustrated document, resembling a technical essay rather than a patent specification, is chiefly interesting because of the diverse industrial knowledge which it reveals; but the idea had to be abandoned because of the pressing demands of the block-mill. The problem of feeding this plant provided a sufficient stimulus to his inventiveness. Saws to rip elm with speed and precision were needed—circular

---

[*] Demolished in the early 1960s.
[†] Records of baptism fail to reveal the children's dates of birth.

saws through which the logs would be propelled on carriages—and in May 1805 he filed a specification (No. 2844) which showed the way and bore the customary hallmark of detailed refinement.

He proposed a saw made of several segments 'in order to obtain a great diameter'—over 5ft in the illustration. The leading edge of each segment was to be given a 'V' profile, and was locked, at the radius line, into the notched trailing edge of the preceding segment. The complete blade was to be secured to the driving belt's drum on the saw's main shaft, and would reach down almost to the surface of the carriage or 'drag' which was to be propelled by the sawyer along rails in a pit below. One side of the log would be secured to the carriage by vertical clamps and, after a plank had been cut, the carriage would be returned, the saw and its shaft moved 'collaterally' (sideways) and the process repeated.

Brunel produced working drawings, and ordered a complete saw from Maudslay. It arrived at the dockyard late in 1806, along with the second 30 hp steam engine of Murray and Wood manufacture, which had undergone tests at the bustling Margaret Street shop.

A more prudent man might not have considered official encouragement a satisfactory substitute for a firm order; but naval expansion had already prompted the authorities to sanction expenditure on block machinery which greatly exceeded the early estimates, so Brunel installed the saw. He knew that failure to feed the block mill would curtail his reward and believed it had commercial possibilities outside the service.

Another prospect beckoned. Maudslay had made to his design a model saw to cut the curved staves for casks. This probably resembled the vertical reciprocating saw described in the block machine patent, and promised to revolutionise barrel-making. This too, Marc tried at Portsmouth, and visited the master cooper at the Deptford Victualling Yard to sound out the market.

As his resources dwindled the ideas blossomed, and in the lengthening spring days of 1806 these two processes received a potent stimulus. He wrote in his Journal, 'On the 9th of April, at five minutes before one o'clock in the morning, my dear Sophia was brought to bed of a boy.' The child was named Isambard Kingdom and became the apple of his father's eye.

The day-to-day problems of the block mill would have been a sufficient preoccupation for most men, as Brunel's letter book of the period bears witness. We find him writing in November to Goodrich that the machine hands would prefer to have half-an-hour for lunch and to finish at 8 p.m. as formerly, rather than having three-quarters-of-an-hour and finishing at 8.15.

Then there were the perennial supply problems, one of which prompted another November letter to Goodrich. 'I will thank you to give directions that he [the foundryman] may have the means of furnishing the present orders and to prepare for casting the larger coaks ... . We shall soon be ready to send in store larger blocks' (probably 'made' blocks).

Additional machines had to be installed to expand production, and the purchase of one, a 'machine for rivetting coaks' (riveting hammer) is recorded under the date May 1806 in the Portsmouth Woodmill's 'Account of Store Book'. The recording of the transaction in this book, which was reserved for consumable stores, suggests an attempt by Bentham's office to by-pass the Navy Board's accountants.

That same year, on 23 September, Brunel filed yet another patent specification, this time describing 'A New Mode of Cutting Veneers or Thin Boards by Machinery'. A two-foot-thick slab of wood was to be glued to a flat table which could be raised, lowered or propelled sideways by hand-operated gearing. Beyond each end of the table, and a little to one side, were depicted bipod supports with Tuscan capitals and astragals (a Brunel trade mark). A knife, reciprocating along rails between these columns, would cut a thin veneer from the top of the slab when the table was moved sideways.

At this stage the results achieved by Brunel's industry and resourcefulness since reaching England already made an impressive list. There were the block machines—one day he would be rewarded for the work he had done—and there was the further prospect of selling blocks to the merchant marine. The stave-cutting saw might transform cask-making. The great circular saw, which had been proved at Portsmouth, might make a fortune for a sawmill owner. And lastly there was the veneer machine, which promised to produce raw material for hat-box and furniture makers at a fraction of the then current cost.

His objective was to derive an income from these inventions, and probably as the result of an introduction by Maudslay, he formed a partnership with one Farthing, to whom he wrote in October, commending a sawmill site at Battersea 'four hundred and seventy-six feet along the river and contiguous to two turnpike roads ... [whence] the bridge will always be a clean walk to Chelsea market'.

There were difficulties. The executors of the late owner did not wish to part with the river frontage, and on 5 November 1806 Brunel wrote again to Farthing suggesting that they should obtain permission to cut a canal through the ground 'where the sluice now is, and to extend it between the old lady's ground and Watson's premises ...'.

After suffering the inevitable legal delays, and contemplating the purchase of some land at Vauxhall owned by Lord Spencer, the Battersea site was bought; but the transaction, and the corresponding discussion regarding the most profitable machinery for the proposed sawmill, involved Brunel in voluminous correspondence with Farthing and with Maudslay, which did not end until the following spring.

It is clear that Brunel contributed the patents and ideas, and Farthing the cash. The financier scrutinised his partner's schemes most carefully, particularly one for making blocks for merchant ships, which was vigorously canvassed after some East India Company Directors had visited Portsmouth in November 1806. 'They have made the most favourable report of the work produced in it' (the block-mill), wrote Brunel to Maudslay, and he expressed his readiness to sell two-thirds of the block machine patent, providing the purchaser would invest £16,000 in a factory. But at the end of the letter there was a cryptic reference to Farthing, 'whose confidence in the new scheme is once more shaken'—evidently by a machine's teething troubles—for he had written to Brunel and recounted 'many fruitless and discouraging tryals on several of the principal engines [block machines] here during a space of nearly eight months'.

The idea had to be abandoned because of the pressing demands of the block-mill, but Farthing liked the circular saw and veneer machine better, and in December Maudslay was asked to quote for another circular saw and carriage 'with friction rollers for bearings and a cast iron spindle'.

Brunel was a tireless correspondent: 2 February to Farthing: 'The circular saw [at Portsmouth] does answer to the greatest perfection, both in celerity and exactness. ... I have performed several cuts of twelve feet long and nine-and-a-half inches wide in forty seconds; I hope it will still exceed this and do it in thirty seconds.' And the following day: 'Do hurry Maudslay about the great circular saw. We ought soon to determine on what terms we are to enter for the sale of such saws. I imagine that the five-foot-six-inch diameter will be more saleable than the other.' Again, two days later: 'The veneer engine cannot be put up at Battersea before the 23rd of March—yet I am desirous of trying it by hand with two or more cutters ... .' (A reference to projected experiments with knives of different lengths.)

On 9 February he cautioned his partner to be particular about the steel for 20 circular saws ordered from Maudslay. 'I should have sent drawings and directions for the connecting apparatus at Battersea if I had not been prevented by the illness of my dear little Sophia.' Three days later he reported that the great saw at Portsmouth had ripped a 13-inch-square baulk into half-inch planks at the rate of 12 feet a minute, and the following day Maudslay was sent directions for making three more saws and carriages.

In March 1807 both the Board of Revision for the Merchant Marine and the Admiralty were sent letters singing the praises of circular saws: 'I do not hesitate to say that the price actually paid for sawing will be reduced from three shillings per hundred [feet] to sixpence.' Circular saws could rip timber for cask staves—a plan which had 'the approbation of the Master Cooper of the Victualling Yard at Deptford'. Should the Admiralty decide to establish circular saws and sawmills at dockyards it would 'be necessary for me to prepare drawings and estimates'.

Although there was no immediate response to these approaches, Brunel continued to keep Farthing informed of developments and we find him writing a few days later, 'the new veneer cutter exceeds my expectations', and he added that he had cut veneers from one eighth to one inch in thickness during trials at Portsmouth.

The first batch of timber sent to the new Battersea mill for conversion was full of nails and gravel, but the lessons were soon learned, and the partners prospered, thanks largely to Farthing's prudent management. At first they converted timber, cut veneers and sold saws. Later, as Brunel's fame spread, they received commissions to engineer improvements to primitive sawmills up and down the country.

The early difficulties at Portsmouth had been ironed out by the time the Battersea mill started work, so Brunel sought a more convenient residence, and in the summer of 1807, brought his darling Sophie and young family to a fine house, 4 Lindsey Row, Chelsea. This stately terrace of seven dwellings had been formed by subdividing Lindsey House, one of the 'village of palaces' which here adorned the river's northern bank. Built by Sir Theodore Mayerne, James I's physician, and rebuilt by Charles II's Lord Great Chamberlain, Lord Lindsey, the house had lofty and spacious rooms whose pleasing proportions survived the subdivision. Next to the Brunels lived the novelist Anne Manning, who wrote of her neighbours,

> There was always something intellectual going on in their home. The two Miss Brunels had just left school, and I looked on them as models of everything young ladies should be, and thought myself blessed indeed when Ellen, the pretty housemaid, used to come in with 'Miss Brunel's love, and would you like to walk with them to Lavender Hill? Or would you take your drawing in for an hour or two?'

In front of the house were steps leading down to the river, and here Isambard learned to swim, for at that time the Thames at Chelsea was a wholesome river, and a pleasant one to travel on when there were friends to visit. The boy's first memories were of this riverside home, and when he grew older he revelled in the parties with which the Row's residents celebrated birthdays and the New Year. There were too, he noticed, many famous visitors to his father's house.

Understandably, Brunel was not loved by the numerous body of sawyers, who complained that the Government had encouraged a foreigner's 'expensive, strap-breaking, crank-breaking, machines'. Nor was Samuel Taylor one of his growing band of admirers; indeed, on 5 January 1808, we find Brunel writing to Goodrich scouting Taylor's allegation that the Portsmouth block-mills could not meet the Navy's needs. After referring to painstaking investigations, he concluded:

> I do not hesitate to state that the woodmill is now, and has been since the 1st November last ... if properly supported with all materials ... capable of making all the blocks and other articles of the blockmaker's contract—except those which have already been pointed out to you—so as to supply the whole of His Majesty's Navy.

In 1808 130,000 blocks were produced at Portsmouth and the claim was certainly justified. Unfortunately for Brunel the Navy Board's accountants seized upon it. If his work was done then his allowance must cease, they decided. And cease it did—despite continuing calls upon his time—of which their chiefs were repeatedly reminded.

As always, the accountants were victorious, and the final quarter's allowance, paid on 21 May 1808, was reduced to £110 5s. because of a never-before-heard-of deduction of £50 for 'income tax'.

Brunel revolutionised the industry with his combinations of powered saws. Richard Beamish, writing some fifty years later, dwelt on the perfection of the circular saws and the speed with which veneers were produced. 'To these important economic advantages to the public was added,' he continued,

> the high gratification to Brunel himself of being able to employ children[*] in the manufactory. The love of the young was a distinguishing and abiding feature in Brunel's character; and now, after a few hours' instruction and one day's practice, he had the happiness to reflect, that for a large number of these special objects of his sympathy he had provided the means of earning an honest and sufficient livelihood.

Napoleon had not been idle during the five years preceding the Brunel's move to Chelsea. On 11 September 1802, less than five months after concluding the Peace of Amiens, the French army invaded Piedmont and entered Switzerland the following month.

On 11 May 1803 Britain declared war and resumed her blockade of France. Napoleon seized Hanover a fortnight later and then began concentrating an army along the French shore of the English Channel. And there, in their homeland, the French troops remained for two years and two months, while spies and diplomats sought inexpensive victories.

Britain had been financing the Duc d'Enghein, a Bourbon prince living in Germany, who was planning a coup to overthrow Napoleon. On 21 March

---

[*] The Health and Morals of Apprentices Act of 1802 forbade the employment of children under the age of nine, and limited their hours of work to twelve out of twenty-four.

1804, while visiting France, the Duc was captured and, soon after, tried and executed.

During April William Pitt became Britain's Prime Minister again and Russia became Britain's ally once more when Tsar Alexander declared war on France. Napoleon proclaimed himself Emperor of France during May and began planning a splendid December coronation. On 9 August 1805 Austria declared war on France and the Third Alliance of Britain, Russia and Austria was formally proclaimed. But at the end of the year, following Napoleon's coronation, Spain became France's ally when her King declared war on Britain.

On 27 August 1805 a re-invigorated and re-equipped Grande Armée marched east and crossed the Rhine. The Austrian General Karl Mack misread Napoleon's intentions and concentrated his forces at Ulm, where the Lech joins the Danube. After being surrounded, he was forced to surrender and nearly 30,000 of his men were taken prisoner.

Napoleon entered Vienna on 14 November and early in December achieved what he later considered to be his greatest victory at the battle of Austerlitz. The Russian army withdrew into Poland after this battle, while the Austrians, who secured a truce, ceded Venetia, Dalmatia and Istria to Napoleon's Kingdom of Italy and subsequently accorded royal status to his allies, the principalities of Würtenberg, Baden and Bavaria—to the last of which the Tyrol and Vorarlberg were ceded when the Treaty of Pressburg was concluded on 26 December.

The invincible Grande Armée's eagerness for battle during 1805 was matched by the French and Spanish fleets' anxiety to avoid it. However, at 6 a.m. on Saturday 9 October, fearful of being replaced by another admiral, Villeneuve, with 33 capital ships of the combined navies of France and Spain, crept out of Cadiz intent on entering the Mediterranean. But their departure was noted. 'How would your heart beat for me, dearest Jane,' wrote Edward Codrington, captain of the *Orion* 'did you but know we are under every stitch of sail we can set, steering for the enemy?' The battle of Trafalgar began on 21 October just before noon. Within four hours 15 enemy ships had surrendered, many of the remainder had been disabled and their combined fleet had ceased to exist as a fighting force. Nelson and his band of brothers had won their greatest victory; but Nelson was dying,

Three months later, on 23 January 1806, William Pitt died and was succeeded as Prime Minister by Lord Grenville. On 1 April, perhaps appropriately, Napoleon crowned his older brother Joseph 'King of Naples' and on 20 June honoured Louis, his younger brother, with the crown of Holland. Three weeks after these pleasantries, he proclaimed the Confederation of the Rhine—a collection of client principalities which included Bavaria—and demanded territory from Prussia.

King Frederick William III responded with a 'retract-or-fight' ultimatum which Napoleon ignored.

The subsequent Prussian mobilisation marked the beginning of the Fourth Alliance of Britain, Russia, Sweden and Prussia and on 7 October, almost a year after the battle of Trafalgar, the Prussian army moved into Saxony. The armies of Prussia's allies were far away, however, and King Frederick William's army, which had deployed along too long a front, was decisively defeated on 14 October at the battle of Jena-Auerstadt, and one year and six days after the battle of Trafalgar, the Grande Armée entered Berlin.

During the winter two powerful Russian armies commanded by Levin Bennigsen and Friedrich Buxhöwden moved into Poland and threatened the Grande Armée, which was handicapped by supply difficulties that only the capture of Danzig could resolve. After the bloody battle of Eylau on 8 February 1807, the combatants withdrew and regrouped while the ultimately successful siege of Danzig began. On 14 June, the hard-fought two-day battle of Friedland ended with a French victory and on 7 July, on a barge on the river Nieman, Napoleon and Tsar Alexander concluded the Treaty of Tilsit, which reduced Prussia to the status of a client state, stripped her of one third of her territory and marked the beginning of an alliance between Russia and France with the Tsar agreeing to cease trading with Britain.

This treaty, which marked the high point of Napoleon's career of conquest, was preceded by a peaceful event—the succession of Lord Grenville by the Duke of Portland as Britain's Prime Minister—and followed by a second Royal Navy strike at Copenhagen which was invested by 18,000 troops on 16 August as a prelude to a bombardment by 20 warships which began five days later on 2 September 1807. The Danes surrendered their substantial fleet and Napoleon's plan to seize it was pre-empted.

The French ban on continental ports trading with Britain was, at best, a leaky bucket. Britain, Europe's workshop, needed food for her town-dwellers and raw materials for her factories which she could pay for by exporting manufactured products, including arms. The ban did not curtail trade with Sweden, Denmark, most other Baltic countries and Portugal. Increasing quantities of Russian oak for planking warships flowed into Chatham's dockyard and there was a considerable trade, even with Spain, whose fleet had been sacrificed to the alliance with France and which lacked the means—and, perhaps, the will—to defend her long coastline.

Napoleon pressed the Spanish King to grant free passage across Spain to a French army commanded by Marshal Junot which would attack Portugal and seal her ports. Next, 'to protect Junot's long supply line' he dispatched General Murat with another, larger army which occupied strategic fortresses in central and northern Spain before entering Madrid in March 1808. He then forced the Spanish royal family to abdicate, crowning in their place his older brother Joseph—previously King of Naples.

The actions, which did not endear him to the Spaniards, resulted in an uprising in Madrid on 2 May, which was forcibly suppressed by Murat who was rewarded with Joseph's used Neapolitan crown. But the insurrection spread and a French force of 18,000 men, marching towards Cadiz, was attacked at Bailén on 20 July and forced to capitulate. Europe was stunned and King Joseph fled from Madrid to a safe haven north of the river Ebro.

On 1 August Sir Arthur Wellesly—hereafter called Wellington—landed in Portugal with an army of 15,000 men. He defeated Junot at Viniero three weeks later but was recalled to England to attend a court of enquiry investigating a decision by others to transport French prisoners back to France. During his absence General Sir John Moore deputised as commander in Spain.

Although the strength of French forces in Spain increased by 150,000 during the summer, because of the insurrection their prospects deteriorated. In November, having persuaded Tsar Alexander to restrain Austria, which had become threatening, Napoleon assumed control of all French forces in Spain—more than 250,000 men. Having defeated the Spanish army—save for a few scattered units in the south—he arrived in Madrid early in December and, on the 20th, moved against Moore who withdrew fighting to Corunna whence the Royal Navy evacuated his army—but not General Moore, who was killed on 16 January 1809.

THE NAVY BOARD PAYS UP

The three years, 1808, 1809 and 1810, were a time of ceaseless and original endeavour, but we cannot look back on any single achievement and say, as we could of the block machines, 'this was a milestone'. The period is interesting for a personal reason. The letters which Brunel wrote about his work and aspirations reveal his character and show us what drove him on—and it is at once apparent that money-making was not the mainspring of his efforts; indeed it bored him.

In the sense that his inventive ability had been acknowledged, and his patents accepted by a financier as solid capital, he had become rich. He was the dominant partner in the prospering Battersea Mill. He knew that the sum eventually awarded for the block machines would be substantial—indeed, if expressed in mid-20th-century money values, it was to exceed Whittle's award for the jet engine. Yet, in the multitude of letters which were sufficiently important to justify a retained copy, there is scarcely a reference to the day-to-day business of money-making. Brunel gave the fruits of invention to Farthing, in the same way that the young Winston Churchill gave the fruits of authorship to his stockbroker saying, 'Fatten my sheep.'

He referred to money either to acquaint a prospective client with the advantage of, say, circular saws or, more often, to plead for payment; and in these cases one senses that, mingling with righteous indignation at tardiness, or small-minded prevarication, there was more than a modicum of irritation that his time should be wasted when there were more interesting and worthwhile matters to think about.

Money-making was a boring necessity but inventing was delightful, and he crowned the development of the circular saw with another patent specification filed in March 1808. The preamble was succinct—thin boards should be cut 'with as little waste as appears practicable. In order to obtain that end, a saw requires to possess two essential qualities, viz. a very thin edge, and at the same time, a great degree of steadiness.'

The saw illustrated was ten feet in diameter, made from a single piece of steel, and fastened to a spoked, cast-iron wheel which became thinner as its circumference was approached. The face of this great saw was flat, and its back was a shallow cone, from which a newly cut board could easily be prised clear. The 'drag' or timber carriage was power driven and ran above the level of the saw's drive shaft in the modern manner. It could also be moved sideways so there was no need to move the saw 'collaterally'.

Ten-foot saws made from a single piece of steel, and timber carriages with lateral adjustment, were developments which Brunel did not exploit outside the Battersea mill for several years, but the patent accurately forecast the shape of saws to come, and prompts the question—where did Brunel acquire the basic knowledge for inventions that transformed Fox and Taylor's primitive circular saw into the machine we know today? An explanation is suggested by a letter which he wrote to James Borthwick in January 1810; but before considering it, a few words are needed to introduce this worthy Scot.

Borthwick was a sawmiller who assiduously planned alterations to the family mill at Leith, with a view to gaining the greatest profit from the available water power. Other mill-owners sought Brunel's advice, and considered the engineer's propositions, but Borthwick was no transient, fleeting figure. A trickle of letters in 1806 had become a steady stream by 1811, and accompanied by his friend Moncrieff, Borthwick visited the Brunels at Portsea before their move to Lindsey Row.

Everything that Brunel developed, Borthwick considered—including, of course, the veneer machine. In March 1808 Brunel wrote, and after apologising for not having sent samples of veneer earlier, mentioned that the machine had cut over 50,000 square feet of mahogany and could then work without an attendant. 'I have never met with so much trouble in one single machine,' he continued; 'all obstacles seem, however, to be removed, excepting those which proceed from want of trade, which appears to be severely felt here.'

The Scot's reply contained further questions and a firm decision to modernise, and it is in his response to this letter that Brunel hints at the source of the saw technology. 'Now that it is your intention to set aside the whole of your old works to be replaced by others on an improved principle; whether my terms meet with your approbation or not, I cannot too strongly recommend you to be very cautious in the selection of the means you are about to adopt.' British elm and oak were irregular in shape, and he warned against installing saws that were supposed to deal with all types of timber: 'The apparatus is likely to be too heavy in some instances and too light in others.' Full use should be made of the available water power:

> It is not enough that logs should be brought near the carriage by the assistance of machinery. I have introduced the use of a windlass of a new construction which saves all labour in the disposition of the logs on the carriages.
>
> In the act of sawing in common sawmills much time is lost for want of proper means of regulating the speed of the carriages. With you in particular,

whose moving power is limited, the water should not be wasted without having obtained from it all the effect it is capable of, and when the saw is sharp, or resistance decreases, progressive motion should be proportionate. As to the sawing and polishing of marble, *I am already acquainted with that sort of mill having erected one in America.** I have seen the mill you mention at Derby and one at Liverpool. I think the old mill which was at work about nine years ago at the former place, ran on a better principal than the new one you have seen.

The confidence you place in me makes me regret that the distance which separates us is so great, the more particularly so as I am at present engaged in the settlement of my affairs with Government, and also, in extending my concern here in the way of cutting veneers, which I have accomplished by means of circular saws of nine feet in diameter in the most perfect manner and with very little waste of wood.

As to the terms on which I could agree to furnish you with plans for a mill, on the scale you have projected, I could not do it for less than two hundred and fifty pounds including the journey, and one hundred pounds without it.

I have lately been called upon for giving plans for a very extensive sawmill for Government [Woolwich] for cutting British timber particularly elm.

Mrs Brunel joins me in kind remembrances.

Within a week Borthwick enquired about stave-cutting saws, but the remark regarding the American marble mill is interesting, because there is good reason to believe that the use of power saws was already well established in the USA. Another letter, which Brunel wrote in September 1808, to the Board of Ordnance requesting a £100 fee for drawings for a sawmill at Woolwich Arsenal, included this significant paragraph.

Although I cannot claim the merit of original invention in sawmills, I would beg leave to observe that the sawmills such as those used on the Continent or in America are confined to uniform work and entirely to deals. They could not be used with any degree of advantage in the service of His Majesty's Carriage Department for wheels in which elm, ash and oak timber, varying in its length, are indiscriminately used, to be converted into scantlings of different dimensions. ...

The author's suspicion that power saws were already established in America, and that the circular saw was not Walter Taylor's invention, but a seaborne idea, was reinforced by this recently published letter.[†]

... The earliest boat timbers were cut from thin trees with two-man pit saws, and from these, clinker boats, like the old Viking boats, were made. When

* My italics.
† R.D. Leakey, *Yachting Monthly*, October 1966, the writer is the distributor of the dory boat which, in 1966, was rowed across the Atlantic by two enterprising soldiers.

the circular power saw was invented in Germany in the fourteenth century, wide timbers could be cut. By bending three timbers, one above the other, round the pointed floorboard of a dory floor, the double-ended dory shape is produced. ... It is said that the reason why dories never took on in England is because the old pit saw men rioted against the introduction of the circular saw, which delayed their use in this country. So there were no wide timbers to make dories. But dories were made wherever the circular saw was used, particularly on the American continent, and they were used by the Portuguese for long-line fishing on the Newfoundland Banks, because they could be carried across the Atlantic one inside another on the decks of a schooner. ...

Subsequently Mr Leakey was good enough to confirm the American source of his information* and even if we question the date given for the German invention, or doubt whether Luddite sawyers delayed progress in Britain, it still seems certain that water-powered circular saws were ripping wide deal planks in the United States before Marc Brunel arrived there. Almost certainly the circular saw and its timber carriage was another of the cargo of 'great ideas' with which he sailed from New York.

The 'settlement of his affairs with Government' had become a pressing concern. In a letter of November 1808 to a Mr Poole of the Navy Board, he pointed out that ten months had elapsed since the block mills had been pronounced capable of supplying all the Navy's needs; '... an imperious duty, the duty of a father whose anxiety is for the welfare of a young family, prompts me to reiterate my solicitations, and at the same time to represent to their Lordships the uncertain and unsettled state I am left in ...'

The Navy Board replied that Brunel should himself prepare an itemised estimate of the economies resulting from a year's working of the block machines. Since the price of all materials except iron had risen sharply during the previous decade, it was necessary to compare the cost of machine-made blocks with the cost of imaginary blocks made by contractors from raw materials at the then current price. When Brunel asked what prices had been paid to contractors for earlier hand-made blocks the Navy Board remained dumb, and they were equally reticent regarding raw-material prices. Brunel had to enquire in high places before the information was vouchsafed.

The whole business was most distasteful and, since a settlement was not yet in sight, Brunel requested that his allowance be restored. This the Navy Board promptly declined, and their negative rejoinder provoked a further letter on 20 January 1809. After observing that between 1797 and 1801 the Navy had consumed 100,000 blocks worth £24,000 annually, Brunel turned to his work at Portsmouth:

* *The National and Maine Coast Fisherman.*

> In consequence of the increase of the Navy I have, after the work was already very forward, found it necessary to give such a disposition to the buildings and the machinery so as to enable it [the block-mill] to supply a much greater proportion of work than was at first calculated.
>
> Instead of increasing the number of engines in order to obtain that desirable end, I have added several material improvements ...

He pointed out that delays and rising labour rates had inflated the cost of the machines, which in 1809 produced 150,000 blocks, worth, at then current prices, £54,000. He had spent over £2,000 of his savings and much time to produce models of machines—whereas an officer employed in an engineering capacity would have drawn on public funds. He had sought a substitute for costly lignum vitae, and conducted experiments with 107 species of tropical wood: 'On the 14th of October, being at Portsmouth, and being informed that the Portuguese ship of war from South America was alongside the jetty, I went on board to collect some specimens of the Brazil wood.'

He enclosed a statement of the expenses incurred since the termination of his allowance, observing that if the Navy Board could not pay him, he would be obliged if they would transmit it to the Lords Commissioners of the Admiralty, 'and kindly beg them at the same time to inform me if my services are in any way further required'. Although payments 'on account' were authorised, his allowance was again rejected, his request for raw material prices was again ignored, and the costings he eventually submitted were disputed. Eventually, after endless letter writing and argument, in March 1810, he sent in the final itemised claim—but a letter written later that month to Borthwick and Company, who were now at last on the move, reveals how the long wrangle had hamstrung his work.

> You may perhaps already imagine that I have made little progress with your plans, it is with great regret I find a considerable portion of my time still taken up in the settlement of my business with Government to the very great detriment of my private concerns, and although the public is now deriving a saving of above £16,000 a year, I am still unrewarded. The business is, however, to be brought to some determination in the course of the next week at the Navy Board, and from them it is to be referred to the Admiralty where I have every reason to expect it will not lay long, my absence at such a period might make a difference of several thousand pounds to me, yet as I have undertaken your concern you may rely as soon as the plans are ready no time shall be lost on my part before I commence the journey [to Leith].

The Scot's long-delayed decision had come at a doubly inconvenient time, for Maudslay was moving to larger premises in Westminster Bridge Road. 'Never,' wrote Brunel to Borthwick three months later, 'was there a complication of controlling circumstances more unfavourable both for your concern and my own. To add to all this, I have been engaged in a settlement of my public accounts which have undergone a third investigation.'

Shafting for Borthwick was made by Fenton, Murray and Wood of Leeds, but only after Farthing had been despatched thither as a resident spur; Bryan Donkin, of paper-making machinery fame, made a water-wheel; but it was at Maudslay's new works that the bulk of the machinery was eventually constructed.

In June, despite the continuing absence of his partner, Brunel journeyed to Leith; but when he returned he found that the contractors had made little progress with the plant. Moreover, his 'affairs with Government' were still unsettled.

Now Borthwick, who had taken five years to make up his mind, became impatient with the delays and the absence of firm promises from his engineer. 'I cannot put up much longer with your procrastination,' he wrote in August, to which Brunel could only reply,

> If you think you could obtain the result in a speedier way by applying to others, I am willing to give you the drawings and models for buildings without making any charge for them, nor for my journey ... You have only to make up your mind. For in everything I undertake I consider my credit of much more consequence than the pecuniary advantage likely to be derived. In the meantime I will attend to the work as before.

But a fair wind was coming. The following day he noted, with evident relief, the receipt of the outstanding balance of the £17,093 18s. 4d. which he had at last been awarded 'in full compensation of my invention of manufacturing blocks ... The Lords of the Admiralty have further ordered a sum of a thousand pounds (for models)' which he promptly but fruitlessly pointed out was £221 10s. below cost.

Borthwick relented. At the beginning of October his friend Moncrieff called on Brunel again, and by 24 November the engineer could write,

> The whole of the apparatus requisite to give motion to the sawmill is now complete, and would have been forwarded had the Berwick smack been capable of taking it; their hatchways are too small to admit a twelve-foot wheel and rings of the water-wheel in their hold. A vessel is expected every day from Leith, which they call a Company vessel, and she will be able to take the whole, which amounts to about six tons.

Throughout the winter parcels of machinery were shipped to Leith, and the following April Brunel despatched thither a millwright named Brown to install the circular saws, frame saws and their attendant shafting on two floors of Borthwick's mill. Brown was paid four guineas a week (including all extra time and travelling charges) and we may imagine Brunel's relief as the job neared completion; for Borthwick's questioning continued. 'Would the saws cut crooked timbers for boat knees?' 'No,' replied Brunel. 'Would the frame saws rip Norwegian timber?' 'Yes,' the engineer replied, '... the smallest frame, which is calculated for Norway baulks particularly, is capable of despatching five thousand baulks in the course of the year providing you slab your boards afterwards by running the edges with two small circular saws.'

The early months of 1811 were a busy and rewarding time. The Navy Board had paid up; Borthwick's business neared conclusion and, as if to prove that good things come in threes, the Board of Ordnance pulled from their pigeonhole his plans for the Gun Carriage Department of Woolwich Arsenal. They ordered a 20 hp Murray and Wood beam engine, two wrought-iron boilers—'with fire apparatus ... (the whole on the most improved construction)', and four reciprocating frame saws, through which the logs would be propelled mechanically.* This was a sophisticated and valuable plant which eventually earned its designer £4,500.

At last, after the years of struggle and disappointment, the harvest was coming in.

* This seems the most probable plant, although one drawing shows six frame saws, and circular saws were mentioned in correspondence.

9

BOOTS FOR THE ARMY

B runel seized upon and developed ideas more quickly than fellow mortals could execute them, and invariably immersed himself in a new endeavour before an earlier work had fructified. Two years before the millwright Brown travelled to Leith, an incident occurred which started Brunel along a new road, and although he would embark on other schemes before he reached this journey's end, we must go back to its beginning because his work affected the course of history.

In February 1809 Brunel visited the woodmill, and found Portsmouth bedecked with welcoming flags for the survivors of Corunna. He hurried to the docks and watched the disembarkation.

What he saw was to trouble him deeply. There were wounded—the inevitable victims of war—but much of the suffering was needless. The men were unshod. They dragged themselves along the quay on lacerated, festering, rag-bandaged feet.

Brunel's enquiries led him to conclude that as many casualties had resulted from faulty boots as from enemy action; but an annual expenditure of £150,000 on footwear seemed to absolve the Army from a charge of blind economy.

Soldiers complained of boots that broke up on the first day's march. Why? He obtained a few pairs, cut them up, and at once their defects were revealed. Between thin outer and inner soles was a filling of clay. The boots were heavy, but their substance dissolved in the first puddle.

Here, Brunel perceived, was a splendid opportunity for mechanical production. If ships' blocks could be machine-made to an unvarying standard of precision and quality, then so could boots. Again he pondered the manufacture of the separate components before mentally assembling them—this was the habit of thought that had brought him to England—but boot manufacture was different from blockmaking. The components were easily made, it was their assembly that raised problems. His personal attitude had also changed since 1802 when Bentham nodded his approval of the model block machines.

Seven years had passed, but the Navy Board had not yet paid him. The Board of Ordnance had just shelved his plans for Woolwich Arsenal. He had three young children. This time, he decided, manufacture should be a private venture, like the 'Battersea concern'—as he called the busy sawmill—and he made his plans accordingly.

This decision deprives us of the carefully husbanded records which illuminate his Government work; but the patent specification entitled *Shoes and Boots* which he filed on 2 August 1810 shows how the invention took shape. First, thick leather would be compressed in a clamp and then, with a common knife, cut to the shape of the clamp's horizontal jaws, which served as a template for the outer sole. On the table-height baseplate of the principal machine, there would be a collapsible last which could be rotated and slid bodily for a limited distance. The thin inner sole of the boot would be laid on top of this last, the upper leather secured around it by means of special clamps, and the previously cut heavy outer sole then pressed into place, thus sandwiching the edge of the upper leather between the outer edges of the two soles.

Next a peripheral row of holes would be punched through this sandwich by an awl protruding from the flat end of a vertical reciprocating rod. The operator would place a nail in each newly punched hole, and this would be driven home and clenched against the inner last by the next stroke of the treadle-driven rod.

When all the nails were driven, the last would be collapsed and the boot removed and finished off by hand.

Brunel and Farthing set up their factory on a site near the Battersea mill and employed 24 disabled soldiers to operate a series of machines which produced good, strong boots and shoes in nine sizes.

A pair of common shoes were sold for 9s. 6d., water-boots for half-a-guinea, half-boots for 12s., 'superior' shoes for 16s., and Wellington boots (for this was a name to conjure with) for 20s. a pair.

Brunel's foresight, and attention to apparently trifling design details, again paid off. His machines made disabled soldiers more productive than craftsmen and the footwear found a ready market. Even the Army authorities made a few cautious purchases.

Soon influential visitors to the 'Battersea concern' found their tour extended to include the new shoe factory, and by the time they left, they had become salesmen for Brunel's ideas. Lord Castlereagh, in particular, sang the praises of 'Brunel boots', and in 1812, when Foreign Secretary, persuaded the inventor to expand production so as to satisfy all Army requirements. This was done, and output increased to 400 pairs of boots and shoes per day.

A subsequent patent filed on 12 March 1814 which describes a *New Method of Giving Additional Durability to Certain Descriptions of Leather*—meaning sole leather—confirms that Brunel's interest in making boots did not flag. It would have been surprising if it had. All of Europe was marching and it would be difficult to name another product for which demand seemed so certain to continue to increase.

On 8 February 1809, following a Crown Council decision, Austria declared war on France and mobilised. An army commanded by Field Marshal Archduke Charles invaded Bavaria on 10 April, but after suffering several defeats, withdrew to the east of Vienna which Napoleon entered on 13 May. Then followed the battles of Aspern Essling, at Wagram at which the Grande Armée was repulsed, and Raab and Wagram at which the Austrian army was defeated having suffered and inflicted very heavy casualties.

On 14 October 1809 the Peace of Schönbrunn marked the end of Napoleon's eastern campaign. Austria paid compensation and ceded its Illyrian province to France, ceded Salzburg to Bavaria and parts of Galicia to the Grand Duchy of Warsaw and to Russia.

But Napoleon had another—relatively minor but still distracting—war on his hands. At the end of April Wellington had returned to Portugal with a reinforced army. On 12 May he surprised and defeated General Soult at Oporto thus clearing the French from almost all of Portugal. At the end of July, having marched into Spain, he fought a successful defensive battle at Talavera, south west of Madrid before returning to Portugal where construction of the impregnable lines of Torres Vedras, between the coast and the Tagus estuary north of Lisbon, had begun.

In London, meanwhile, Spencer Percival—a lawyer—became Prime Minister but his term of office was destined to end abruptly on 11 May 1812, when he was succeeded by Robert Banks Jenkinson, later Lord Liverpool, who served until February 1827.

The French command in Spain was reorganised during April 1810. General Soult retained command of the 'Army of the South' but on the 17th Marshal André Massena was given command of the 'Army of Portugal'. After taking the frontier fortresses of Ciudad Rodrigo and Almeida, Massena attacked Wellington's army at Bussaco Ridge, a strong defensive position. Wellington repulsed several assaults but, in danger of being outflanked, withdrew to the lines of Torres Vedras which his rearguard entered on 10 October. Massena could not penetrate these defences and in March of the following year withdrew with a hungry army that had lost 25,000 men.

Wellington followed deliberately, fighting over the frontier fortresses of Cuidad Rodrigo and Almeida and fighting another successful battle at Fuentes de Oñoro. Further south General Beresford fought Soult's 'Army of the South' at Albufera before retreating towards Seville after inflicting and suffering heavy casualties.

Once again Wellington withdrew to Portugal for the closing months of 1811, while Napoleon, who had occupied Holland during 1810, prepared to invade Russia. On 8 January 1812, encouraged by the eastward withdrawal of French units, Wellington surrounded Ciudad Rodrigo which was stormed 11 days later. He then stormed Badajos before advancing into Spain early in April and separating the 'Army of Portugal', with its new commander Marshal Auguste Marmont, from Soult's Army of the South.

Wellington's and Marmont's armies subsequently confronted each other near Salamanca, but believing the arrival of French reinforcements was imminent, Wellington prepared to withdraw whereupon Marmont made an outflanking move—to cut off Wellington's retreat—but, in doing so, over-extended his left wing which Wellington destroyed, inflicting 14,000 casualties. This very successful defensive battle opened the road to Madrid, which Wellington entered on 13 August—King Joseph, much frightened, had already fled to a northern sanctuary.

The French abandoned southern Spain and Wellington besieged Burgos, a strategic road junction, making four unsuccessful attempts to storm its citadel. Then, threatened again by French reinforcements, he evacuated Madrid and on 19 November withdrew to Ciudad Rodrigo for the winter.

10

THE CHINESE ENCHANTER'S CAR

Having noted the timely birth of the modern footwear industry, and Napoleon's weakening hold on Spain, we must again go back five years and return to the plant which Brunel designed and installed in the Royal Arsenal, for it marked the beginning of a period of frame-saw development and the burgeoning of mechanical handling.

The saws, which reciprocated between graceful, Tuscan, cast-iron columns, were arranged in a line across the centre of the shop. They were driven by connecting rods actuated by crankshafts in the basement, each of which was belt-driven from the main driveshaft.

The logs, supported in notched chocks, were drawn over the stout, smooth timber floor, through which the frame-saws reciprocated and cut them into planks. The steam engine did more than power the saws and propel the timber; it turned windlasses on the floor which drew in logs from the yard outside, and other windlasses near the ceiling which lifted away the newly cut boards.

In his first saw patent, Brunel had mentioned the possibility of mounting a number of circular saws on a common shaft, so as to cut a log into several planks in one pass. This idea was abandoned, but at Woolwich each reciprocating frame carried a number of saws, and, although these were slower cutting than the circular variety, their power requirement was less, and they were easily adjustable to produce boards of differing thicknesses—an important consideration as irregularly shaped hardwood logs were being converted.

Although later in date than Borthwick's, the Woolwich mill, being near to home, was the first in which Brunel could regularly observe his frame-saws at work. The windlasses, as he had predicted to Borthwick, certainly 'saved all labour in the disposition of the logs' within the mill, but there remained a formidable timber handling problem outside. Brunel knew from experience that in shipyards this problem was immense, and he knew from Lord Spencer that it was a matter of concern to the Admiralty—particularly at Chatham.

In 1807 Bentham's office of Inspector-General of Naval Works had been abolished, probably as a sop to the Navy Board, but Bentham had subsequently been appointed a Commissioner of the Navy, and in this capacity continued to innovate and modernise the practice of shipbuilding. Our wealden oak forests had been depleted long before Trafalgar, and although English oak was still preferred for framing warships, imported timber, particularly oak from the forests of southern Russia, was used for planking. Two thousand oak trees, each one hundred years of age or more, went into every new 74-gun ship, and it is not surprising that the efficient use of this ever more costly material became Benthain's chief preoccupation. At Chatham he planned a lighted cover over a slipway so that construction might proceed in dry conditions which were comfortable for the shipwrights, and beneficial for the timber; for he had already introduced a thorough timber-seasoning regime.

Newly sawn planks were stacked in stick* for two or more years, depending on their thickness, and then removed to new timber sheds from which the shipwrights were supplied. In the long run, this sensible procedure resulted in more accurate construction and more durable ships, but, in the short run, enormous quantities of oak were needed to fill the seasoning yards and at the same time provide for the shipwrights' day-to-day needs. By 1810 12,000 tons of Russian oak were being landed annually at Chatham Dockyard.

Handling and converting this great mass of timber was a subject near to Brunel's heart. He estimated that the cost of dragging it around the Chatham yard with horses exceeded £4,000 a year, and it was all sawn by hand. He formulated plans, which he pressed upon members of the Government and the Admiralty. 'The imperfection of the various mechanical contrivances ...' he wrote,

> led me to direct my views to the invention of such machinery as should be the means of obviating these difficulties, and I foresaw that the field would be open to me of rendering service to the naval establishments of the Kingdom of a magnitude much exceeding that which had been derived from my improved system of making blocks.

Again Bentham was beset with difficulties, and again Brunel was striving to overcome them. Eventually, in January 1812, Brunel received an official request from the Admiralty for plans embracing a log-handling and sawmilling plant for Chatham Dockyard. By this time he had decided how to transport the timber, and it is probable that his preliminary drawings depicted frame-saws resembling those at Woolwich. However, the saws that were later installed almost certainly incorporated improvements described in two patent

---

* Stacked horizontally, to lose moisture, with an air gap of about 20mm formed by transversely placed sticks between each plank.

specifications, both entitled *Certain Improvements in Saw Mills*, which he filed in January 1812 and January 1813.*

The earlier specification proposed using a form of screw adjuster to tension saw blades within their frame instead of wedges and nuts, and then described a device for sharpening the saw blades accurately. The second patent developed this saw-sharpening theme, and proposed improved and stiffer saw frames; but the most notable innovation was a subtle mechanism for imparting an oscillating motion to the frames; their descent—the cutting stroke—remained unchanged, but before ascending they would move backwards, and so the saws would rise with greatly reduced friction.

That Brunel's revolutionary proposals for Chatham were accepted within eight months is a measure of his standing at this time, and he at once engaged two assistants, one named Bacon, and the other a former curate named Ellacombe, to supervise construction by the Royal Engineers' labour force, which consisted, in the main, of French prisoners-of-war.

The building which he designed comprised a pitch-roofed sawing hall with two open sides—supported by the customary columns—which was flanked by three-storey wings. The western wing housed two boilers and a beam steam engine, and the eastern wing supported a large iron water tank beneath its roof. The wings, though iron-framed, were in the best Regency style; the centre hall had a Moorish aspect; and the building adorned a site between the old and new dockyard walls on a low chalk hill overlooking the Medway.

In front of the water tank wing, an oval, masonry-lined shaft, measuring 92 feet by 72 feet, was driven downwards some 60 feet into the chalk. From its base a tunnel was dug towards the South Mast Pond—a lagoon linked to the Medway. The tunnel was driven 400 feet, and then became a cutting or canal for 150 feet more before reaching the lagoon.

The completed cut and tunnel formed a waterway through which logs could be floated from the Medway to the base of the shaft in front of the sawmill. The good taste of Brunel's architecture, and the boldness of his civil engineering, were matched by the ingenuity of his mechanised timber handling.

---

* An earlier patent specification, which Brunel filed in October 1810 on behalf of 'a certain foreigner residing abroad, has not been mentioned. It described a 'Machine for Obtaining Motive Power'. Air was to be forced into a vessel containing cold water by an Archimedes screw within a tube. The bubbles would be trapped by an inverted funnel and carried by a pipe to the bottom of an open-topped vessel heated by a fire. The inverted buckets of a water wheel, which dipped into this great cauldron, would trap the hot ascending air, and thus the wheel would be made to turn. It was claimed that the hot water in the boiler would cause the air to 'become greatly enlarged in its dimensions' and therefore 'the mechanical force imparted to the water wheel' would be greater than the power absorbed by the Archimedes screw. Brunel's later work was to reveal a profound understanding of heat and mechanics, and it is surprising that he consented to be godfather to this natural child of the steam engine and the water wheel.

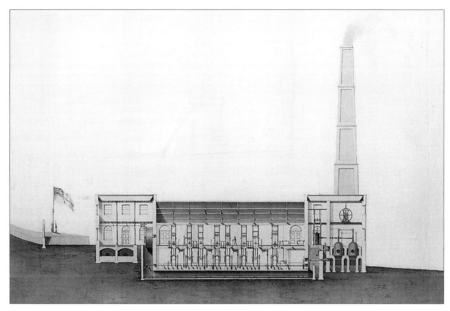

The Chatham Woodmill. A tinted drawing by Brunel.

An open topped iron tank hung by two chains above the oval shaft. The chains passed over pulleys and then descended to a cradle submerged in the water below the shaft's base. When a cargo of logs—up to 60 feet in length—had been floated onto the cradle, the hanging tank would be filled with water from the tank in the sawing hall's eastern wing, thus becoming a counterpoise which raised the log-laden cradle above the top of the shaft.

A pair of rails were supported sleeper-fashion, by transverse brick walls of varying heights, so that they descended the hill in front of the sawing hall at a constant rate in a northerly direction for 860 feet. A rope-hauled crane travelled on this railway which was flanked by stacking areas or 'berths' for logs and, lower down the hill, by seasoning berths for planks.

The crane driver could collect logs from the cradle and place them in a stacking berth. He could then pick up a dry log from another berth and place it in a flat car which would be winched up one of five sidings to the sawing hall's floor in front of a saw frame. When the log had been 'converted', its planks, again on a flat car, would be lifted away by the crane and placed in a seasoning berth.

Eight vertical saw frames, each with up to 30 saw blades (depending on the plank thickness required) formed a line across the sawing hall and reciprocated through its floor at a rate of 80 strokes per minute. The tension of the blades was adjustable and the frames oscillated so that the saws cut while descending and then rose freely. The logs, guided by chocks, were hauled through the saws by windlass-powered ropes.

There were two circular saws in the hall, which trimmed sawn planks to the widths required; machines for making oars; and devices for tilting baulks of timber so that frame saws could produce weatherboards with thick and thin edges.

Besides driving the saws and their attendant windlasses, the sawmill's steam engine pumped water into the high tank, which supplied the counterpoise, winched flat cars into the saw-mill and provided power which enabled the travelling crane's driver to position the crane and perform all the out-of-doors timber handling operations that were needed.

Charles Dickens, whose childhood was punctuated by periods of distress, has left a word-picture of some happy moments at Chatham:

> ... but for a whisper in the air suggestive of sawdust shavings, the oar-making and saws of many movements might be miles away. Down below here, is the great reservoir of water ... Above it, on a tram road supported by pillars, is a Chinese Enchanter's Car, which fishes the logs up and rolls smoothly away with them to stack them. When I was a child (the Yard being then familiar to me) I used to think that I should like to play at Chinese Enchanter, and to have that apparatus placed at my disposal.*

'It was,' Brunel observed, 'a case of untried combinations being brought to act in unison and harmony.'

But the Navy Board struck a characteristically discordant note, for, after acknowledging Ellacombe's exemplary services, they dismissed him for reasons of economy. 'May you, my good friend,' wrote an enraged Brunel, 'be as great an ornament to the Church as you have been in that most arduous career in which you leave your very sincere friend, with one of his lights out.' However, Bacon saw it through and remained in charge of the plant for many years.

Fifty years ago there was still something to see at Chatham; the building and its splendid chimney were well preserved, although the sawing hall was a store and the boiler house a laundry. Parts of the saw frames remained (bearing the imprint 'J. McDowall and Sons, Johnstone') and outside several of the transverse walls which had supported the rope railway still stood, with the square iron bars—which secured the rails to longitudinal battens—pointing heavenwards. Great Western enthusiasts should note that Marc Brunel, not Isambard, originated the broad gauge—these iron bars were exactly seven feet apart.

---

* *The Uncommercial Traveller*

II

THE REGENT

———◦•◦———

The year 1812 was the high point of Marc's early career. The Portsmouth blockmills were the Navy's pride. The Battersea concern produced a golden harvest. On highways and by-ways of England and the Peninsula marching infantry slowly but surely wore out their machine-made boots; and mules drew field-guns whose sturdy limbers were made from timber converted in the new mill at the Woolwich Royal Arsenal. Blocks, veneers, boots and gun-carriages were the engineer's children. Brunel was their father, mother and nurse, and their sterling services redounded to his credit. Now, on a hill overlooking the Medway at Chatham, another brainchild was growing up.

Professional satisfaction was matched by domestic contentment. 'Darling Sophie' ruled the home, and his family was happy and healthy, though Emma was not a strong girl.

In the evening, when not travelling or busy at his drawing-board, he would visit friends, taking Sophie with him when possible, or there would be a dinner party at home. Good talk—shop or otherwise—delighted him, and although Beamish says, 'All he seemed to desire was leave to work out the conceptions of his mind in the quiet of his study; his drawing board before him,' yet he was an adventurous talker and his gift for prompt and pointed reply—heavily accented, it is true—seemed the mental counterpart of a physical agility which was often attributed to 'double joints'. The society of cultivated and elegant women gratified him, and once, while engrossed in an after-dinner conversation, he fondly caressed a lady's hand; but Sophie, knowing he believed it to be hers, understood his absent-mindedness.

A love of music, combined with a keen ear, resulted in many commissions to buy harps and pianos for French and American friends; and even amongst that surprisingly numerous and most impractical body of inventors, to which he was a magnet, he retained a reputation for courteous accessibility.

This, then, was Brunel—artist, mathematician, inventor, engineer, a fountain of enthusiasm, a man who revelled in conversation, enjoyed good food, upheld the rule of law, and was a devoted husband and father, though caring little for 'religionists' and not at all for money-making.

Probably his hours at home were his happiest. All children pleased him, but Isambard, his 'gifted and precocious little son', was his favourite. Marc romped with him, explained that drawing was the engineer's alphabet, drew perfect freehand circles (whose centres he indicated precisely) and found the boy a ready pupil. The construction of a cart-wheel was explained to Isambard, and he was told how perfectly it was suited to its purpose; and then his mother would come into the nursery to tell stories about her uncle Thomas Mudge who had invented the lever escapement before becoming the King's watchmaker. At the age of eight, when he started at a nearby day school run by the Reverend Weedon Butler, Isambard had mastered Euclid and after a short period at this school, where he revealed exceptional mathematical and artistic gifts, he transferred to Doctor Morell's boarding school at Hove.

Isambard had all his father's early attributes, and his father was delighted; but Sophie seems to have been a little disturbed by his inclinations—perhaps she foresaw the heartaches that could come in the wake of great ideas—for by 1813 there was already a small cloud in the sky.

Farthing had withdrawn from the 'Battersea concern'—probably because he had made enough money to live comfortably and no longer wished to be harnessed to whatever whirligig Brunel might add to the sawmill and the shoe factory. Whatever Farthing's reasons—and relations between the ex-partners remained cordial—the shrewd and trustworthy associate had gone, and the commercial management of the enterprise was in new hands. Sophie, knowing Marc's distaste for commerce, hoped the new partner would prove reliable. The business was the family's main support—the mill alone yielded a profit of about £8,000 a year from an annual turnover of about £11,000—but she knew that slow-growing plants could wither quickly, and at any time Marc might spend prodigally to develop some new invention.

During 1813 Brunel was fully occupied with the Chatham installation, but inevitably his thoughts turned to new fields—this time to steam engines and their applications. A stimulus was provided the following year by an order received from the Duc de la Rochefoucauld for a steam engine for the Conservatoire des Arts et des Métiers in Paris. Unhappily the transaction proved long-winded, and ended in an unhappy wrangle about payment, but Brunel seized upon the weight-saving and power-gain possible with steam engines of the double-acting type, and had one manufactured (probably by Maudslay), which was installed in a specially constructed mail boat, *Regent*. The vessel was built to ply between London and Margate, and there was great excitement among the younger Brunels, who assembled on a pier below London Bridge to wave to their father as the new paddle steamer bore him away on her maiden run. It was a great success, although the landlord of the *York Hotel* at Margate took a gloomy view of the new-fangled ship and refused Brunel a room.

Perceiving that steam-powered tugs could tow men-o'-war from harbour and provide them with an offing despite unfavourable winds and tides, and confident that the naval advantages must be self-evident, Brunel presented the idea to the Admiralty but the battle of Trafalgar and the subsequent action at Copenhagen had ended France's naval threat and the Navy Board soon replied '... their Lordships feel it their bounden duty to discourage the employment of steam vessels as they consider the introduction of steam is calculated to strike a fatal blow at the naval superiority of the Empire'.

The era of 'paddles churning river-wrack to muddy greens and browns' had not dawned. Only *Regent*'s regular passage-making pointed the way and it was not until June 1822 that Brunel filed one of his most significant patent specifications describing Marine Steam Engines.

Napoleon, by contrast, had pressed on and on 24 June 1812 had led the Grande Armée out of the Duchy of Warsaw and over the river Nieman to invade Russia. Six hundred thousand men, including reserves and line-of-communication troops, crossed the bridge, and fewer than half of them were French. The central force comprised three 'armies'. One Napoleon commanded directly, one was commanded by Eugène de Beauharnais, his stepson, and the third was commanded by his younger brother Jerome. The force's left flank was shielded by General Alexandre MacDonald's corps and its right flank by Prince Schwarzenberg's Austrian auxiliary corps.

Napoleon planned to encircle and destroy the Russian armies one at a time, but the Russians withdrew too quickly and the hot June was followed by five days of heavy rain which made dirt roads impassable for horse-drawn supply wagons. Then, because of a communication failure, Jerome quit his command and returned to his kingdom of Westphalia. It was not an auspicious beginning.

The Russians fell back in good order to Smolensk on the Dnieper—roughly halfway to Moscow. The three-day battle for the city, which ended on 19 August, cost Napoleon 10,000 casualties and reduced his effective fighting force to 130,000 men. He pressed on to Borodino, a village 65 miles from Moscow, where Prince Kutuzov's army confronted him on 7 September in a well-fortified position. Its central redoubt was stormed after a day's fighting at a cost of 30,000 casualties—but the Russians slipped away to Kaluga.

Seven days later, with 95,000 men, Napoleon entered the largely deserted city of Moscow and stayed there for five weeks. The long and terrible march back began on 19 October. Napoleon had planned to withdraw along a more southerly route but an indecisive attack by Kutuzov five days later at Maloyaroslavets induced him to retrace his steps.

Bitter weather weakened his undisciplined, loot-laden army and, when the first snow fell early in November, guns and wagons were abandoned while starving soldiers, foraging for food, were killed by Russian peasants and by Cossacks. Nearly half the men who had entered Moscow failed to reach Smolensk, but the collapse of discipline ruled out a pause and Marshal Ney's shielding rearguard forced the army to march on.

On 17 November the shadowing Kutuzov struck again at Krasnoi, 25 miles beyond Smolensk, but was repulsed by Ney's old guard. Five days later, the Russian army of Moldova captured Napoleon's supply depots at Minsk and seized the only bridge over the flooding Beresina river. Kutuzov joined up with this army and the French were encircled. Napoleon ordered Marshal Oudinot to re-take the bridge with his advance corps. Oudinot failed but fought the Russians for four days and distracted their attention from French engineers building two wooden bridges across the icy river 11 miles further upstream. By 29 November, when these bridges were destroyed by the engineers, 35,000 men had crossed the Beresina, but 50,000 who died or were captured did not cross.

Napoleon left his army and made for Paris on 5 December, and nine days later Marshal Ney, 'the bravest of the brave', was among the last French soldiers to recross the Nieman bridge and leave Russia.

The political fallout from this disastrous campaign began five days earlier at Vilna where well-stocked food depots were looted by starving troops. Fearing a Russian attack, Marshal Murat abandoned his rearguard and marched his main force to Kovno and thence through Poland and East Prussia—decamping on 11 January 1813 to his kingdom of Naples where he signed alliances with Austria and Denmark.

On 30 December General Johann Yorck, commander of the Prussian Auxiliary corps, signed the Convention of Tauroggen thus releasing his force from Prussia's alliance with France and inducing Frederik William, his king, to flee Berlin with its French garrison. The King concluded an alliance with Russia two months later.

On 30 January 1813 Prince Schwarzenberg was ordered to extricate his Austrian Auxiliary Corps, which had lost 11,000 men. He duly signed a convention granting it neutral status pending the Habsburg Empire's accession to the alliance against France on 26 June.

On 3 March Prince Bernadotte of Sweden concluded an alliance with Britain. Two months later elements of the Swedish army landed in Pomerania.

On 4 March the Russians entered Berlin and 13 days later Prussia formally declared war on France.

British money and arms influenced these events, but the decisive catalyst was distrust of Napoleon. At 44, however, he could not be idle. France and the territories she still controlled could be made to yield enough conscripts to nourish an army of 600,000 men. And nourished the Grande Armée was. Its resurrection during the spring of 1813—following its near destruction and the subsequent defections—must surely be reckoned Napoleon's most extraordinary achievement.

The Grande Armée fought eight battles against the alliance in the course of that year—achieving four victories, accepting one draw and suffering three defeats. This was an outstanding performance against an alliance that could field 800,000 men, after Austria's accession, but it was not sufficient. The penultimate four-day October 'Battle of the Nations' at Leipzig—the greatest battle of the Napoleonic wars—was a disaster. Seventy thousand men retreated across the Rhine with Napoleon at its close, but 120,000 others did not reach the western bank.

Inexorably the tide flowed towards the setting sun, bringing the front line nearer and nearer to France. And, to make matters worse, there was the annoying distraction in Spain. On 21 May 1813 Wellington had once again advanced into Spain causing King Joseph, with 50,000 men, to hasten to a defensive position at Vitoria which Wellington outflanked on 21 June, after a hard fight, routing the King's army and capturing his treasure.

Command in Spain was then given to Soult, who assembled a force in France and crossed the western Pyrenees to reinforce San Sebastian and Pamplona, both of which Wellington invested, capturing San Sebastian on 31 August and Pamplona during the second half of October. On 11 November Wellington attacked Soult's force, which had withdrawn across the river Nivelle, and after breaking through its line advanced into France.

But Blücher's Prussians and Schwarzenberg's Austrians were much nearer to Paris and the city would fall to them.

12

THE NEVA BRIDGE

———◦·◦·◦———

The early months of 1814 were full of promise for Brunel. His work at Chatham was nearly finished and there would be time for family outings—even, perhaps, for a day in Lord Spencer's library. He had been blessed with several new and fascinating ideas to weigh and perhaps develop. And there were a few interesting official and professional engagements.

On 15 January he had the unusual pleasure of speaking French with Tsar Alexander who was being given a glimpse of the Royal Navy while touring Portsmouth, its dockyard and block-making factory. The Tsar expressed his admiration for Brunel's achievements and, just before he departed, placed on his finger a gold ring, embellished with a large ruby encircled with diamonds. Marc could not have foreseen how reassuring this token would be.

Two months later he was elected a Fellow of the Royal Society. Then, at the end of the first week of April, there was good news from France. Napoleon had abdicated, and the way had at last been cleared for Louis XVIII to receive his crown.

The year's closing months were less reassuring. During the early evening of Tuesday 30 August 1814, a destructive fire occurred at Bank Side in the City. Many business houses were razed, and the surface of the Thames was covered with a film of burning oil which ignited moored coal barges.

By some evil chance, at half-past ten that very night, when the puny fire-engines were almost all committed to the Bank Side conflagration, an observer at Chelsea espied another blaze at the Battersea Mill. *The Times* correspondent reported that the observer

> immediately directed the watchman to give the alarm at Mr Brunel's. Mr B., being at Chatham on public service, his servant was sent to Battersea, but before assistance could be obtained, the fire had made such progress as to threaten entire destruction. Two fire-engines, one from Mr Noble's and one from Chelsea, were the only ones that came; all others being detained at the fire at Bank Side; but for want of water, the tide being quite low, the right wing of the building and the steam engine was all the could be saved. The greatest exertions were made to save the stock of wood and veneers, and this object was effected at the risk of the lives of those who strenuously exerted themselves upon the occasion.

'Thus,' commented the correspondent of the *Gentleman's Magazine*:

> in two hours, these most valuable machines, which, in point of execution and perfection, exceeded everything we know, and which have been visited by some of the most illustrious characters in Europe, presented the awful sight of a heap of fragments; the fruits of six years of exertion and ingenuity, attended with an expense of about £20,000. were destroyed.

Brunel was not dismayed. A good part of his £20,000 had been spent on machines like the 'Veneer Engine', which were subsequently abandoned. Here was an opportunity to rebuild the mill with yet more perfect machinery. Probably he was insured against fire, but he could not have hoped to recoup the loss entirely, to say nothing of the consequential loss of business. He called for his bank statement and, to his dismay, found a balance of £865. The previous October it had stood at £10,000. Now the loss of Farthing was keenly felt.

A third daughter, Harriet,* was born to Sophie during the month following the fire. Brunel had every reason to bestir himself, and during 1815 divided his time between Battersea and Chatham; and there is little doubt that he was paid for his work at the dockyard before the year ended. He had earned £4,500 for designing and installing the earlier Woolwich plant, and we may suppose that he received £10-15,000 for this more extensive and sophisticated installation. This, and whatever fire insurance compensation he received, was the capital he had to work with.

During the first week of March 1815 there was startling news from France. Napoleon had escaped from Elba and landed at Cannes with 1,100 men and four guns. It is doubtful if Napoleon was aware of Marc Brunel's activities but Marc, his senior by 14 weeks, was aware of Napoleon and must have been alarmed and fascinated by the brilliance of his collapsing career.

All the troops sent to oppose Napoleon's march to Paris defected to him and on 20 March, when he reached the capital without a shot being fired, he had acquired a considerable force which was greeted with cheers.

His return resulted in the exile of King Louis and prompted the allies at the Conference of Vienna to resolve their differences. The Seventh Coalition was proclaimed and the allies pledged an army of 700,000 men dedicated to Napoleon's overthrow. Peace, which Napoleon had claimed to want, was not an option.

Displaying undiminished energy, Napoleon assembled an army comprising five army corps, a cavalry reserve, the Imperial Guard and 358 pieces of artillery. Pitted against this force were three allied armies. One under

---

* The hair of another child (initials SB), who died in infancy, is preserved in a locket. Probably Harriet was Sophie's fifth child.

Schwarzenberg was marching from Austria while, two, under Blücher and Wellington, were already in Belgium.

The three-day battle of Waterloo began in the morning of 16 June when Napoleon attacked Blücher at Ligny while Ney, with the army's second corps, tried to take the strategic crossroads at Quatre Bras from the British. Neither attack succeeded but at 8 p.m., following an attack by Napoleon's Imperial Guard, the Prussians withdrew under cover of darkness, having lost 16,000 men.

This indecisive victory was Napoleon's last. Late the following morning, having received from Blücher a promise of support with two corps, Wellington fell back northward 12 miles to the ridge of Mont St Jean, a strong defensive position with two fortified areas—the chateau de Hougoument on the right and the farm La Hay-Sainte to the left of the ridge's centre.

The following day, having decided that this position could not be outflanked, Napoleon launched a series of frontal assaults, none of which was successful, although Wellington's cavalry suffered heavy losses. A final attack by the Old Guard, led by Ney personally, also failed and the French army started to disintegrate as the Prussians joined the British. The combined armies then advanced and Napoleon left the field for Paris. He abdicated on 22 June and was taken by a British warship to exile in St Helena, where he spent the remaining 14 years of his life.

Louis XVIII returned to the French throne in Paris and in London, on 23 October, Marc and Sophie's little daughter Harriet died.

Although the army was rapidly disbanded following Wellington's victory at Waterloo, the Government urged Brunel to continue boot production on the former scale, and he unwisely agreed to do so without firm orders. By the time he called a halt the following autumn, £5,000 worth of footwear lay on the shelves, and this stock had to be sold off to pay for new equipment for the sawmill. A loss-making clearance sale was Brunel's reward for his contribution to the victory.

The Battersea mill was rebuilt and re-equipped, and in 1816 it started up again. Visitors thought they glimpsed a new and wonderful epoch.

'I beheld the planks of mahogany and rosewood sawed into veneers the sixteenth of an inch thick, with a precision and grandeur of action which was really sublime,' wrote Sir Richard Phillips. 'The same power at once turned these tremendous saws, and drew their work upon them.'

All Brunel needed was a shrewd and steadfast partner to control the enterprise, for he was busy with new schemes.

The first of these was a Tricoteur or Knitting Machine, an invention which, the patent specification of March 1816 tells us, was communicated to him by a 'certain foreigner residing abroad'—a friend in France. At the base of the machine there was to be a horizontal spoked wheel, which had a series of closely spaced needles, 'similar at their ends to those used in the common stocking or weaving loom', radiating from its rim. A vertical spindle arising from the wheel's hub would support a second slightly smaller, rotating, wheel. This upper wheel would carry a bobbin, and one or more sets of four arms which, by means of small wheels at their extremities, would manipulate the woollen strand around the hooked radial needles of the lower wheel, thus forming cylindrical knitting suitable for stocking-making. A machine was built and found to be efficient but, because of the low cost of Lancashire cotton goods, knitted woollen hose proved unsaleable and no profit flowed from the idea.

The following year, in his capacity of engineer to an English company tendering for works to supply Paris with pure water, Brunel took his family to France. The scheme was supported by Louis XVIII, who looked upon the engineer as 'a good Frenchman lost',* but the city's water porters were united in opposing the project which eventually foundered despite royal support.

When their French ship slipped out of Calais and set course for England Brunel could not have known the disappointing outcome; indeed, as they cleared the land, and the violence of the south-west gale became apparent, all thoughts of steam engines and waterworks deserted him.

Clearly the ship must bear away and run before the wind. But despite tumultuous seas, panic-stricken passengers, and Brunel's representations, the captain held his course. The crew, seeing his folly, grew sullen and refused his orders, and it seemed that the wave-lashed ship must founder, when a passenger hit upon a decisive argument. He offered the captain a bribe to hand over his command. This was readily accepted, and Brunel sailed the vessel safely into Deal.

An enquiry awaited him on his return home. It was for a bridge to cross the Neva at St Petersburg, and bore the seal of his admirer, Tsar Alexander.

The difficulties, which became increasingly apparent as details were received, attracted Brunel to this project more even than his client's royal status. The Neva's width exceeded 800 feet at the chosen spot, and to this engineering challenge was added the problem of communication, for although French was appropriate for correspondence with the Russian Government, the bridge-builders would use their native tongue—and this Brunel could not speak. But the greatest obstacle was presented by the climate. In winter the Neva is covered with a thick sheet of ice, and no work is possible between its banks.

---

* While in France, according to Lady Noble, Brunel made an unsuccessful attempt to sell his stock of boots to the French Government.

Because a suspension bridge could not then be built with a sufficient span, and because building a masonry bridge would be a labour of several seasons, Brunel considered a tunnel. It would need to be longer and more capacious than the subterranean canal at Chatham, but instead of chalk, he would have to mine soft, alluvial strata, compressed only by the river's weight. Reluctantly, despite the nagging pull of half-formed ideas, he abandoned this solution.

The plan which he eventually submitted through Prince Lieven, the Tsar's ambassador, was for a bridge with a clear span of 880 feet. The huge arch, resembling that of Sydney Harbour Bridge, and more than half as long*would rest on massive abutments on either bank, and carry a suspended roadway across the stream. Because the Neva was an important waterway, the centre section of the roadway would open, Tower Bridge-fashion, to provide a passage for ships, whose tall masts would pass below the soaring arch. Only a visionary could have designed such a bridge a century and a half ago—but the building plan was as daring as the conception. The bridge would be timber. The great arch would be prefabricated and then floated onto its abutments with the aid of four pontoons.

In this way, more than forty years later, Isambard would erect the arched tube girders for his bridge across the Tamar which carries the railway into Cornwall.

Visions rarely butter parsnips. Child-labourers made the Lancashire cotton kings safe from competition by the Tricoteur. Paris water porters defeated Louis XVIII's scheme for a piped supply, and Russia's treasurers spiked the plans for the Neva bridge. It was a bad time for Brunel, for profits from the shoe factory and the mill at Battersea were disappointing, and he asked Sansom, a city banker friend, to investigate. Sansom was aghast at the commercial confusion which he found.

'It was,' he reported, 'a most extraordinary jumble which you have certainly not understood, and I should have wondered if you had. I should hardly have been more surprised than I am if one of your saws had walked to town.'

What a sorry state of affairs! What had happened, in five brief years, to the splendid success of 1812?

It is easy to point to the remedy. The mill and the shoe factory were viable. All Brunel had to do was to ensure their prudent management. If he had devoted three months to their commercial well-being, and to finding a dependable partner or manager, and if he had eschewed inventions that consumed his treasure, he could have faced the future without anxiety.

---

* The arch of Sydney Harbour Bridge has a span of 1,650 feet.

But he could no more engross himself with ledger entries or credit ratings than an accounts clerk could design a bridge or found an industry. His ability to concentrate his energy and attention exclusively on work in hand—and a 15-hour working day was often divided amongst three or more separate projects—was in this respect a disability. Commercial administration he excluded completely from his thoughts, and only when affairs went desperately awry did he grudgingly allot two or three hours to looking at the Battersea books.

Already he was maturing new schemes; sometimes at Chatham he would be engrossed for an hour by a mollusc, which he minutely examined through his magnifying glass. On Sundays, with his family, he liked to visit Barge House, Lambeth, the home of his good friend, Ben Hawes—an enthusiast with whom it was delightful to discuss novel ideas. Isambard too looked forward to these visits, for the younger son, William, was the favoured friend to whom boyhood's most daring exploits could be confided; while Benjamin, William's elder brother, was an understanding if slightly remote hero, six years his senior.

Later, long after Isambard had adopted Barge House as his second home, Benjamin would represent the new Borough of Lambeth in Parliament, launch the Fine Arts Commission and, later still, become an Under Secretary of State for War and send a hospital Isambard designed to Florence Nightingale.

But it was Sophia, the elder daughter, who most eagerly accompanied her parents to Lambeth on Sundays, for Benjamin was her sweetheart.

13

'THE MISFORTUNE'

———◆·✦·◆———

The family was growing up. 'I have passed Sallust* some time,' wrote Isambard from his school at Hove, 'but I am sorry to say I did not read all, as Doctor Morell wished me, to get into another class. I am at present reading Terence and Horace.

> I like Horace very much, but not as much as Virgil. As to what I am about, I have been making half a dozen boats lately, till I have worn my hands to pieces. I have also taken a plan of Hove, which is a very amusing job. I should be much obliged if you would ask Papa (I hope he is quite well and hearty) whether he would lend me his long measure. It is a long eighty-foot tape; he will know what I mean. I will take care of it, for I want to make a more exact plan, though this is pretty exact, I think. I have been drawing a little. I intend to take a view of *all* (about five) the principal houses in that great town, Hove. I have already taken one or two.

There was an almost uncanny resemblance between Isambard and his father in boyhood. Both had common interests and enthusiasms. Both had large heads, nimble hands, small, lithe bodies, and quick wits. The bilingual Isambard spoke English without accent, but his olive complexion and dark eyes betrayed his French ancestry.

Richard Beamish described later how his chief reacted prophetically to a drawing of Navier's first suspension bridge across the Seine. 'You would not venture, I think, on that bridge unless you would wish to have a dive.' And on another occasion, as they walked past a new warehouse at Deptford, Brunel tugged at his sleeve, exclaiming, 'Come along, come along; don't you see, don't you see? ... it will fall!' And that night it fell.

Isambard inherited this seemingly intuitive ability to gauge forces. 'That will fall,' he told his schoolmates, noting a gathering storm and the faulty construction of a partly-built house. Next morning only rubble marked the building's place; but Isambard's commercial instincts were acuter than his father's. He laid a wager on the collapse.

While the boy studied, his father invented. He foresaw the development

---

* Gaius Sallustius Crispus, a Roman historian (86-34 BC) who accompanied Caesar during his African war and became governor of Numidia.

of decorative packaging, and in December 1818 filed a patent specification describing *A New Species of Tin Foil, capable of being Crystallized in Large, Varied, and Beautiful Crystallization*. He noted in the preamble that tin's naturally crystalline appearance was destroyed when it was made into foil for the looking-glass trade, but if the foil were melted, it would, on cooling, regain its crystalline surface. He therefore proposed first that the foil should be heated to just below its melting point by being laid in a smooth, flat tray which floated in a bath of molten alloy. Then it would be liquefied by heating its surface with a portable gas burner which 'renders the flame as manageable as a pencil'. After solidifying, the crystalline foil could be removed from the tray merely by blowing on its surface. The following treatment would produce the finished article:

> Take one part by measure of sulphuric acid, diluted with five parts of water. Take also one part of nitrous acid of commerce, diluted with an equal bulk of water, and keep each of the mixtures separate. Then take ten parts of the sulphuric acid, diluted in the manner before stated, and mix it with one part of the diluted nitric acid, and then apply this mixed acid to the surface of the tin foil with a soft brush or sponge, and repeat the application of the said mixed acid until the result you expect proves satisfactory. When this has been done the foil must be well washed with clean water and immediately dried. It may then be covered with a varnish or japan more or less transparent, colourless or coloured at pleasure.

With decorative tinfoil he hoped to effect his financial salvation, and he entrusted its manufacture to Shaw, the latest partner at Battersea. The pretty wrapping material became a popular novelty, and since the cost of developing the process had been comparatively modest, we may conclude that he was not unduly sanguine.

The work with molten tin led him down a fascinating new road. For centuries printers' sons had perpetuated their fathers' craft, but at this time daily newspapers were proliferating and an era of innovation had arrived. Hardly a month passed but new developments were proposed, and it is noteworthy that many came from French and German inventors. Brunel was familiar with all this. In particular he knew of König's work, and of his improved steam-driven press which *The Times* had installed in 1810, for a printer named Taylor had financed König, and Taylor's brother was a partner in the engineering firm of Taylor and Martineau in Whitecross Street with which Brunel had dealings.

But in 1820, despite the exertions of many gifted men and a considerable expenditure by their several backers, no one had successfully printed newspapers in the way that Lancashire cloth was printed—on a rotary press. Printing plates were the difficulty. Until a reliable means could be discovered of casting accurate stereotype plates from moulds carrying the impression of composed pages, the rotary newspaper press would remain a pipe-dream.

Throughout 1819 Brunel experimented at Battersea, using different mould materials. John Walter the second, son of the founder of *The Times*, took an active interest in the work, but did not consider the results an unqualified success. However, it is clear that Brunel thought they were promising, for on 25 January 1820 he filed a patent specification entitled *Certain Improvements in Making Stereotype Plates*, with the declared objective of providing a means of 'multiplying printing plates for the purpose of accelerating the printing of daily papers'.

First, type (or woodcuts) would be set up in a galley fitted with a perforated lid made from flexible steel sheet. The type would be covered with several layers of thin calico, and the inside of the lid would be coated with a paste made with water and 'pipe-clay seven parts, chalk or burnt clay pounded very fine twelve parts, and starch one part in bulk, not by weight'. By closing the lid and passing a roller over it, a series of impressions would be made in the mould material, a layer of calico being removed after each impression. When the last layer had been removed, the type would be lightly oiled and the final impression taken. The lid and mould would then be baked at a temperature below 500°F.

The mould, impression side uppermost, would next be put in an iron tray with a perforated base and, after being heated, would be charged with molten type metal. The thickness of the cast would be controlled by the tray's lid, and the metal cooled by water injected through its perforated base. After trimming and washing, the stereotype plate would be ready for the press.

As an alternative, Brunel suggested that the flexible steel plates might be disposed around a cylinder and, after being coated with mould material, rolled mechanically over galleys containing the type—impressions being obtained in the manner previously described. In this way curved stereotype plates could be produced which would be suitable for rotary presses.

Finally, almost as a postscript, he noted that perfect plates 'possessing all the qualities of a stereotype plate' could be made by coating a flexible steel sheet with shellac, and then baking it and subsequently dipping it into molten type metal. While this 'tinning' was still fluid, the plate would be pressed against a baked mould and left to cool under a press. 'The impression thus obtained is remarkably perfect. The same plate may be made to take another or successive impressions, by repeating at each time an immersion into type metal, and proceeding as stated before. This mode of obtaining stereotype plates is very expeditious and may prove of great benefit.'

The final paragraph, which seems to anticipate gravure printing, may have been a shot in the dark, for Brunel concentrated his attention on perfecting

the mould-making and casting techniques. But it must have been clear to
him that, even if he solved the problem of stereotype plate production, he
could expect little profit until the rotary press was brought to a similar state
of perfection, and this inevitably would be a slow and costly process.

While their father experimented, the younger Brunels bestirred themselves. Sophia married her Benjamin, and crossed the Thames to her new
home at Barge House. Isambard left Dr Morel's establishment, sailed for
France, and entered the college of Caen early in 1820, transferring in the
November to the Henri Quatre Lycée in Paris. There, in the following year,
he obtained what his father shrewdly judged to be the best available mathematical education.

As the year 1820 drew to its close, Brunel must have reflected that his
chickens were a long time coming home to roost. The performance of the
sawmills, the shoe factory, and the tinfoil enterprise was disappointing. (Despite
the patent, the process of manufacturing decorative tinfoil was promptly
pirated.) He had founded three industries, and had been robbed of his profit
by lax bookkeeping, bad debts and dishonesty. The idea of managing the
'Battersea concern' personally never occurred to him, but he paid increasingly
frequent visits to Sweet, his solicitor, and to Shaw's fecklessness was added
the burden of professional fees. So, since printing presses required a lengthy
period of gestation, he produced, in December 1820, from his conjurer's
hat, what he hoped would be an instant invention. To his credit, he did not
entrust this to Shaw, but persuaded his former partner, Farthing, to sell the
device, which was a portable duplicator, *A Pocket Copying Press*.

Outwardly it was a small, narrow box, with a lever along its top. When
the lever was raised, the box's top and two long sides were lifted, and a
slot appeared above its substantial wooden base. The base was hollow, and
contained a stoppered tube, within which was a thin cylinder wrapped around
with several layers of calico—all kept damp by a sponge.

To duplicate, a sheet of manuscript was laid in the slot, and on top of
the manuscript a sheet of thin transparent paper, a sheet of damp calico, and
a sheet of oiled paper, in that order. Further sheets could be added in the
same sequence, or the sheets of manuscript, calico and oiled paper could be
interleaved between blank, rice-paper pages of a book. When the device had
been loaded, the lever was pushed down and, after a series of pressures, the
writing was transferred to the blank paper.

This invention, which was manufactured by Taylor and Martineau, produced copies like the mirror images left on blotting paper, but these were
easily read from the reverse side of the thin sheets,* and the copier was well
received.

* The 'spindle' type duplicator which was still in use early in the 20th century produced similar
copies.

Early in 1821 an enquiry for a bridge to link Rouen with the island of La Croix provided further encouragement, and Brunel set to work with a good heart, for there was no better place for his work than Rouen where, as a boy, he had roamed the quays and gazed in wonder at the beam engine; where he had fought with the mob and met his Sophie; whence he had fled in the early dawn on a cantering horse.

He had scarcely despatched his plans, when he received some bitter news from nearer home. Sykes and Company, his bankers, had become insolvent and had put up their shutters. At once his normally deferential creditors grew brusque and pressing. They pressed at a bad time; Brunel's business enterprises were sickly and his printing press imperfect—only the Rouen bridge held out the hope of profit. He did not have long to wait on this account; the French authorities wrote regretting that his design could not be considered because he was not a member of the Government Corps of Engineers.

This was the *coup de grâce*. The creditors closed in, and on 18 May 1821 Marc and Sophie were arrested for debt and consigned to prison, he for the first and she for the second time.

King's Bench Prison, where they were immured, closely resembled nearby Marshalsea, which has been graphically described in *Little Dorrit;* but even in prison it is possible to make friends, and when friendship germinates in chill adversity, the bond usually endures. One stout-hearted visitor, Admiral Sir Edward Codrington—captain of the *Orion* at the battle of Trafalgar—gave his friendship, and many years later recalled the scene of his first meeting, 'the small room, in one corner of which was Brunel at a table littered with papers covered with mathematical calculations, while seated on a trestle bed in the opposite corner sat his wife mending his stockings'.

It was a time when fair-weather friends discreetly withdrew, and the mild Emma, alone at home with Ellen the housemaid, who had become almost a member of the family, must have been shocked to find herself on the brink of the half-world of paupers, from whom the well-to-do averted their eyes.

Marc was fortunate in his Sophie, in his friends, and in his intellect, which roamed beyond the confines of the cell in search of new ideas. But friends had to be circumspect, lest in offering sympathy they offended against the timeless ethos sanctifying wealth. The couple's plight was euphemistically termed 'The Misfortune', and as the months dragged by a feeling of helpless isolation grew within Brunel. 'It is now ten weeks,' he wrote to Lord Spencer, 'that I am in this cruel position. I have called to my aid all the forces of my soul; but I feel that I cannot longer support that which may compromise my name in the eyes of the world.'

He was a migrant imprisoned in a land whose people were not his own folk and, although this situation aggravated the sense of loneliness, it also kindled a flame of indignation. If the English did not want his services, others did; nor would he return, a ruined man, to his own country. He resumed the correspondence with Tsar Alexander, which had been suspended with royal expressions of regret when the Neva bridge plan had been abandoned; and by some strange and fortunate chance news of the Russian dialogue leaked out.

'No sooner,' wrote Lady Noble, 'was it rumoured that "the unfortunate Mr Brunel" was going to shake the English dust off his feet, than his friends bestirred themselves.' Now the National Interest was involved. Ben Hawes, young Benjamin—Marc's son-in-law—and Lord Spencer perceived a feeling of anxiety at the Admiralty and, when the Duke of Wellington asked the Prime Minister what his penny-pinching Chancellor of the Exchequer was doing to ensure Mr Brunel's services were retained for Britain, the embarrassment was unmistakable.

The Chancellor discreetly enquired about the prisoner's intentions.

'I must starve,' replied Brunel, 'or get employment here, or go to Russia, but if I see honourable and permanent employment here, you may be assured that I shall not be wanting in zeal, but shall devote my future services and talents to the benefit of the country.'

An influential, informed minority began to express its anxiety in public. The fabled blockmills, the boot factory and the dockyard works were recalled; and after an agonising official reappraisal, £5,000 was entrusted to Mr Bandinel, a Foreign Office official, who was instructed to place the money in his friend's hands, 'there being strong public grounds for the Government to avail themselves of Mr Brunel's extraordinary talents'.

The creditors were paid, and early in August Marc and Sophie walked out into the sunshine.

Following the liberation, he wrote to the Duke of Wellington:

My Lord Duke   August 10th, 1821
    I was very much disappointed at being deprived, through Your Grace's absence from England, of the opportunity of returning in person the thanks I owe to Your Grace for the favour shown to me by the British Government in the adjustment of my affairs, and in the consequent liberation from my confinement.
    Sensible as I may be at the happy termination, I cannot find expressions to say how much pleasure I feel at the peculiarly fortunate circumstances of having been deemed worthy of the notice and patronage of the most distinguished character of the age—a circumstance not only flattering and most honourable, but which has materially contributed in softening the gloom which so distressing a reverse would otherwise have left on my mind. The only way by which I could make a suitable acknowledgement to Your Grace is by employing my time in preparing plans for the service of the British Government.

The spirit of initiative had survived.

14

ISAMBARD AS PARTNER

———◆•••◆———

Brunel put his affairs into a better shape. Shaw was replaced by two brothers named Hollingsworth, and by one Mudge, a relation of Sophie—probably her cousin. Brunel divested himself of the boot and tinfoil enterprises, and retained only a half-share in the sawmill—the Hollingsworths gaining a substantial stake for what we may suppose was a modest investment. But, at any rate, Brunel could hope that his partners would behave responsibly. They had either bought their shareholding, like his good first partner Farthing, or were related by marriage.

In France, Isambard completed his studies at the Henri Quatre Lycée, and in the autumn of his parents' liberation, began a year's apprenticeship with Abraham Louis Breguet. This was a happy period for the youth, and he later realised that he was greatly privileged. Although the renowned Swiss watchmaker was nearing the end of his life, he took care that his young apprentice lacked no opportunity to learn his craft and improve his skill.

With memories of the prison cell fresh in her mind, it is not surprising that Sophie viewed her son's inclinations with mixed feelings. But she treasured the memory of her uncle Thomas Mudge, and when Breguet—on whose shoulders Mudge's mantle had fallen—wrote in November, 'I think it is important to cultivate with him [Isambard] the happy inventive tendencies which he owes to nature or to education and which it would be a great pity to see wasted,' she proudly accepted the career Isambard had already chosen; for, like his father, he was determined to be an engineer.

After an abortive attempt to enter the École Polytechnique, from which he was disqualified by foreign birth, Isambard returned to England on 21 August 1822 and started work in the small office which his father maintained at home. No would-be engineer could have been given a better formal education, and the three years in France had sharpened his appreciation of the arts and given him a penchant for works of grandeur. Best of all, he could call himself 'élève de Breguet'. Finding his father busy, the youth joyfully immersed himself in professional affairs, and a most effective partnership was forged between Marc, who was 53, and Isambard, who was sixteen.

Having freed him, the Government had to find work for Brunel, and in the year following his release he completed plans for a sawmill for the island of Trinidad in the West Indies. But it was work for the French Government which preoccupied him when Isambard returned. His plans for two suspension bridges for the Ile de Bourbon (now called Réunion) had been accepted and they were being constructed by the Milton Ironworks in Sheffield.

Each bridge would have two 8ft 9in teak roadways, which would be given lateral support by eight bracing chains capable of withstanding winds of hurricane force. The smaller St Suzanne river bridge would have a span of 131ft 9in, and each of its roadways would be carried by three suspension chains, which would pass over iron towers arising from stone piers on either bank. The similar bridge for the river du Mât was to have two 131ft 9in spans—one each side of a tall mid-stream iron tower.

A drawing by Brunel of the bridge to span the river du Mât in the Ile de Bourbon (now Réunion).

The Milton Ironworks proved unsatisfactory contractors, and the thankless task of supervision involved Brunel in many journeys to Yorkshire; but eventually, during the summer of 1823, the bridges were erected at Sheffield. They were then dismantled and shipped to London, where their chains were tested to the satisfaction of two French engineers. At last, with a feeling of profound relief, Brunel wrote in his diary on 29 November: '—A SHIP WITH THE BRIDGES SAILED THIS DAY FROM GRAVESEND FOR THEIR ULTIMATE DESTINATION'.

Isambard had plenty of variety in the busy office; there were plans for paddle tugs on the Rhine, plans for a cannon-boring mill for the Netherlands Government, plans for a new bridge across the Serpentine and other projects. The Dutch cannon-boring mill was built subsequently. The Rhine tugs were not, and John Rennie's design was selected for the Serpentine bridge. Along with this work, the development of a rotary press at Taylor and Martineau's premises continued—John Walter and others showing encouraging interest. Isambard was often left in charge, for at this period Brunel received frequent retainers to appear as an expert witness in patent actions, and the law is no respecter of a man's time. Brunel père also travelled about the country, when possible calling on Lord Spencer at Althorp, where he knew a welcome awaited him—although on one occasion he was refused entry because he sent in a visiting card that was not his own. At Althorp he loved to browse in the library, which contained some 35,000 volumes: 'Found in an old book on machines by Ramilly that the circular barrel for a pump was then (1588) employed, and also several other inventions, but very unsuccessful.' He would leave with commissions to procure French ducks for Lady Spencer's pond, or to introduce an expert on warmed-air central heating, for the house was cold.

Besides these affairs, and the Battersea concern, and some business resulting from the pocket copying press, Brunel found time to invent. His thoughts had returned to double-acting steam engines, and 18 months before the Bourbon bridges were finally shipped, he filed a visionary patent specification entitled *Certain Improvements on Steam Engines*. The drawings accompanying it are marvels of draughtsmanship, and clearly illustrate the developments, which were directed at marine applications. The lessons of the successful *Regent* mail boat had been well learned.

The engine was to be in the form of an inverted 'V', its crankshaft would double as a paddleshaft, and its governor would act against a spring instead of gravity and so be reliable in a rolling ship. Another notable innovation were metal piston rings, which were described probably for the first time. To eliminate the risk of a fire tube being uncovered when the ship rolled, the two boilers would be completely filled—steam being drawn off through domes and, after powering the engine, condensed for re-use. The furnaces would be fuelled by mechanical sprinkler stokers.

Bearing in mind its date, the content of this patent is remarkable. Isambard later used the inverted 'V' or, as the Brunels called it, the triangle-frame engine, to power the *Great Britain*—the first screw-propelled trans-Atlantic steamship. Still later, he referred to the specification when designing governors for the engines of the *Great Eastern*.

Father and son were kept busy; in 1823, in addition to the ventures already mentioned, there were added a swing bridge for Liverpool Docks* and, by way of contrast, work on improved treadmills. In the December Brunel moved his office to No. 29 Poultry, and thither the clerk and his son transferred. Isambard's tasks were as varied as the projects; before assisting with the patent drawings for the steam engine, he had undertaken a series of tests on governors, sprinkler stokers and condensers at Maudslay's works

---

* The Dock Committee's minutes record the receipt of Brunel's plan for a 'swing bridge for foot passengers ... to be erected over the Old Dock Cut', and the Committee resolved that preparations be made for 'Introducing the Bridge at any future convenient opportunity'. It is probable, therefore, that the bridge was built, although the minutes provide no positive confirmation.

and, six months before the office move, more experiments began.

An entry in Marc's diary of 30 May 1823 marked the birth of the new dream. 'Met Sir H. Davy who adverted to the discovery of a carbonic gas to be used as a power—which he denominates a differential power ...' He lost no time, and sensing the need for strong materials, called the same day on another old friend. 'Saw Mr Faraday upon the alloy of iron with nickel, but the metal is too expensive.'

Throughout the following decade Brunel's diary is sprinkled with cryptic references to hair-raising experiments and tests on the 'gaz engine', most of them conducted by Isambard. Thus, on 8 April 1824: 'Isambard was so far ready with the Proving Apparatus that he charged it to forty-five atmospheres; but no condensation took place notwithstanding the reduction of the temperature to ten degrees or about below freezing point. This is a very unfortunate result.'

Pressures soared yet higher and, by June of the following year, condensation had been effected and the Proving Apparatus became a Differential Engine (or Gaz Engine—the two appellations were used indiscriminately). 'June 4th ... Isambard engaged in charging the condenser of the Differential Engine; but one of the packings being crushed by the pressure—ninety-six atmospheres—it burst at once, without any injury to any other part of the apparatus. The result of this day's proceedings upon the whole satisfactory.'

A patent specification filed the following month explains how the engine was to generate power by means of liquefied gas.

> There are several [possible] gases ... some of which are treated upon by Mr Faraday in the papers read before the Royal Society of London in one thousand eight hundred and twenty-three. I give the preference to Carbonic Acid Gas. This gas, at the temperature of freezing water, requires a pressure of about thirty atmospheres to condense and retain it in the liquid state.

The power would be derived from a double-acting piston which would reciprocate within an oil-filled cylinder. Each end of this cylinder would be connected by a pipe to a pressure vessel half-filled with oil. The top of each pressure vessel would be connected by another pipe to a cylindrical liquid gas container through which a cluster of heat-exchange tubes, like miniature boiler smoke tubes, would pass. Thus the work cylinder would be flanked by two oil-containing pressure vessels, and outside these would be the two cylinders filled with liquid gas at just below its critical temperature.

When hot water was passed through the heat exchange tubes in the first liquid-gas container, and cold water through the tubes of the second, a pressure differential would arise and be transmitted hydraulically to the work cylinder, thus raising the piston. By reversing the water flows, the piston would be forced down. The piston would, presumably, be coupled to a crankshaft, from which a water-flow reversing valve could be actuated. Thus, given a hot and cold water supply, the gaz engine could provide power to drive machinery.

Brunel's faith in the gaz engine was unshakable. He was supported by Dr Faraday and Sir Humphry Davy, and even the Admiralty subscribed £200 to help with development. It proved an expensive mirage, which cost him £15,000 before it was finally abandoned; but the absence of casualties during the work is a tribute to his engineering acumen.

Only rarely did Brunel decline work, and he would accept interesting commissions that a more hard-headed engineer might have rejected as being inadequately backed. In 1824 he undertook a study for a canal across the isthmus of Panama. He designed a suspension bridge to span the Thames at Kingston, and two smaller suspension bridges for the Huddersfield Canal Company. For the Grand Surrey Canal Company he designed new coal docks called South London Docks and, for a group of financiers, new cargo docks at Bermondsey. There was a sawmill for the county of Berbice in British Guiana, and a subterranean aqueduct to supply Hampstead with Thames water from Hammersmith. Only the sawmill—a Board of Ordnance project—was built.

The following spring he collaborated with Gay-Lussac over a process for refining tallow to make candles, contemplated rope-hauled railways in France and London, and designed a diving bell crane for some adventurers who planned to salvage Spanish treasure in the Bay of Vigo. The summer saw him busy planning a canal to link Fowey Harbour with Padstow on the North Cornish coast, which would eliminate the hazards of the passage around Land's End. In the autumn he returned to bridges. He submitted proposals to the Chester Bridge Committee for a rubble version of the 200 ft span, single-arch Grosvenor Bridge across the Dee, which Thomas Harrison had planned to build in stone. And for the Duchess of Somerset he designed a graceful new three-arch bridge to carry the turnpike road across the Dart at Totnes. Despite Brunel's claim that a 'rubble' (meaning brick or stone set in mortar and reinforced with iron) bridge across the Dee would cost no more than £10,000, Harrison's bold stone design was adopted, and in 1833 the bridge was completed, on a different site nearby, at a cost of approximately £50,000. In 1826, after visiting Liverpool Docks, Brunel designed a new floating passenger embarkation pier for the port. The Dock Committee minutes are even less informative about the floating embarkation pier than about the swing bridge. However, an article in the *Liverpool Echo* of 16 July 1926 states that no floating pier was built until *circa* 1835 when 'a very small floating stage ... approached by a moveable bridge on a slip' was installed near the Princess Dock. This was undoubtedly Brunel's embarkation pier, which

Totnes Bridge.

remained in use at least until 1847, when William Cubbitt built the larger George's (floating) landing stage to designs of Joseph Simpson.

The Cornish canal proved too expensive with the new power of steam on the horizon, but the Liverpool embarkation pier was a great success, and a new bridge was built at Totnes, whose flat arches and classical proportions suggest its designer more credibly than the print in Totnes Guildhall.*

He found time in summer to snatch a few days at Brighton with Sophie, and filled his diary with notes about the tunnel at Black Rock, and the settlement of the chain pier, 'which may be considered a striking ornament to the town and, exclusive of the piles on which it is raised, a beautiful object ...'.

During the more frequent business trips, he made detours when possible to view interesting buildings. York Minster pleased him but, 'I never saw choristers so filthy,' and the toll collectors at the Berwick Bridge across the Tweed provoked a similar reaction: 'the dirtiest people that can be met with— filthy indeed!' Returning home he would take up his pen and write to the innkeeper at Euston, 'for the purpose of tracing my cloak which must have been left either there or ... at Stratford, Warwick, or Leeds'.

---

* The print bears this inscription: 'Drawn on stone by D. M. Baynes, London, from an original drawing by Mr C. Fowler, the architect'.

Dirt and disorder he hated, especially when graveyards were disfigured, and with the architect Augustus Pugin he designed a cemetery fit for good folk to rest in, which he called 'The Necropolis of London'. Children with clean faces could rely on him for a halfpenny, and their grubby brothers would be similarly rewarded if they promised to go home to mother and wash. Another abuse which roused him was the way stagehorses were driven to death, and he would angrily cite Mr Waterhouse, 'who loses a horse in every run of two hundred miles'.

How he found time to campaign for horses and cemeteries is a marvel. He kept afloat and financed his inventions only by prodigious industry. Although he received £2,500 in 1822 from the Battersea concern, the Hollingworths cheated him shamelessly, mainly by pocketing the receipts, and Mudge proved to be a soundly sleeping partner.

The tricoteur was sent back to M. Furneaux in France, but the steam engine patent promised to be as useful a source of royalty income as the several sawmill inventions, and work on the gaz engine never ceased.

'Would you like to know how many letters there are in a single page of *The Times*?' wrote Princess Lieven to Metternich.

> Two hundred and fifty thousand. I am very learned. I got that from the engineer, Brunel, inventor of *The Times* presses ... I had him to dinner yesterday. He gave me a lecture on engineering which rather bored me, and of which I remember scarcely anything. All the same, he is the cleverest man at his job.

For once, the lady, who was said to know more state secrets than the King's Ministers, was wrong. *The Times* did not install the Brunel rotary press which Taylor and Martineau had built. He had not, after all, found the perfect mould material for casting stereotype plates, and it was not until the advent, some years later, of flong, the wet papier-mâché mould material, that rotary presses became a practical proposition.

The reader may be forgiven for concluding that Brunel was working himself into his tastefully designed grave; and that succeeding generations, if they remembered him at all, would do so because of the blockmills, or the Chatham Dockyard works, or because he was the father of Isambard. Nothing could be further from the truth. By 1826 the projects which we have mentioned occupied less than half his time.

His greatest work had begun the year before. He was building a tunnel beneath the Thames.

15

'AN UNINTERRUPTED
COMMUNICATION'

In May 1798, at about the time he projected the Grand Surrey Canal, Ralph
Dodd addressed to the gentry of Kent and Essex a paper whose preamble
contained these words: 'In the course of my professional travelling, I
have observed the want of a grand, uninterrupted line of communication in
the south-east part of the Kingdom, which would easily be obtained if the
River Thames could be conveniently passed.'

Dodd's observation was timely. A highway east of London across the
Thames would expedite the Army's deployment along the Dover coast and
its potential commercial advantages increased each year.

The East and West India Docks, London Docks, and St Katharine Docks
clung to the northern shore by Wapping, whose ancient link with the sea was
still recalled by Execution Dock, where, in living memory, pirates were hanged
about the low-water mark and left swinging from the gibbets until three tides
had overflowed them. Opposite, on the southern bank, mills and warehouses
had sprung up and were nourished by a stream of carts and wagons which
plied between the docks across the stream and their gates. Their journey was
slow and tortuous. Through the narrow streets to the Tower, onwards to old
London Bridge—where a toll was collected—across the broad river, down
Tooley Street, through the labyrinth of Southwark, and into the marshlands
of Rotherhithe, their destination. By the 1820s more than 4,000 wagons,
carts and drays crossed daily over London Bridge and, during working hours,
half the southbound stream turned off down Tooley Street. Wags claimed it
cost more to carry skins across the Thames from Wapping than across the
Atlantic from Hudson Bay.

Each working day 350 watermen ferried ten passengers apiece in their
'graceful wherries' back and forth across this reach of the river. Upstream,
nearer London's heart, the footbridge at Waterloo yielded a toll revenue of
£12,000 a year. Even at the turn of the century, it was beyond dispute that a
highway for carts and foot passengers across the lower Thames would earn
an ample revenue.

Ralph Dodd had foreseen an opportunity; his handsome paper solicited support, not for a bridge—the river was too wide, and in any event could not be obstructed—but for a 900-yard-long tunnel between Gravesend and Tilbury fort.

The correspondent of the *Gentleman's Magazine* thought that

> the souterrain about to be formed between North and South Shields, near the mouth of the Tyne, seems to have suggested to Mr Dodd the notion of a like aperture beneath the Thames; and its practicability is inferred from the supposed rock of chalk which is imagined to pass under the whole bed of that river and into the marshes on either side.

A cylindrical tunnel 16 feet in diameter was proposed. It would be driven from the base of an access shaft and would accommodate a roadway 'of sufficient capacity to admit carriages passing'.* It was estimated to cost £15,995. Money was subscribed, a steam engine erected, and a shaft dug to a depth, according to one account, of 146 feet; but the chalk proved elusive and, when funds neared exhaustion, a fire in the engine house brought the venture to an end.

Dodd had failed. His estimate of the cost of the tunnel and its shaft seems wildly optimistic but, if thirty or forty feet down, he had found the 'rock of chalk that was imagined to pass under the whole bed of the river', he might have succeeded. The Wylan Colliery driftway below the Tyne, the Whitehaven offshore colliery workings, and the Cornish tin mine galleries off St Just were all hewn through rock. He knew that a tunnel through clay, silt or gravel must be crushed by the river's weight. There was no chalk, so he abandoned the attempt to dig the highway.

Indeed, at that time there was but one example of a tunnel having been driven successfully through a river's soft bed; but, as a contemporary translation of Diodorus the Sicilian's account reveals, the building plan had limited applications.

> In the low ground of Babylon, Semiramis [a legendary Assyrian queen of great beauty, who, after succeeding her husband Ninus, builder of Nineveh, founded Babylon and other cities in the seventh century BC] sunk a square pond, thirty-five feet deep, each side being three hundred stadia in length [34 miles square], and the banks whereof were lined with bricks well cemented with bitumen. She then turned into it the water of the Euphrates. Across the channel of the river, thus made dry, she then made a passage in the nature of a vault from one pass to the other. The arch was built ... of firm and strong bricks, plastered all over on both sides with bitumen. The walls supporting the arch were twenty bricks in thickness, and twelve feet high from the floor to the springing of the arch, and the breadth of the passage was fifteen feet.

* Very small carriages.

This work was finished in two hundred and sixty days, and the river was turned into its ancient channel; so that Semiramis could go privately from one palace to the other, under the river. She made also two brazen gates at each end of the vault, which continued to the time of the Kings of Persia, the successors of Sirus (from Samuel Ware, *A Design for a Public Road from the Tower Under and Across the Thames, 1827*).

Semiramis's scheme would have cost more than the gentry of Kent and Essex would have cared to subscribe, and Dodd made no more plans to molest the Thames; but in 1802 Robert Vazie, an intrepid Cornish mine engineer nicknamed 'The Mole', circulated proposals for a shorter tunnel between Rotherhithe and Limehouse.

Being nearer London Bridge, Vazie's plan did not offer a short cut between Kent and Essex, but for every country squire's coach and four there were a dozen city merchants' drays, and his proposal attracted greater support than had Dodd's earlier project. Eventually, in 1805, the Thames Archway Company—for such was the grand title the promoters assumed—was empowered by Act of Parliament to build a tunnel according to Vazie's design.

The most surprising feature of this enterprise was the failure of the engineer to give a credible explanation of how the tunnel proper would be built. First he proposed building a shaft near Lavender Lane, Rotherhithe, which would be 330 feet back from the river's bank; then, from the shaft's base, a closely timbered driftway would be driven beneath the river to connect with a north-bank shaft to be built later. There is barely enough room for two men to pass each other in a miner's driftway—this passage was to be three feet wide at its floor, tapering to two feet six inches at its roof, and five feet high—so there seemed no reason to doubt that the timbering would support it and, if worked by a skilled miner, the small face might not prove too great a hazard. So far, so good.

Finally, the tunnel would be built above the drift, which would serve as a drain for the larger work. This drain would undoubtedly be necessary, but how the tunnel's extensive working face and the adjoining unlined strip of wall were to be supported, Vazie did not say.

He may have been uneasy about the nature of the ground, for he requested a 50 hp steam engine for pumping, but the Directors thought this extravagant and persuaded him to accept a 14 hp engine of 'imperfect construction'. In due course this engine was erected and work began; but when the 11-foot-wide shaft had been carried to a depth of 42 feet, a stratum of gravel was encountered, water poured in, and the pumps were overwhelmed,

The Directors were badly shaken, but fortunately for Vazie a major shareholder accepted responsibility for the cost of completing the shaft, and

by means of a caisson the engineer passed through the gravel and carried
it to a depth of 76 feet below Trinity High Water, although at the reduced
diameter of eight feet. At this level, borings through the shaft's base revealed
a great bed of quicksand, and Vazie decided to begin his drift without going
deeper.

Once again the Directors hesitated. The shaft's cost had exceeded all
estimates, so Vazie cooled his heels while they consulted John Rennie and
William Chapman. These gentlemen could not agree, so on the advice of
Vazie and Davies Giddy* the board called in Richard Trevithick, who was
close at hand dredging gravel from the Thames.

Trevithick was born at Illogan in Cornwall and was the first surviving
son of a mine manager. The boy was his mother's darling, but his Camborne
schoolmaster found him obstinate, slow, disobedient and spoiled, and
complained that he was frequently absent, invariably inattentive, and
inclined to draw on his slate instead of working with the class. Yet the youth
developed an extraordinary flair for mathematics and engineering which
was complemented by immense determination and physical power. By 1807
the 36-year-old Cornishman had established a formidable reputation. He
was more than a match for the hesitant Directors of the Thames Archway
Company. A letter to his friend Giddy sheds some light on their meeting:

> Last Monday I closed with the tunnel gents. I have agreed with them to give
> them advice, and to conduct the driving of a level through to the opposite
> side ... to receive five hundred pounds when the drift is halfway through, and
> five hundred pounds more when it is holed out on the opposite side. I have
> written to Cornwall for more men for them. It is intended to put three men
> on each core of six hours' course. I think this will be making one thousand
> pounds very easily ...

Trevithick was now in charge. On 17 August he directed a disgruntled
Vazie to commence the driftway, and a few days later, from the *Plough Inn*,
Kidney Stairs, Limehouse, wrote again to his mentor:

> Tuesday last was a week since we began to drive our level at the bottom of
> the engine shaft of the archway.... . The first week we drove twenty-two feet.
> This week I hope we shall drive and timber ten fathoms. As soon as the rail-
> way is laid I hope to make good twelve fathoms a week. The distance we have
> to drive is about one hundred and eighty-eight fathoms. The ground is sand
> and gravel; and it stands exceedingly well, except when we hole into le-areys,
> and holing into such houses of water makes the sand very quick. We have
> discovered three of these holes which contained about twenty square yards.

* Man of letters, mathematician and later, after changing his name to David Gilbert, MP for
Bodmin.

It is very strange that such places should be in the sand at this depth. When we cut into such places we are obliged to timber it up closely until the sand is drained of the water, otherwise it would run back and fill the drift and the shaft.

I cannot see any obstacle likely to prevent us from carrying this level across the river in six months. The engine throws down a sufficient quantity of air [by means of a bellows], and the railway underground will enable us to bring back the stuff, so as to keep the level quite clear, and the last fathom will be as speedily driven as the first. There is scarcely any water in the level—not above twenty gallons per minute.

The drift was extended northwards horizontally, but the Directors were dissatisfied with progress, which averaged six feet per day, and after a stormy meeting the unfortunate Vazie was dismissed, and Trevithick assumed direct control. Thenceforth over eleven feet were added each day to the passage until, having passed below the middle of the river, it began a gentle ascent. Almost immediately a stratum of calcareous rock was encountered, which descended perceptibly and opposed the driftways' climb. It proved to be seven feet six inches thick, but after much hard work with cold chisels, the top half of the drift emerged into a stratum of saturated sand containing bands of shell. At once the roof collapsed in front of the timbering. Working on their knees, almost a thousand feet from safety, the miners cleared the blockage, timbered up the hole, and drove pipes forward from the top of the face so as to drain the sand.

The ground continued treacherous, but early in the New Year the low-water mark on the northern shore was passed, and success seemed almost within reach when, on 26 January, the face was breached by an exceptionally high tide. The miners fled, back along the dark drift towards the shaft 1,026 feet distant. The muddy water of the Thames rolled in behind them, slowing their hurrying feet, dragging at their knees, always rising as they stumbled slower and yet more slowly, along the tomb-like corridor to safety. Richard Trevithick was the last to emerge, and the waters had reached his neck.

He plugged the hole in the river bed with bags of clay and gravel, pumped the driftway dry, and resumed the work within a week. He continued to build the drift's floor at the same inclination but, to reduce the area of the face, he kept the roof level for a short distance until the height inside the timbering was a bare three feet. Despite this expedient, frequent bursts of water made conditions impossible, and soundings revealed that the river bed was sinking around the site of the breach and also over the place where the drift had broken through the belt of rock.

Trevithick concluded that the passage could be completed only from above, and proposed excavating the bed of the river from within a series of coffer dams and then laying a sectional cast-iron tunnel in the trench.

Instead of seeking capital for this bold, but then unproven, plan, the Directors sought to make a scapegoat of their engineer. A faction had already reported him to the Lord Mayor, who accused him of breaching the bed of the Thames, and subsequently, when he plugged the hole, of obstructing the navigation. Now the Board offered £500 for another plan, and in due course the most promising 49 schemes were submitted to Dr Charles Hutton and William Jessop, mathematician and civil engineer respectively. These arbiters found none to their liking and concluded their report with these words: 'Though we cannot presume to set limits to the ingenuity of other men, we must confess that, under the circumstances which have been so clearly presented to us, we consider that an underground tunnel, which would be useful to the public and beneficial to the adventurers, *is impracticable*.'

The report marked the end of the Archway Company's attempt. Trevithick's gloom was lightened by his wife's pleasure at leaving the murk of Rotherhithe, and although various schemes were aired, no more companies were formed to build another 'grand uninterrupted line of communication'.

Brunel pondered the problem. The drift's success would not have surprised him, but he saw no hope of building the tunnel unless its face and the portion in front of its masonry lining were somehow supported.

One day, whilst at Chatham Dockyard, he chanced upon a piece of keel timber newly removed from a ship. It was punctured by a series of tunnels; he took out his glass, and found in one a living shipworm of the species *teredo navalis*, that had reputedly sunk more ships than all the cannon ever cast.

This lowly mollusc is nine inches long and half an inch in diameter. Its head is encased by two jagged, concave triangular shells, between which a proboscis protrudes, like the centre pin of a carpenter's bit. The boring shells oscillate about the axis of the proboscis, grinding the hardest oak into a nourishing flour, and from this unvarying diet the worm derives its power, and its smooth tunnel lining of petrified excreta. The flimsy ship-worm is completely protected; its head by the strong boring shells and its transparent body, in which the beating heart is visible, by a tunnel lining of its own manufacture. To imitate the action of the ship-worm became Brunel's preoccupation.

'From these ideas,' he said, 'I propose to proceed, by slow and certain methods, which, when compared with the progress of works of art, will be found to be much more expeditious in the end.'

16

THE IRON SHIP-WORM

—◆•➤◆•—

The Thames Archway Company was wound up in 1808. Seven years passed, Brunel rebuilt his burned-down sawmill, completed the chalk tunnel at Chatham, and began his study of the ship-worm. The Tsar's enquiry in 1817 regarding the Neva bridge stimulated this train of thought, and while he worked on plans for the great bridge, the first faint glimmerings of a workable tunnelling machine dawned in his mind. By the following year these had fused into a clearly perceived idea, which was revealed to the world with the publication of his patent specification of 20 January 1818, for *Forming Drifts and Tunnels Under Ground.*

Inventive achievement can be measured in terms of subsequent utility—a test which would put the water closet in the front rank of original ideas—or, with greater difficulty, by reference to the quality of the inventor's conception. The latter evaluation is now fashionable, and Leonardo da Vinci is respected as much for inventiveness as for artistry. Brunel's block machine patent and this specification for a tunnelling shield must command our admiration on both counts. The first opened the door to mass production, the second made tunnels through mud, and London's tube railway, possible. Both proved useful and both were inspired.

He prefaced his ideas by defining the problem 'which consists in finding efficacious means of opening the ground in such a manner that no more earth shall be displaced than is to be filled by the shell or body of the tunnel, and that the work shall be effected with certainty'. After explaining that 'certainty' depended on supporting the unlined portion of the excavation, he turned to the relative magnitude of a drift and a tunnel; the former involved 'an opening of eighteen feet area; whereas the body of a tunnel on dimensions sufficiently capacious to admit of a free passage for two carriages abreast cannot be less than twenty-two feet diameter, consequently about twenty times as large as the opening of a small drift'.

The body of the specification described two 'modes' of driving tunnels with 'certainty'.

The first involved subdividing the circular working face by means of a series of iron cells, with rollers between them, each of which would accommodate a miner in what was tantamount to a separate driftway. The cells' curved outer walls, which were in contact with the sides of the excavation, would extend backwards to overlap behind the tunnel's masonry lining. Each working face would be supported by boards which a miner would remove to dig out the ground. When a face had been excavated, the cell would be advanced by an hydraulic ram.

Referring to the second 'mode' of tunnelling, Brunel observed,

> The combination of mechanical expedients by means of which I perform the same, I denominate a teredo or auger, from its great analogy to that instrument and also the vermes, known under the name of Teredo Navalis. This insect is capable of perforating the toughest timber by the power and organisation of its auger like head worked by the motion of the body inclosed within its tubular cell, which cell may be supposed to represent a tunnel.

In fact there would be two concentric augers. The small one, like the ship-worm's proboscis, would be located in the centre of the working face; it resembled a three-foot-diameter corkscrew working inside an open-ended drum. The annulus between this drum and the tunnel wall which, in this 'mode', was to be spirally lined with bolted together cast-iron segments, constituted the second, larger auger or 'teredo'. This outer auger would not rotate; instead, the annular working face would be supported by 12 segmental *radiant pieces*, each with an inner end connecting with the drum and an outer end fixed to a curved iron plate or *stave* which would extend back along the tunnel wall behind the cast-iron lining. The radiant pieces would be arranged spirally, and at the edge of the spiral a slice of ground would be exposed, which a miner, working at right angles to the face, could excavate. This done,

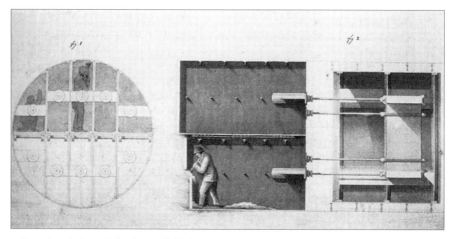

Drawings by Brunel showing a divided circular tunnelling shield; one of the two types envisaged in his patent of 1818.

the radiant piece would be advanced into the space, and the ground behind the next radiant piece would be excavated. Once again hydraulic rams would supply the propulsive force.

Brunel had not then decided which form of shield he would use, but the idea of a 'grand, uninterrupted line of communication' had fired his imagination. It was the bed of the Thames that his 'Great Shield' would pierce.

Great undertakings had a fascination for the Brunels which their fondness for the adjective confirmed. Marc had talked of his *Great Saw*, now it was his *Great Shield*, soon it would be his *Great Descents*. A railway and a ship of Isambard's were named *Great Western*, another ship *Great Britain*, and his fatal third *Great Eastern*. Royalty caught the fashion; the Prince Regent's banquets were prepared in the Royal Pavilion's *Great Kitchen* and, for Hyde Park, Albert arranged the *Great Exhibition*.

'We may soon anticipate,' Brunel wrote, 'a speedy and total change in the face of the maps of this great metropolis—in that portion of it which has hitherto presented nothing but swampy desert—namely the parish of Rotherhithe … This parish will soon display a scene of activity that is not to be witnessed anywhere else.'

17

THE THAMES TUNNEL COMPANY

D uring the experiments with decorative tinfoil and stereotype printing plates Brunel's thoughts returned again and again to the bed of the Thames. The Archway Company's attempt had revealed a variety of strata below the river, and some of them were unsuitable for tunnelling. At a depth of 42 feet, water from a bed of gravel had flooded their Rotherhithe shaft, and at 76 feet Vazie had been within probing distance of an immeasurably deep and treacherous quicksand. To stand any chance of success, a new tunnel would have to be built in the 34-feet-thick layer of sound ground between these hazards. Since a tunnel to carry two streams of traffic needed an inside diameter of at least 22 feet, there would be little room to spare.

In 1821 'the misfortune' provided Brunel with an opportunity for undisturbed reflection, and the more he studied what had been learned about the river bed, the less hospitable it appeared to be. Halfway across, at a depth of about 70 feet, Trevithick had encountered a vein of calcareous rock which descended perceptibly in a northerly direction. What if the gravel also descended? How big a tunnel could be driven beneath the river in reasonable security?

Reluctantly he concluded that a cylindrical excavation would run the risk of being flooded from above—for the gravel must surely be that which Trevithick had dredged from the river—or of being engulfed in the quicksand below. The excavation would have to be flattened; instead of being circular, his Great Shield must be rectangular.

The second 'mode' envisaged in the patent—the teredo or auger shield—was not adaptable to an angular shape (it suffered from the additional handicap of providing a very restricted work-face which would have been too small for more than one or two miners). But the first 'mode'—which involved the subdivision of the face into separate drifts—was adaptable; indeed a rectangular shield would be simpler to partition.

The thin layer of good ground determined the shape of the excavation into which the shield must fit, and in the two years following his release from King's Bench Prison the details of an oblong shield matured in Brunel's mind.

Instead of advancing each iron drift or cell independently, he decided to unite three cells into a vertical iron frame. The Great Shield would resemble a row of hollow books—each book representing a frame containing three cells—and each capable of being advanced independently.

Working drawing of a frame.

An article by Brunel, published in the *Mechanic's Magazine of* September 1823, described a shield of 11 frames, each about 19 feet high and three feet wide, in which

> intrenched and secure, thirty three men may be made to carry on an excavation, which is six-hundred-and-thirty feet in superficial area, in regular order and uniform quantities—with as much facility and safety as if one drift of only nineteen square feet was to be opened by one man ... If we examine the nature of the ground we have to go through, we observe under the third stratum [clay underlying the gravel], which has been found to resist infiltrations, that the sub-strata to the depth of eighty-six feet are of a nature that present no obstacles to the progress of the tunnel.*

---

* i.e. above the quicksand—the difference in depth, 86 feet instead of 76 feet, is probably accounted for by ground level instead of Trinity high water being used as the datum line.

Like Vazie, Brunel intended to drive his tunnel from the bottom of a shaft sunk into the Rotherhithe bank; but since the excavation would be 33 times larger than the earlier drift, the volume of spoil to be removed would be proportionately increased. He therefore proposed a shaft 50 feet in diameter. When the tunnel reached Wapping, a second, similar shaft would be sunk to connect with it.

These capacious shafts were not an extravagance. As soon as the tunnel had been completed they would be fitted with gently rising stairways, and serve as access points for pedestrians wishing to cross beneath the Thames. In this way, he contended, the tunnel would be earning money before the Great Descents, which would serve as entry points for wheeled traffic, were constructed.

Section showing the scale of the tunnel.

The Great Descents were another novel conception. Instead of taking a gently descending roadway down to tunnel level by means of a long cutting, he proposed building a pair of concentric shafts on the landward side of each 'Foot Passengers' Shaft'. The inner shaft of each pair would be 180 feet in diameter, and the outer shaft, surrounding it, 250 feet across. In the annular space between these shafts, a spiral roadway would be built which would descend to a short tunnel linking the base of each Great Descent with its neighbouring Foot Passengers' Shaft. In this bold and ingenious manner wheeled traffic would be led below the river from compact and inexpensive sites on the surface. Like the tunnel, the Great Descents would accommodate double carriageways and there would be pavements in the tunnel itself for pedestrians.

The plan was a two-phase scheme. First, the Rotherhithe Foot Passengers' Shaft would be sunk. From its base the Great Shield would march under the river, pressed on by the miners, and the supporting bricklayers, who would build twin horseshoe tunnels or *Archways* in its wake. After travelling 1,250 feet, four-fifths of the way below water, the shield would meet the second Foot Passengers' Shaft newly sunk at Wapping.

The second phase involved the construction of the Great Descents and the link tunnels on either bank.

The plan would be expensive, but unlike Dodd's or Vazie's earlier proposals, it was a *complete* plan, and only the minimum amount of money would be expended before the hazardous part, the tunnel proper, was built. And every year the need for a 'grand uninterrupted communication' grew more pressing.

Before he wrote the *Mechanic's Magazine* article, Brunel had prepared his plan in detail. He had decided exactly how the great and intricate shield would

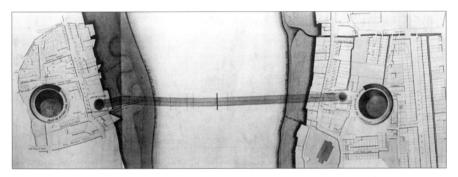

Plan of the projected Thames Tunnel.

operate. He had evolved a novel mode of building the access shafts—which would be larger subterranean structures than had previously been attempted in similar soil conditions. He had estimated the quantity of bricks, the weight of iron and, from these and other calculations, could offer credible estimates of expenditure and toll revenue.

Except in old age, when he consulted Isambard, there is no record of Brunel seeking the assistance of any notable contemporary. His versatility, originality and theoretical insight had made him the doyen of his profession, but he enjoyed cordial relations with fellow engineers and scientists, was receptive to ideas and equally ready to expound his own plans; especially this tunnel plan, which would require finance on a grand scale and could easily founder on the rock of expert criticism.

From February 1823 onwards, ever more frequent 'tunnel' entries are interspersed in his diary amongst others regarding the Bourbon bridge, the printing press, the steam engine and, later, the gaz engine. They record a growing expenditure of effort—much of it Isambard's—to make small-scale drawings, to prepare engravings for booklets, and to gather support—for Brunel was an accomplished lobbyist.

Probably either J. Wyatt or I.W. Tate, promoters of the earlier Archway Company, introduced Brunel to William Smith, MP for Norwich, and parliamentary spokesman for slave traders, the three Christian denominations, and—when he thought fit—for builders of roads and bridges.

Brunel called on Smith on 11 July 1823 and left him with two pamphlets. A fortnight later he visited the Duke of Somerset and Admiral Codrington. He canvassed business men, bankers and directors of canal companies.

A week before Christmas he saw Robert Humphrey Marten, Deputy Chairman of the Commercial Dock Company, with two co-directors, and James Walker, their engineer. 'After a long conference with them I asked them whether they were likely to oppose the measure. *'Oh, no, Mr B. The Commercial Docks will not, of course, oppose a project of communication between the two shores of the river.'* He circularised friends, fellow engineers and members of the Government, and from all sides offers of support flowed in. Even the directors of the Surrey Dock Company were in favour of the 'new communication'.

By the end of the year the campaign for the tunnel had acquired a momentum of its own, and on the 8th of the following January the well-wishers gathered informally at the *King's Head*, and appointed a small committee to organise a public meeting to launch the venture.

Now the drive for public support was intensified still further, reaching a climax on 17 February when Brunel addressed the Institution of Civil Engineers. His Journal of Transactions provides us with a clear account of what transpired the following day, at the *City of London Tavern*, where 'upwards of one hundred persons met from private advertisements and notices'.

'Mr W. Smith, M.P., was called to the chair and after having opened, by a very suitable speech, the business of the day, Mr Wollaston read an exposé of the various points bearing upon the execution of a tunnel across the Thames, and submitted a series of resolutions for the consideration and sanction of the meeting.

'The different resolutions being proposed, etc., they were all agreed upon by a unanimous show of hands.

'A committee was instituted, and the business ended by Mr Wollaston proposing to open immediately a list of subscriptions for £50 shares with a deposit of £2 per share.

'Mr G. Wollaston opened the list, taking five hundred shares, and afterwards fifty shares more, besides his brother, the Doctor. Thus in the course of an hour one-third of the subscriptions were filled, namely, one thousand-two-hundred-and-fifty shares.

'Mr Williams was proposed as treasurer.

'On this occasion Mr P. T. Taylor spoke in very flattering terms of both the scheme and its projector.

'Mr Donkin's sentiments could not be more gratifying.

'Mr Bramah likewise—.

'The meeting ended at about four o'clock, having been opened at half-past-one.

'Dined at the City of London [Tavern] with Mr Sweet, Mr Mayelstone, the proposed Secretary, and Isambard.'

They were off to a flying start; the following day he noted: '767 shares were taken today, making 2,128 shares [altogether]'.

The meeting fired the public's imagination. Within three days 3,874 shares were spoken for, and even after deducting the subscriptions of 276 well-wishers who subsequently defaulted, the sum pledged amounted to £179,900.

There was much to do. Pending the acquisition of suitable premises, the new committee moved into the Poultry office, and immediately began drafting the necessary parliamentary Bill; meanwhile Brunel found temporary accommodation, and busied himself arranging for a geological survey, selecting a tentative site for the Rotherhithe shaft, and gathering support in high places.

> March 5th .... Waited on the Duke of Wellington by appointment, the object of which was to have the plan of the mode of proceeding with the tunnel explained to him. His Grace made many very good observations and raised great objections; but after having explained to him my Plan and the expedients I had in reserve, His Grace appeared to be satisfied and to be disposed to subscribe.

The new Company's powers were defined in a Bill for 'Making and Maintaining a Tunnel under the Thames', which had a smooth passage through Parliament and received the Royal Assent on 24 June—less than six months after the inaugural meeting.

The tunnel was to run 'from some place in the parish of St John of Wapping in the County of Middlesex to the opposite shore of the said river in the parish of St Mary, Rotherhithe, in the County of Surrey, with sufficient approaches thereto'.

The 'Thames Tunnel Company' was empowered to issue £50 shares to a total value of £200,000, subscribers to be given votes in proportion to the number of shares held, and later a further £50,000 might be solicited.

Lest a quarter-of-a-million pounds should prove insufficient, the Company was further empowered to make limited borrowings, but payment of interest was to take priority over dividends to subscribers.

The Act vested the Company with authority to construct the tunnel, and to acquire the necessary property on either bank, but stipulated that tenants should be given three months' notice to quit, and that landlords should be compensated for any damage to their premises. The access shafts were to be raised three feet above Trinity High Water.

The Company might erect turnpikes at either end of the completed tunnel, and charge the following maximum tolls:

Foot passengers	2d.
Six-horse carriages	2s. 6d.
Three- or four-horse carriages	2s. 0d.
Two-horse carriages	1s. 0d.
One-horse carriages	6d.
Horse-drawn wagons and carts	4d.
Wheelbarrows	2½d.
Horses, mules or asses without carts	2d.
Not more than 1s. for every score of cattle.	
Not more than 6d. for every score of calves, sheep or lambs.	
Not more than 6d. for every score of geese, ducks or turkeys.	

Redundant watermen were to be compensated to an extent to be settled later by jury. Finally, the authority vested in the Company would lapse if the tunnel had not been completed within seven years.

Installed in their new premises at 2 Walbrook Buildings in the City, the Company's officers next prepared for the first General Meeting, which was duly held on 20 July, once again at the *City of London Tavern*.

William Smith took the chair, and informed the assembled subscribers of the arrangements already made, then Robert Marten outlined the terms of Brunel's appointment.

> ... Your Directors have made arrangements with Mr Brunel for the use of his patent, for which they have agreed to pay him £5,000 when the body of the tunnel shall be securely affected, and carried sixty feet beyond each embankment of the river, and a further and final sum of £5,000 when the first public toll under the Act of Parliament shall have been received for the use of the proprietors.
>
> To effect the work Mr Brunel has received the appointment of *Engineer to the Company*, with the salary of one thousand pounds per annum for a period of three years, the utmost limit which the Directors contemplate at this stage as necessary for the execution of the work; the whole of which sum the Directors have agreed to give him in case the work should be accomplished to their satisfaction at an earlier period.

The subscribers unanimously endorsed all arrangements, including the fee of £1,000 per annum which the Directors collectively awarded themselves.

The composition of the *Court*, as the Board of Directors was grandly styled, must have been a source of satisfaction for Brunel. It included the engineers Bryan Donkin, Timothy Bramah and Thomas Brunton. Commerce was represented in the persons of Thomas Brandram, Richard Peckover Harris and Robert Marten of the Commercial Docks. A close friend, the scientist George Hyde Wollaston, was Deputy Chairman, and Ben Hawes and Hugh Gray, the brother of a family friend living in Brighton, were directors. Mr Sweet's firm were the Company's solicitors, and the Clerk, Charles Butler—for Mayelstone did not secure the appointment—was practical and positive.

It would have been difficult to have imagined a Board more closely linked with their engineer, but this satisfactory outcome merely reflected the realities of the situation. The tunnel was possible because of the Great Shield, Brunel's invention; it would be built according to his grand design, and the lustre of his name had conjured up unprecedented financial backing.

Given time, the Chairman might possibly become his rival for public esteem, but Smith's support had been unswerving, his parliamentary *savoir-faire* was invaluable, and his ability to talk at great length, as the occasion demanded, was well known:

> At length, when the candles burn low in their sockets,
> Up gets William Smith with both hands in his pockets,
> On a cause of morality fearlessly enters,
> With all the opinions of all the Dissenters.

18

CLEARING THE DECKS

W hile the Company's professional officers busied themselves with minutes, Bills and resolutions, Brunel attended to the earthier matters that are the lot of engineers. Chief amongst these was the geological survey, for the practicability of the venture depended entirely on the strata below the river, and even if borings justified the projectors' optimism, local aberrations might be revealed which could entail varying the provisional line of the excavation.

The illustrated booklets which the Company had issued showed the tunnel crossing to Wapping by the shortest route from a foot passengers' shaft at Cow Court, Rotherhithe—a site which lay 140 feet back from the southern bank. This line, which Brunel had chosen after a reconnaissance of both banks, was three-quarters of a mile upstream from Trevithick's ill-fated drift.

To confirm its feasibility, Brunel put in hand three surveys. First, Montague, a City surveyor introduced by Sweet, was instructed to make a schedule and valuation of all properties that would be affected. Secondly, Francis Giles, a canal engineer, was engaged to make soundings across the river to establish precisely the level of its bed. Finally, Joliffe and Banks were instructed to make a series of borings across the river, on each side of the tunnel's proposed path, and to investigate the strata below Cow Court and at Wapping.

The early signs were favourable. Sir Edward Banks, who had developed special augers, reported that his firm's earlier borings for Rennie's new London Bridge had revealed a 'strong bottom' below the gravel at a depth of 40 feet—a little nearer the surface than Vazie had found it when sinking his shaft.

The surveys proceeded, with Isambard in frequent attendance, and at Cow Court a sizeable well was dug through the gravel with the object of boring downwards from its base.

Brunel visited the well diggers on 19 April, and found the 30-feet-deep well full of water, which rose and fell 18 inches with the tide. 'It is manifest from this,' he noted in his Journal, 'that unless the tunnel is inclosed in the stratum of clay [below the gravel] it would be unsafe to drive through the bed of gravel.'

Sound strata were found below the well's base, and the borings across the river proved reassuring. The Company was able to inform subscribers that in each bore 'a stratum of strong blue clay of sufficient depth to insure the safety of the intended tunnel' had been encountered.

Subsequently a pamphlet written by Brunel gave this more detailed picture of the ground below Cow Court.

STRATUM 1, to a depth of nine feet. Brown clay.

STRATUM 2, to a depth of thirty-five feet, eight inches. Loose gravel with a large quantity of water, twenty-six feet, eight inches thick.

STRATUM 3, to a depth of thirty-eight feet, eight inches. Blue alluvial earth, inclining to clay, three feet thick.

STRATUM 4, to a depth of forty-three feet, nine inches. Loam five feet, one inch thick.

STRATUM 5, to a depth of forty-seven feet, six inches. Blue alluvial earth, inclining to clay, mixed with shells, three feet, nine inches thick.

STRATUM 6, to a depth of fifty-five feet. Calcareous rock in which are embedded gravel stones, and so hard as to resist the pickaxe, and to be broken only by wedges, seven feet, six inches thick.

STRATUM 7, to a depth of fifty-nine feet, six inches. Light-coloured muddy shale in which are embedded pyrites and calcareous stones, four feet six inches thick.

STRATUM 8, to a depth of sixty feet. Greensand with gravel and a little water, six inches thick.

STRATUM 9, to a depth of sixty-eight feet, four inches. Greensand, eight feet, four inches thick.

This account makes two things clear. First that the third stratum, which had been described as 'strong blue clay of sufficient depth to insure the safety of the intended tunnel', was in fact a three-foot-thick band of blue alluvial earth inclining to clay. It was evidently impervious, and would provide a roof over the shield. Second, if the greensand is assumed to be Vazie's quicksand, there was a twenty-four-foot thick band of reasonably impermeable strata between it and the loose gravel through which the tunnel could be driven.

It is also a fair assumption that the bores through the river bed and at Wapping were not driven as deep as that at Cow Court, so the possibility of lower strata dipping in a northerly direction—as Trevithick had reported—was not ruled out; this, however, was not a matter of great concern; the depth of the gravel had been established, and no one had suggested that the lower strata might ascend.

As a result of the survey, two changes were made in the original plan. First, the face of the proposed excavation was enlarged from 630 to 834 square feet by using a shield 37 feet 6 inches wide, made up of 12 frames, each 22 feet 3 inches high. Secondly, to lessen the risk of perforating the clay ceiling, the tunnel would not be driven level but would descend gently to a low point below the middle of the river.

With the survey completed, Brunel recruited a second draughtsman named Pinchback to assist with the drawings of the Great Shield, for which he had proposed seeking tenders from Maudslay's, Donkin and Company, and Bramah and Company. However, the Court rejected this idea, because the principals of the latter firms were Directors of the Tunnel Company, and instead the drawings were submitted to Sturgess and Company of Bradford, and to Maudslay's. To Brunel's relief, Maudslay tendered the lower price and won the order.

The construction of Vazie's earlier shaft had been all but abandoned because of the influx of water from the bed of gravel. What had been a crisis with an 11-foot shaft would have been a disaster with one of 50 feet diameter; Brunel therefore decided to prefabricate at least the upper half of the shaft, and then to sink it bodily into the soil of Rotherhithe by mounting it on an iron curb and excavating the ground within it.

A steam engine would be required to power a bucket chain elevator, pumps, and later, a rope railway and gear to lift spoil from the tunnel. This engine was to be mounted on timbers across the top of the shaft, and had to be powerful, light in weight and vibration-free. Since Brunel's triangle-frame engine met these requirements exactly, Maudslay received additional orders for the curb, the bucket elevator and a twin-cylinder, 30 hp engine, together with a boiler whose working pressure was to be three atmospheres.

We may suppose that many a knowing head shook, and many a respected voice was heard, in private, to express misgiving at the notion of sinking the gigantic shaft—and with the aid of an engine working at three atmospheres of pressure! Brunel gave them not a thought, he had many other matters to attend to. He negotiated the lease of a wharf from the incumbent of St Mary's, Rotherhithe, for £200 a year; arranged to divert a sewer, hired a pile-driving machine, and bought timber, bricks and cement.

Brick and cement supplies were a continuing preoccupation. The volume of the solid walls of the upper half of the Rotherhithe shaft was calculated to be 17,700 cubic feet, and the tunnel itself would consume 71 million bricks. Eventually, after protracted enquiries, half a million bricks of closely specified quality were ordered from a factor named Townsend, and arrangements were made to organise a 'Company' brickfield on land near by.

Brunel knew every detail of the basins at Chatham Dockyard where a quick-setting cement had been used. He determined to use this mis-called

'Roman' cement* for the Thames tunnel works, and justified its cost by pointing out that the tunnel brickwork must set rapidly so as to support the excavation after the shield had advanced. Similarly, the newly built shaft would be subjected to great stress during its descent, and might well crack if the cement failed to set quickly.

Bryan Donkin and Timothy Bramah were sceptical, but during July and August another new assistant named Smith made a series of experiments with various makes of Roman and other cement, extending brick cantilevers from a wall until they collapsed, and making cubes of brickwork which they then crushed with jacks. This work proved beyond question the superiority of Roman cement for structures that were stressed when newly built, and Messrs Turner and Montague, Messrs Francis and White, and Wyatt Parker and Company were given initial orders.

Even by Brunel's standards, 1824 was a busy year. The preparations for the tunnel had to be fitted in with work on the Dutch cannon-boring mill, the Serpentine bridge, the printing press and the gaz engine; and he had to continue his struggle for a fair return from the wily Hollingsworths at Battersea.

Much was delegated. Working drawings were produced by Pinchback and a draughtsman named Bordège, and by Isambard who, when his father was otherwise engaged, kept in touch with Joliffe and Banks, or supervised Smith and Chilcott, another junior assistant. Despite this staff of unwonted size, there were many matters requiring personal attention. Sketches had to be produced; the Directors, collectively and severally, had to be attended to—as did Maudslay and other suppliers—not to mention important officials like those of the Thames Navigation Committee, whose permission was needed before the boring crews could begin their work. The assistants had to be organised, supervised and paid, and no one but Brunel could recruit the skilled hands and responsible officers who would form the nucleus of the Tunnel Company's labour force.

After abortive talks with Pritchard and Hoof, the contractors responsible for the Thames and Medway canal, it was provisionally decided to build the tunnel with directly employed labour, and on 25 August William Armstrong was engaged as resident engineer. This young man was commended by Bryan Donkin and John Rennie, and secured a salary of £300 a year, a house and, eventually, although the Court demurred, an allowance for coals and candles. In November a clerk of works named Litchfield was recruited, and in December a smith named Redman, who had offered to make over a thousand

* Cement produced from limestones containing clay by a process patented in 1796 by James Parker.

small screw-jacks for the shield and to set up a shop near Cow Court. Also in December negotiations began with a craftsman named Stewart, who applied for the post of chief brickmaker.

By the end of the year preparations were well forward, but Brunel had earlier realised that the tunnel would make heavy demands on his time for some years to come. Accordingly, on 10 June he leased a house, No. 80 Bridge Street, Blackfriars, and the following day transferred thither his staff* from the Poultry office, which he vacated. Stabling and a coach-house in Water Lane were included in the lease, and when the premises had been cleaned and decorated, Brunel put his old house up for auction† and brought Sophie to Blackfriars.

---

* The staff consisted of: Pinchback, a draughtsman paid £62 10s. per quarter; Smith, a young engineering assistant paid £3 10s. per week; Bordège, a draughtsman paid 30s. per week; Chilcott, a junior with some surveying experience paid 15s. per week; Isambard, paid £7 10s. per quarter (soon to be increased to £12 10s. per quarter).
† The Chelsea house did not sell, so Brunel let it.

PART III

THE LABOURS OF HERCULES

And what thing soever besides cometh within
the chaos of this monster's mouth, be it beast,
boat, or stone, down it goes all incontinently, that
foul great swallow of his, and perisheth in the
bottomless gulf of his paunch.

PLUTARCH
Mortals

19

THE ROTHERHITHE SHAFT

PROJECTS ARE ON foot for Fowey and Padstow Canal and the Bermondsey Docks. I am preparing plans for South London Docks in case my father should be named Engineer. I am very busily engaged with the Gaz Engine, and a project is likewise made for a canal across the Panama. Surely *one of these* may take place!

It may be curious at some future date to read the state we are in at present—I am most terribly pinched for money. Should receive barely enough next quarter to pay my debts, and am, at this moment, without a penny. We keep neither carriage, nor horse, nor footman, only two maid-servants. I am looking forward with great anxiety to this Gaz Engine—building castles in the air about steam boats that go fifteen miles per hour; going on a tour to Italy; being the first to go to the West Indies, and making a large fortune, building a house for myself, etc. etc. How much more likely it is that all this will turn out to nothing! The Gaz Engine, if it is good for anything, will only be tolerably good, and perhaps make us spend a good deal of money; that I should pass through life as most people, and that I should gradually forget my castles in the air, live in a small house, and, at most, keep my gig. On the other side, it may be much worse. My father may die, or the Tunnel may fail, and I most likely in such circumstances, cut my throat or hang myself. But whatever may turn out, I should, in imagination, have enjoyed my fortune for at least a year or two without doing anybody harm.

Thus wrote Isambard on 9 March 1825, but the Brunels presented a public face of confident assurance—as, for instance, at the celebration a week earlier, which was recorded, with evident pleasure, in Marc's Journal.

Mr Smith, our Chairman, attended by most of the Members of the Court of Directors, and a very numerous cortège of friends invited for the occasion, proceeded from the Tunnel wharf to the ground [Cow Court] where they were received among the cheers of a great concourse of people. Mr Smith addressed the assembly in a very eloquent speech, suitable for the occasion, and performed the ceremony of laying the first stone. From this day dates the beginning of the work.

Rotherhithe was en fête, and after the ceremony two hundred people sat down to a 'sumptuous collation', a dozen bottles of wine were laid away to celebrate the completion of the work, 'the bells from the steeple of Rotherhithe rang out their joyful acclamations, and success to the undertaking was echoed from a thousand voices'.

Earlier the site had been cleared, and the 48 segments of the cast-iron curb bolted together. This curb was 40 inches high, pointed at its cutting edge, and had an inward-facing ten-inch-wide flange, to which a ring of timber one foot thick and three feet wide was bolted. This upper 'timber curb' rested on the shoulders of 24 short piles which carried the weight of the whole assembly. A circular trench had been dug below the curb during the week preceding the celebration, and then the piles had been driven down until, at the time of Smith's speech, only the timber ring remained above the surface. The following morning, after clearing away the bunting, Brunel loaded the curb with dry bricks to a height of seven feet and then judiciously drove down the piles until the 215-ton load rested on the ground—and there it remained for a fortnight until the overnight settlement decreased to one-sixteenth of an inch. It was the middle of March before work on the tower started. The stone laying ceremony with a silver trowel had marked neither 'the beginning of the work', nor the commencement of the shaft.

The tower was built to a height of 35 feet (40 feet if the iron and timber curbs are included), and the cavity between its inner and outer skins of carefully laid brickwork was filled with rubble thrown into a thin grout made with Roman cement and sand. The yard-thick wall was reinforced with hoops of three-inch-square timber, as well as with 48 vertical timber ties half of which encased inch-square wrought-iron bars, whose threaded ends carried nuts which united the brickwork to the timber curb and to a similar member placed on its top. When the last brick had been laid, the shaft was made smooth and impermeable with an external rendering of Roman cement.

The structure was built in three weeks without difficulty, but unfortunately Townsend delivered only 58,000 of the half-million bricks he had contracted for, and Brunel had to send young Smith round the local brickfields to procure alternative supplies. These were obtained, but at a greater cost than Townsend's original price of 43 shillings per thousand, and since the Company's brickfield was not yet functioning, the additional expense was another stick in the hands of Bryan Donkin, who continued to jib at the use of Roman cement. A Journal entry of 31 March reveals Brunel's annoyance at the public expression of Donkin's criticism. 'Such an observation before strangers and before our men is highly reprehensible for a Director who has the opportunity of requiring any explanation he might wish from the work.'

Donkin continued to argue that newly burned lime should be substituted for Roman cement which cost 1s. 8d. per bushel. Brunel agreed that lime-mortar was cheaper but reminded the Court that he had proved that new brickwork was stronger when laid in Roman cement mortar. Eventually, to placate Donkin, he agreed to an experiment and despatched a 'young but intelligent hand' named Morgan to Bridport to obtain lime samples. Morgan's marching orders illuminate the manner of doing business before the hurried railway age.

> Morgan,   April 4th, 1825.
> You are to set off today at two o'clock by the coach *The Regulator* and proceed to Bridport in Dorsetshire.
> On your arrival there, tomorrow morning between nine and ten, you will immediately call at The Bull inn on Mr Giles, the chief engineer of the works carrying on in the harbour of that town.
> Having already communicated with Mr Giles respecting the object of your mission, you will accordingly act from his instructions or from those of the person he may recommend to you.
> You will bear in mind that you are expressly sent for the purpose of obtaining lime of the best quality that can be had from Lyme Regis or its vicinity. If there are two sorts equally well recommended, you will purchase twenty-five tons of each sort, or fifty tons of one and the same quality, if there is but one.
> You will apply to some shipowner there and agree with him for the immediate conveyance of the stone in question to London, and enquire at the same time on what terms the same may be procured in future to be delivered at the Company's wharf at Rotherhithe.
> You will take your quarters at The Bull inn, where I shall direct my letters to you.
> You are not to leave Bridport until you have seen the limestone shipped for its destination.
> You will write and report as early as possible what you have done, and how soon you can effect the object of your mission.
> You are requested to send by wagon, one cask of lime of the best quality and newest burnt. Let it be a light cask of about thirty-six gallons, and have it directed to the Thames Tunnel office, Walbrook, London.

While Morgan was carrying out his instructions in Dorset, carpenters threw a platform across the top of the tower and rigged on it a large hand windlass, which would serve as a hoist until Maudslay delivered the steam engine and bucket chain. The shaft was perfectly stable, so Brunel dispensed with the supporting stays which he had planned to use, and prepared to lower it.

By 20 April the shouldered piles had been removed, and after ramming earth under the timber curb, navvies began excavating inside the shaft and loading the spoil into buckets, which were hoisted by the windlass gang and tipped overboard into carts. The shaft descended 8¾ inches, with perfect regularity, during the first day.

The extraordinary sinking tower was a magnet to the Iron Duke, who came with Lord Somerset and General Ponsonby on 22 April. The trio clambered inside the structure, and watched the operations with evident fascination. In the Duke's wake came the flower of the aristocracy, and during the following month the work was visited by the Duke and Duchess of Cambridge, the Duke of Gloucester, Prince Leopold, the Duke of Northumberland, Lord Spencer, the Austrian Ambassador, Prince Lieven and Mr (later Sir) Robert Peel and his lady. 'The crashing sound produced by the entrance of the iron curb into the gravel ... being reverberated from the walls of the tower had,' writes Beamish, 'a striking, not to say startling effect; while it tended to deepen the impression which the greatness of the work was so well calculated to inspire ...'

The tower descended smoothly until 29 April, when an inspection of the ground below the curb revealed large stones on the west side, while on the eastern edge, near a diverted sewer, conditions were soft.

'When everything was ready for sinking,' Brunel noted,

> I went outside in order to watch the progress ... The tower went down all at once about three-and-a-half inches to the west, and upwards of seven inches on the east. Isambard, being on top at the moment, compared it to the movement of a ship. In fact it was a considerable surge, such as would have split the brickwork if not as well bound as it is. The men soon recovered the overhanging of the wall which descended upwards of ten inches.

By the beginning of May the curb had bitten deep into the 27-foot thick stratum of gravel which had so nearly marked the end of Vazie's attempt, and a battery of hand pumps was rigged on the platform to remove water which flooded into the excavation. Other pumps drew water from Joliffe and Banks's well, which was only 12 feet away from the shaft. 'Seventy-two men employed in pumping,' noted Brunel on the 9th, 'thirty-six by day and as many by night, and thirty-two for heaving up the gravel, all of which would have been saved had the steam engine been at work, and that in the course of a week or ten days at the utmost.'

Ten days later the eastern rim of the curb reached the stratum of 'strong blue clay', but water continued to pour in from the opposite side, nearest the well, and after another frustrating week Brunel called at Maudslay's works to remonstrate at the delay in completing the steam engine. He was received by Joshua Field.

'I intimated to him,' Brunel noted,

> that the Court had expressed such feelings upon the protraction in the execution of that order [the steam engine] as to excite some apprehension that they might call upon Mr Maudslay for a compensation of damages. Mr F. stated in reply that, knowing Mr Maudslay as he does, and as I ought

to know him, he feels convinced that if he knew of such intention on the part of the Court, he would not hesitate to lay by and set the Company at defiance at once.

It is expedient, I am sure, to submit patiently.

To drain the shaft, the well was deepened and a driftway was driven from its side to reach a segment of the curb, through which numerous holes were drilled. In this fashion water was diverted from the shaft to the well, whence it was pumped away. This expedient, coupled with the use of sheet piling, brought the flood under control, and by 3 June the top of the tower had sunk to within two feet of its prescribed position. But it was stuck, and only by extending the driftway from the well so as to encircle part of the curb, by loading the shaft with fifty thousand bricks, and by allowing water to rise inside it, did Brunel drive it down the last few inches.

Probably if the tower had continued to descend he would have built it higher and sunk it all the way. This was not possible, but Brunel's bold plan had carried the excavation through the treacherous gravel, through the 'strong blue clay', which lay beneath it, and into the safe ground below. All this had been accomplished in less than seven weeks, and without a steam engine.

Brunel next prepared to finish the shaft by underlaying—that is by extending the excavation downwards and lining its sides with brickwork. Although Vazie's records, and the findings of Joliffe and Banks, promised dry ground below the clay, excavating downwards another ten feet would expose a surface 15,000 square feet in area, and if only a little water oozed from each square foot, the total volume might well be more than hand pumps could remove. This risk could not be taken, so, pending the triangle-frame engine's arrival, a 14 hp steam engine was hired from Maudslay, mounted on the timber platform and coupled to temporary pumps. On 7 June, after rigging internal stages and ladders, Armstrong set his navvies at work to deepen the excavation.

When the pit had been extended eight feet at a slightly reduced diameter, a segment of its curved wall was cut back until perpendicular with the outside of the sunken tower. A panel of brickwork was then built up, from timber foundations, until it reached the tower's base, from which the inner part of the timber curb was first broken away. The new wall was built out hard against the excavation's side and anchored to it with spurs of brickwork but, because flooding occurred each time the fickle steam engine broke down, the ring of underlaying was not completed until the end of June.

The triangle-frame engine and the bucket elevator were delivered at this time and during July all hands were employed installing the machinery and covering the shaft with a timber roof. Greatly assisted by the elevator, Armstrong's men again deepened the excavation and in seven days built a second six-foot ring of underlaying, inserting in its northern side a timber section, which could later be removed to form part of the shield's exit.

When this had been done, digging was immediately resumed, with a view to completing the underlaying with a single deep ring. When the pit had been lowered 12 feet at its circumference, and some three feet more at its centre, a small central well was opened to drain the work, and the pumps were re-positioned to draw water from it; but after four or five feet, the well-diggers broke into a thin band of saturated sand, which boiled up with great force, and all but overwhelmed the pumps.

Stones were flung into the pit and the influx brought under control, but the thin quicksand would clearly be dangerous if pierced by the shield and Brunel decided to drive the tunnel a few feet higher than originally planned. The final ring of underlaying was therefore built 12 feet deep, on concrete foundations some sixty feet below ground level. As in the middle ring, an opening, closed with timber, was left for the shield; but Kentish Rag stone was used to fill the cavity between the inner skin of brickwork and the sides of the excavation, and it was laid in a mortar made with sand, a little Roman cement, and lime burnt in a kiln on the Company's brickfield, which consumed chalk from Lyme Regis and Dorking. This construction proved cheaper than brickwork laid in Roman cement; it was also strong and impermeable, and since the sides of the excavation were firm and dry, its slower hardening was not a disadvantage.

Brunel's diary of 12 July records the first fatality.

> Painter, an old ganger, has been killed by falling from the top of the shaft
> ... He survived about eleven hours. On enquiring, I learned that he went
> out about eleven o'clock and came back at one, rather in liquor. Mr Marten
> examined several of the men who witnessed the accident, and he issued
> directions for inquest and burial.

The engine suffered teething troubles; steam-pipe joints failed, and were found to have been soldered instead of brazed—Maudslay's were too busy evidently—but the underlaying was finished on 10 August, and while the bricklayers built a storage tank at Cow Court to hold 5,000 gallons of Thames water for the engine's boilers, a new gang of Somerset miners were put to work constructing a drainage reservoir below the shaft's base.

The earlier decision to make the tunnel descend to a mid-river nadir had complicated the drainage problem. Brunel had planned a channel below the tunnel floor to lead water from the face to a cistern beneath the shaft; but whereas the first 500 feet of tunnel would descend gently, the drain must ascend so that water would flow back along it. The reservoir into which it discharged had therefore to be sunk quite deep.

Before starting work, Armstrong made trial borings below the excavation. He found, beneath the thin quicksand, fifteen feet of solid ground, but under this, there was another deeper quicksand. The upper band of sand had proved extremely troublesome, so sheet piles were driven downwards through it to form a square well which the pumps evacuated. Next, a 20-foot-diameter iron curb was placed around this well and a nine-foot-tall brick tower built upon it and lowered in the same way as the upper part of the main shaft. This done, the reservoir's base was built in the form of an inverted dome, whose lowest point was some 78 feet below ground level, and six feet above the deep quicksand.* Lastly, the shaft's base was built, also with a downward slope to the rim of the new cistern which, by 15 October, had been fitted with a domed brick cap.

The two months expended on this cistern may be taken as a measure of the difficulties encountered, and Brunel decided to substitute a large cast-iron pipe for the brick drain since, in view of the quicksand, it would be easier to lay beneath the tunnel floor. The first section of pipe was built into the reservoir's northern side, and other pipes pierced its roof and were connected to four force pumps, each with a 12-inch bore and a four-foot stroke, which had been manufactured by Taylor and Martineau.

After the pumps came the components of the Great Shield accompanied by fitters who assembled the frames within the shaft, while the Tunnel Company's hands sealed the joint between the bottom of the sunken tower and the top of the underlaying.

The timbered-up opening was not high enough for the shield now that the tunnel's line had been raised, so men in the shaft and in an external gallery around it removed four feet three inches of brickwork above the aperture, and also the northern segments of the curb, which were raised to the surface through three wells which pierced the gallery's roof.

At last, on 21 November, the shaft was finished, and the Great Shield's 12 frames stood in line like soldiers awaiting their orders to march North to Wapping. This was the end of the beginning, and for Brunel a moment of relief. Shaft, reservoir and shield were finished. The new steam engine had settled down. The ground beneath the clay 'stood exceedingly well'; and upwards from the thin quicksand the strata were sound and free from water for 32 feet.

His Journal records a reaction which is scarcely surprising.

> November 22nd. On getting out of bed I was taken with giddiness and sickness, the same as is experienced by turning or spinning round ... Doctor Morris was sent for. I kept to my room with little or no relief. He ordered

* The depths stated seem the most probable. Brunel's notes are confusing—depths being given 'below ground level', 'below high water', and 'below Trinity High Water' indiscriminately.

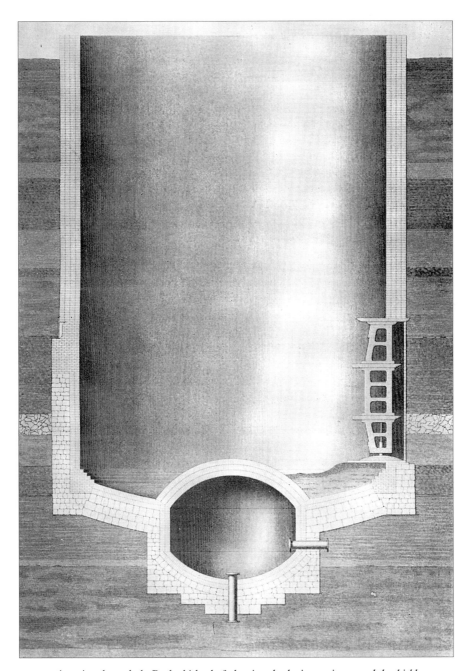

A section through the Rotherhithe shaft showing the drainage cistern and the shield.

ten leeches.' And the following day: 'Very ill, though much relieved by the leeches. I could not attend the committee of the South London Docks. Isambard wrote an apology ...

On the 28th he was 'improving in health but very weak', but two days later he was in the saddle again, attending the Dock Committee, writing to Gay-Lussac, and ordering a second boiler for the tunnel engine from Taylor and Martineau.

The 56-year-old engineer had been overworking. Sunday had been added to his six-day week, and save for a couple of October days in Brighton with Sophie and Emma, he had not rested since the shaft was started. Professional responsibility was a refreshment for him, but the 'Court' was a novel and unwelcome burden—or rather some of the Directors were—Donkin in his brash moments—and Smith and his ambivalent friends almost all the time.

The tempo of work affected the various executives in different ways. Brunel finished the immediate task, had a breakdown and recovered in a week. Armstrong was still active and dependable, but the signs of exhaustion were clear to see. Young Smith, Brunel's junior, had become erratic and would soon be dismissed; Isambard seemed to need no rest.

Indeed Isambard's source of energy was to become a much argued riddle. Perhaps, in return for a celestial overdraft, he had the hours of sleep deducted from his mortal life. Certainly at 19 he displayed exceptional vitality. His occasional leisure hours were spent at the opera (the cheapest seats), or at art galleries, or exploring Lavender Hill with William Hawes, or racing up the Thames with him in their jointly owned *funny boat* (a light clinker-built skiff), and then returning to Barge House in the evening to read Hume's *History of England*.

He was serious on occasions: 'I have just begun again my Journal,' he had written the previous December, 'which I hope to continue, and I think I may even pray to Heaven for strength to continue it.' A February entry reveals the observant guest:

> Dined at Lord Spencer's, where we met Lord Bessborough, Mr Ponsonby, Dr Wollaston, Mr Chantry, etc. This is the first time I have dined there, at least in Town. The etiquette seen here is very great. The servants are all in gloves, and many other little things peculiar to a house of this kind.

At the age of 20 Isambard would be a Fellow of the Royal Society, but he loved to build castles in the air and to flirt with pretty girls. 'Went down in the steam boat with M.C. I do not know what to think of myself. I have made love openly to C.H. and received a return, and doing the same thing with M.C. here—she has made a fool of me, and I of her.'

20

THE GREAT SHIELD

A n ambulating coffer dam travelling horizontally' was how Brunel had described the shield to the Institution of Civil Engineers. Besides supporting the face itself, the shield's 12 frames would fill the seven-foot long gap between the face and the tunnel's brickwork upon which the river and its bed would press with a force of 600 tons—more or less—depending on the state of the tide.

Fifty tons would be borne by a single frame, whose massive cast-iron side members were reinforced with wrought-iron struts. Two cast-iron floors partitioned each frame into three cells or boxes, the lowest housing two extendable articulated legs whose ankles joined them to cast-iron feet or shoes. Rollers above the frame's head would carry two top staves to support the tunnel roof, and the face would be secured by 43 oak poling boards, each three inches thick and propped in place by two poling screws—the small screw jacks that Redman had made.

The rearward thrust from the face would be transmitted through the poling screws to the frame, and then through two large screw jacks, called abutting screws, to the leading edge of the tunnel brickwork.

The frames in the shaft were numbered 1 to 12 from west to east, and they were identical—except for 1 and 12, whose outer side members were equipped with sliding iron side staves, to support the tunnel walls.

The shield was to be manned 16 hours a day by two shifts, each of 36 miners (one per box) and, if we assume that the 12 frames are in place in a straight line, and imagine the labours of the trio in number three, the manner of working can be readily understood.

Each miner removes the top poling board in front of his box, excavates the ground to a depth of 4½ inches, and replaces the board, at the same time lengthening its poling screws; but instead of replacing their ends in the sockets in number 3's side members, he transfers them to spare sockets in the sides of the neighbouring frames. This process is repeated until all the poling boards have been advanced 4½ inches or, in the miners' vernacular, until the faces have been 'worked down'.

The frame, freed from the thrust of its poling boards, is now advanced 9 inches by rotating its two abutting screws with levers called fleeting bars.

The same faces are now worked down another 4½ inches, and the poling screws replaced in their original sockets. Number 3 and its faces is now 9 inches in advance of its neighbours and, since the same operations have been repeated along the line, the six odd-numbered frames, which together may be regarded as the shield's left foot, have all stepped forward.

It is now the turn of the six remaining frames, and when the other miners have worked their faces down, advanced them, and worked their faces down again, the even-numbered frames and faces will have closed ranks and the cycle can recommence.

One might conclude that the miners in half the frames are always idle, but the top staves, the shoes, and the side staves beyond 1 and 12 must all be slid forward with screw jacks, so there is plenty for them to do.

Waiting on the miners is a gang of labourers who carry the spoil from the shield and load it into skips, which are wound up the shaft by the steam engine. The skips return full of bricks and casks of Roman cement, and these materials are carried to the bricklayers, who extend the tunnel lining each time the shield steps forward.

The lengthening brickwork is complex. Its outer edges are built flat against the excavation's sides, but the inner faces are all curved, and since there are two tunnels or archways—each roughly 14 feet wide and 17 feet high—there are two curved floors or inverts and four curved walls—all built with templates—and two arched roofs, which are built with centerings.

Great care is taken with the brickwork. The innermost course is laid in pure Roman cement, and the rest in a mortar made with equal proportions of Roman cement and sand. Each cask of cement is proved by the foreman bricklayer who, every five minutes, adds one brick, mortared with neat Roman cement on its broad face, to horizontal 9-inch-deep cantilevers. The cask is rejected if failure occurs before 12 bricks adhere.

The lining brickwork is nowhere less than two feet six inches thick, and the substantial dividing wall blunts the chisels of a small gang of men, working some distance back from the shield, who pierce it to form 'cross arches' at 18-foot intervals.

This glimpse of tunnel building is sufficient to reveal Brunel's essential ideas. That he carried out this plan with only minor variations is a tribute both to his prescience and his determination. He had to fight tooth and nail for those parts of it which the Company's technically minded directors claimed to understand.

One instance of this sometimes spirited dialogue was the disagreement with Donkin regarding the use of Roman cement. Another was the design of the tunnel brickwork, about which, before accepting Brunel's plans, the Court consulted two independent engineers: One said it was not strong enough; the other claimed it was six times stronger than necessary. Only in one direction, which we will discuss in its place, did Brunel agree to modify his original ideas, and this proved to be a costly mistake.

So far as the Great Shield was concerned, he was on a good wicket. He was its father. No one else had dreamt of, let alone used, such a device; and since the Thames Tunnel Company itself existed because of the shield, he was given a free hand in designing his brainchild.

The shield which Maudslay built differed in two respects from the divided shield described in the 1818 patent. The cells—or frames in this case—were to be advanced by screw jacks instead of hydraulic rams—probably because Maudslay, an hydraulic ram expert, advised that screw jacks would be cheaper. Also the top and side staves and the shoes were not long enough to overlap the tunnel brickwork—no doubt Brunel thought this precaution unnecessary in view of the sound lower strata that had been encountered—and the ground left unsupported when a frame advanced would be very small in area.

The triangle-frame engine and the Great Shield were Brunel's brainchildren, and no one but Maudslay could hope for a hearing on questions of design. But Brunel was sadly mistaken if he thought he could guide this infant in privacy while it took its first tottering steps. The Great Shield was everyone's baby.

A contemporary writer looking ahead and seeing no clouds in the sky described it as

> an engine almost as remarkable for its elaborate organisation as for its vast strength. Beneath those great iron ribs a mechanical soul really seems to have been created. It has its shoes on its legs, and uses them, too, with good effect. It raises and depresses its head at pleasure; it presents invincible buttresses in front to whatever danger may there threaten, and when the danger is past, again opens its breast for the further advances of the indefatigable host.

Just before his illness Brunel submitted detailed estimates for the two Great Descents, predicting that each would cost £45,000, almost half of which would be accounted for by wages. £90,000 for the pair was a greater sum than his original estimates had led the Court to expect. Notions of grandeur were certainly close to some directors' hearts, but although a colour-wash drawing by Brunel showed buildings about the entrance to a Great Descent, which would have been an ornament in ancient Athens, the estimate included neither Portland stone nor marble, and we must assume that surface works were excluded from it. Almost certainly the labour cost of the Cow Court shaft had exceeded expectations, and Brunel adjusted his estimate for the larger works in the light of this experience.

The directors' reaction was predictable. They subjected each item to a searching scrutiny and, finding nothing challengeable, sought economies in the body of the tunnel itself. The shield had already been built and a thinner tunnel lining seemed risky in view of the conflicting opinions tendered by advisers. What could be cut out? Why not the drain?

Why not indeed! The bands of saturated sand had already prompted Brunel to propose a pipe in place of the more capacious culvert he had originally envisaged beneath the tunnel floor. This refinement merely substituted a prefabricated conduit for one of brick—admittedly it would be easier to lay pipes under water than bricks but the thin upper quicksand would still have to be pierced. For almost thirty feet beneath the stratum of strong blue clay the ground was firm and dry. 'Why', asked the directors, 'have a pipe drain if the only water to be carried in it flows from the sides of the trench in which it is laid?'

Brunel pointed out that the ground beneath the river might prove to be wet, and if no drain were laid each drop of water would have to be pumped from the face up the sloping tunnel into the cistern beneath the shaft. Instead of being dependent on one set of pumps, he would be dependent on two sets, and hand pumps at the shield could not match the output of the steam-driven pumps in the shaft. Men's lives and the tunnel would be put at risk.

The directors replied that the money in hand or in prospect was insufficient to complete the work on the original plan, and unless Brunel could suggest a better economy, the drain must go; so, feeling like a general who had been deprived of his strategic reserve, Brunel acquiesced and prepared to break out from the shaft.

Beginning the tunnel was difficult. The shield was designed to enable the miners to excavate a flat face; but there was no flat face for the poling boards— the ground exposed by the removal of the shaft's northern timbered sector was a curve of 25 foot radius. The two abutting screws, which would support each frame, were intended to thrust against the leading edge of the tunnel brickwork; but there was no tunnel brickwork, so 12 timber buttresses had to be erected within the shaft to serve as temporary abutments. But even when a few feet of tunnel had been built, there remained the danger that pressure from the face might force it backwards; so Brunel doubled the thickness of the first fourteen feet of the tunnel's roof and walls so as to spread the load over a greater area of the shaft's brickwork. The roof was a relatively simple problem, as there was already a gallery above the frame's top staves in which the bricklayers could work—it had, of course, to be laboriously widened from three to 14 feet—but beyond the side staves of frames 1 and 12, new headings (i.e. short driftways) had to be dug and timbered to accommodate the thicker walls.

While Brunel sustained his leeches, Armstrong and Isambard directed the labours of the two shifts of miners and bricklayers who toiled unskilfully by the flickering light of candles in the base of the gloomy shaft. Contending with them for the limited working space were carpenters whose lofty buttresses further impeded their movements and those of the labourers who carried cement, sand and more than 12,000 bricks for every foot of tunnel—the thicker walls consumed double rations.

By 29 November the outermost frames had passed through the shaft and their polings bore against the ground, but Brunel had fallen ill at a bad time for, although Isambard and Armstrong worked double shifts, many matters demanded their attention. The steam engine was stopped and its boiler cleaned of the sludge left by the bad water which had been evaporated before the storage tank was built. This had to be done quickly lest water overflowed the cistern while the pumps were stopped. On the surface a culvert with a 12-inch-wide weir was built so that the volume of water pumped from the works could be measured with a floating gauge and recorded half-hourly in a special book. Tasks of this sort, and organising supplies, left little time for supervising the miners, who were mostly illiterate and masters of nothing more sophisticated than picks, shovels and handcarts.

To the miners the great 80-ton shield was a mysterious novelty. They were like farm labourers, whose sickles a genie had transformed into a combine harvester. They could scarcely have been more surprised, more suspicious or more destructive. They misplaced the abutting screws so that the buttresses collapsed and the frames tilted. They ran the screws out of their boxes and stripped the gun-metal female threads. 'They were,' as Brunel observed, 'unused to the management of a machine of such complication in its parts, and of such nicety in its movements, as the shield is'.

The frames crept forward. By Christmas Eve the poling boards of all but the centre pair were in place against the ground. Although the faces were unexpectedly wet, because sinking the shaft had disturbed the upper strata and locally ruptured the yard-thick clay ceiling, and despite increasing difficulties with the abutments which became elastic as they were extended with blocks of wood, the miners showed signs of settling down. They had not achieved a working rhythm, but at least it was something Armstrong and Isambard could begin to imagine. Unfortunately, the growing hopefulness of the engineers met with growing scepticism from the directors.

For the tunnel to be built in three years, 'the utmost limit' which had been publicly contemplated, 400 feet must be built each year or eight feet each week, if shaft building was disregarded. Eight feet was all that had been built in the first month. Of course they had been told there would be initial difficulties, but some members of the Court felt that difficulties

Sections through the Thames Tunnel.

might never be in short supply. Their engineer had been given his shield, and was spending their money prodigally. Each day a miner drew three shillings and a bricklayer four shillings; including the four foremen, who received half as much again, there were more than a hundred such tradesmen—besides labourers, carpenters, brickmakers, millwrights, Tillet the boilerman, and the salaried staff. Funds were ebbing, where was the tunnel?

On 3 January the directors approved a New Year resolution requiring Brunel to obtain their sanction for all future expenditure and to explain the hitherto slow rate of progress. With the second request he complied lengthily, but he declined emphatically to be hamstrung over expenditure—the Court must trust him, or if not him, then someone else.

The directors drew back. During January Brunel travelled to Chester to discuss the bridge and to Liverpool to view the docks, but the tunnel remained his first concern and his lieutenants strove to improve their organisation.

However, the Chairman was not mollified, and on the 20th, when the tunnel walls were 10 feet long, sent for Armstrong and complained about his slowness—an interference which Brunel considered 'not quite handsome'.

On 4 February a young man named Heath was engaged to assist Armstrong, but he proved hopeless and was dismissed three days later. Young Smith, Brunel's junior, was another misfit who left the works 'to relieve himself' at critical moments and was sacked towards the end of the month, his place being taken by Morgan and a stout-hearted miner named Robert Greenshield, who were made responsible for the operation of the shield during their respective shifts.

Despite the frames being sadly out of level, despite an increasing influx of water, despite poor abutments, unskilled hands, and irregular supplies of frequently unacceptable bricks, the tempo quickened slightly. There were 14 feet of tunnel by the end of January.

Before the abutting screws could be repositioned against the new brickwork and the timber buttresses cleared away, an urgent repair had to be made to the boiler feed valve which had lost its float some days earlier. Brunel and Isambard worked to replace it throughout the night of 30 January; but by the time the engine was restarted, at 5.30 in the morning, water, which streamed through the top staves of the centre frames, had risen more than half-way up the archways. The pumps soon cleared it, but the miners' dependence on the steam engine had been demonstrated dramatically, and they exhibited some 'hesitation' which was not quickly dispelled, for when the centre frames were pushed forward, the influx increased dramatically.

It had to be staunched, so a small brick well was sunk over the shield and a heading was run from it which revealed a pocket of gravel in the band of clay. This was dug out and replaced with impermeable material. At once the flow of water diminished and on 7 February the shield resumed its march.

While some of the carpenters dismantled the buttresses, others constructed two timber trunks inside the shaft. The larger of these was a lift shaft in which skips of spoil were raised and skips of bricks and other materials lowered. The smaller was a ventilator whose lower end connected with an opening two feet square, which had been left in the brickwork above the dividing wall, midway between the shoulders of the two arched roofs. The top of this duct was joined to the boiler's furnace; through it the fire inhaled stale air from near the face, and this was replaced, for the miners' benefit, by fresh air drawn down the shaft. Yet other carpenters built two wheeled stages with small hoists, one in each archway, to serve as working platforms for the bricklayers who built the roof, and later, as mountings for their centerings.

February was a bustling month. The miners and bricklayers worked with a better heart and, although water again burst in over the centre frames on the 15th, they stood to their posts and pushed the shield forward while the influx was drawn off by means of a pipe driven through the crown of one archway a few feet back from the shield. The frames were still out of line and tending to drift westwards, but rollers were inserted between them, as an experiment, and thereafter they moved forward more easily.

Isambard could claim much credit for the improving morale. His tireless encouragement and boldness heartened the men. He stood by the brave ones, like Morgan, Greenshield and Huggins, a bricklayer, and they in turn gained authority over more faint-hearted comrades.

By the end of the month the faces were firm and drier. The shield was performing the task for which it was designed. The standby boiler had been installed, and the first boiler moved to let a little daylight into the shaft. On the surface, the earth-laden skips were hauled by the steam engine up an incline and then tipped into a hopper; this in turn discharged into horse carts which carried the spoil to barges or, when good clay was being mined, to the Company's brickfield.

The shaft had been tidied up. The men were organised and in better heart. Each week the tunnel grew a yard longer. They had broken out. The march to Wapping had begun.

It was time to lift the curtain, and on 4 March Brunel escorted a party of directors and shareholders around the shaft and the twenty-nine-foot tunnel. The magnitude of the work impressed them strongly, and at a subsequent board meeting, the Court reaffirmed its confidence in their engineer and its admiration for his achievement.

There was but one dissenting voice at Rotherhithe that March morning. 'Mr Smith showed a disposition to condemn everything. ... He ... betrayed a strong bias against every report that appeared favourable to the work. His son expressed very openly his disapprobation. ... The shield was unnecessary. ... The brickwork improperly formed.'

21

THE FIRST 350 FEET

T he story of Brunel's endeavours and his men's exertions during 1826 is a narrative of difficulties overcome.

Difficulties with the ground; the first travellers to the moon found the way better mapped than these miners who scooped their way Wappingwards through the bed of London's tidal sewer. Difficulties with the shield; an untested machine, that was put to work in conditions from which its inventor would have recoiled had he foreseen them. But worst of all were difficulties with the atmosphere which nourished the labourers' toiling muscles. Nothing, not one frame, one brick, one ounce of spoil, one drop of water, was moved at the face, by any power other than the physical power of men.

Such were the peculiarities of the environment. Is it surprising that the human fabric sometimes cracked? That there was ineptitude, lethargy, drunkenness and panic occasionally? And sickness and exhaustion more often than not?

To the preoccupations of tunnelling was added the petulance of the Chairman. Engineers, directors and shareholders were alike committed to the tunnel. At best, giving up meant failure; at worst, ruin. Most of them trusted their engineer and sought to understand his setbacks. But not William Smith. Like a little boy, he had dreamed of the cheers for the victor—but not of the battle's agony—and he cried loud and often and his plaints received attention because he was Chairman and a Member of Parliament

When the works were inspected on 4 March, the shield and the face were lit by newly obtained gas burners, mounted on cylinders of condensed gas. Ignorant of the danger of their contents, the men handled these flimsy flaring canisters, which belonged to the Portable Gas Company, like casks of cement. However, each was the equal of many candles, so one was retained in each archway, and in their eerie glow the shield was pushed forward five feet during each of the four remaining weeks of March.

At the beginning of the month, Isambard's knee had been injured by a baulk of falling timber, and for three weeks he nursed his leg at home. Brunel could not himself make good the loss of supervision. Although he visited the shield twice daily, he had to attend meetings of the Court, look to other professional engagements, and as his Journal of the 17th reveals, to the brothers Hollingsworth.

'Went to Battersea to examine the books ... observing that Aldrich, Gurney and Simmons had made no payments for several years.' After visiting a number of apparent debtors and discovering that 'they had made many payments and ... only a few pounds were due', he returned home and 'prepared a statement of the circumstances to submit to Mr Sweet'.

Inevitably Isambard's accident threw more work on Armstrong. He had to muster the first shift in Rotherhithe Street, outside Cow Court, at 10 p.m., and for eight hours attend to their needs and direct their endeavours. At 6 a.m. the second shift arrived, and after they departed at 2 in the afternoon he had to organise supplies, superintend repairs, and report to his chief when Brunel made his afternoon inspection.

The exertions of shaft building had left their mark on Armstrong, and the three six-day spells of virtually uninterrupted duty sapped his remaining reserves. He put off ordering replacement parts for the shield 'till tomorrow'; and when Isambard returned he reacted condescendingly, as to an irresponsible boy, instead of welcoming his father's trusted 'coadjutor'.

The shield bore witness to the absence of effective control. The frames were eighteen inches too far to the west and, to accommodate the eastern wall, a chamber of equivalent depth had to be cut beyond the side staves of number 12. On the 25th Brunel found this unsupported excavation in a threatening state.

> Went to the tunnel with Isambard. Found that a considerable fall of ground had taken place at the right side. ... I inspected it, and directed that, after making good, flat bars of iron be driven in at the head of the side staves in order to pin it up. ... It is very bad and extremely dangerous; the ground is evidently the same as that which, in the report of the first attempt, was found so loose as to have dropped upon the works, leaving a large cavity above, when it is said the man ascended and made good the hole.

They had found one of Trevithick's 'le-areys'.

During March Brunel attended two meetings of the Court. The first was on the 14th, and Smith left the room as soon as he entered, but the other directors were friendly. At the second meeting, a fortnight later, Brunel asked the directors to dissociate themselves from the Chairman's allegation that he had deliberately misled them with the estimates for the Great Descents, as he had been 'subjected to very abusive expressions by persons who had heard Mr Smith's sentiments'. The sally embarrassed Smith, and Robert Marten assured the engineer that 'the Court had never expressed any unfavourable opinion upon those estimates, that they had, on the contrary, the utmost confidence in everything he had brought forward'.

Isambard was back by the beginning of April. He had taken lodgings near the shaft in a Company house, one room of which Pinchback and Bordège used when occupied on tunnel drawings. This concentration of effort proved a great convenience, so the 'gaz engine' was taken to Rotherhithe, and Isambard supervised its development within hailing distance of the shaft.

It was fortunate that he returned when he did, for Armstrong was away ill during the first week of the month, as was Robert Greenshield, a miner named Nelson who had superseded Morgan, and Munday, a foreman bricklayer. There was something about the 50-feet-long tunnel which sapped a man's vitality, and on the 7th, when Armstrong returned, Brunel fell ill. For three weeks Doctor Morris kept him at home.

The invalid at Blackfriars sent a stream of sketches and directives to Cow Court. The roof centerings were to be mounted on the wheeled stages, and trolleys were to be made for conveying skips of spoil from the face to the hoist in the shaft. Responding to the Court's pressure for faster progress, he arranged for Maudslay's men to chip out the joints of the frames' legs so that the shield's stride could be doubled. Thenceforth the faces would be worked down in nine-inch bites, and the frames advanced in 18-inch steps. A thousand new long-reach poling-screws were purchased and the lining brickwork was laid in nine-inch, instead of 4½-inch rings. All this was done in April, and each week eight feet were added to the tunnel. By 12 May, thanks to still faster working, it was 100 feet long.

The rapid progress gratified the directors, but Brunel soon had misgivings. One by one the frames' legs bent and their screw jacks jammed. Brunel's calculations indicated that the legs were amply strong, but as they had been trouble-free previously, he was forced to blame the longer stride.

Timber props were used as makeshift legs, while the jacks were repaired, and the frames became difficult to control. By the middle of May they were badly out of level, and a chain had to be slung across the upper boxes to hold them together. The shield was 2ft 8in too far to the west, and Brunel's disquiet regarding its management was increased by the fracture of a frame's head.

On 21 May, while en route for Maudslays, the coachmen told him that the engineering works was in ruins. At once he remembered the cast-iron trusses, and exclaimed, 'It must be the roof!' It was indeed the roof. Sixty workers had been buried, some killed, many injured, and Maudslay himself had had a narrow escape. Back home Brunel filled a page of his Journal with reflections on the treachery of cast iron and its need for wrought reinforcement, noting in passing that the centerings in hand for the tunnel were 'upon the whole wretchedly done for Maudslays'.

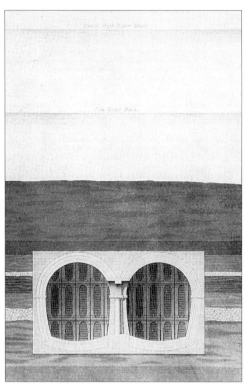

A transverse section through the Tunnel showing the brickwork and the strata beneath the river.

His thoughts turned to the careless working of the frames. Nothing had been done to correct the shield's westerly deviation; on 10 May he had found 20 inches of unlined roof behind the top staves; a house in Rotherhithe Street had cracked as a result of subsidence, and subsidence could occur only if the ground excavated had a greater volume than the tunnel and its brickwork. This should not be. It was contrary to the principles enunciated in his patent.

Armstrong had never spared himself, and his admiration for his chief was unmistakable. Respect of this sort is always gratifying, and it is doubtful if Brunel was fully aware of Armstrong's failure to cooperate with Isambard. At any rate, the sight of his old friend's ruined works was a reminder that disasters arrive unheralded, and Isambard was treated to a stern harangue about the management of the shield. It seemed unfair, and in the young man's Journal that evening there appeared the only reference to a family disagreement that the writer has discovered in any Brunel diary. 'Une dispute avec mon père, qui me menace de me donner un soufflet; je ne le souffrirai pas.'

Amity was soon restored, but Isambard left his father in no doubt about his relations with Armstrong, and on 1 June Brunel noted, 'There is a considerable degree of *laxity* in the service. The work is not carried on regularly. Short of bricklayers in one shift. The resident engineer is too lenient with the men, who do as they please. Isambard is the most efficient inspector we have. He is constantly in the work.'

The shield's deviation caused much wasted effort. At the eastern side of the face a heading had to be cut to accommodate the brickwork, while the ground excavated in front of frame number 1 on the western side was outside the line of the tunnel, and a double thickness of wall was needed to fill it up. The danger inherent in the slowly widening eastern heading was even more serious than the waste of time and material, especially as the face was becoming perceptibly wetter, and Brunel determined to move the shield sideways.

During the first week of June the eastern heading was widened and lined with carefully laid brickwork so as to provide a precise abutment for number 12's side staves when that frame was re-positioned. On the 5th tunnelling stopped and the men began the tedious business of dismantling each frame and moving it sideways. Armstrong was despatched to Leigh in Sussex during this operation, ostensibly to organise alternative brick supplies, for the output of the Company field satisfied only a fraction of the bricklayers' needs and recent consignments from the Patent Brick Company had been of unacceptable quality. His departure left Isambard in control and by the 10th he had moved the shield and resumed tunnelling.

Despite its brevity, the interruption irritated Smith, who had convinced himself that the shield was unnecessary. The upshot of this conviction was renewed pressure for still faster working, which was to be achieved by paying the bricklayers piece rates. Brunel disagreed. Piecework, he retorted, was shoddy work, and the bricklayers would urge on the miners who would take unwarranted risks. It would be more to the point if the directors would restrain their friends from visiting the works without prior warning; the engineers could ill afford the time to wait on them.

Brunel was disenchanted with Smith and his faction. He had complied with their whims and suffered needless anxiety. He had forgone his drain. He had reluctantly awarded the valuable Roman cement contract to a talkative and little-known manufacturer named Wilkes, whose cement varied in quality—but a consignment could not be rejected without protests from Wilkes's 'friends at Court'. But on 19 June Brunel was reminded that discretion was not one of his Chairman's qualities. The bricklayers levanted, and 'on enquiring into the cause', he learned that 'there was no other but to have a libation on the new arrangement of piecework'.

Trouble with bricklayers and the supervision of piecework were burdens Brunel was anxious to avoid. Armstrong was near the end of his tether, and had resisted a proposal designed to simplify laying the tunnel's roadways—a difficult task in the quagmire which had been created when the shield was repositioned. Brunel could not easily replace Armstrong. Except for Isambard there was no other engineer with tunnelling experience. Conditions at the face were becoming more difficult and Isambard needed time to win the directors' confidence.

Towards the end of June the shield's gentle downhill march carried the top staves into a band of silt which lay beneath the clay ceiling. The silt adhered to the staves, which became difficult to jack forward, and several frame heads fractured with reports like cannon shots. The shield was becoming decrepit so, since Maudslays had not delivered the stronger legs and shorter shoes that had been ordered, Brunel reverted to 4½-inch face working, and the frames resumed their original nine-inch steps.

The tunnel was 143 feet long at the end of June, but eight feet a week was not enough for Smith, and a week later Brunel was forced to introduce piece rates for the bricklayers. Well aware that the men would grow careless in their attempt to lay as many bricks each day as possible, Brunel sought to replace the much-dented portable gas lamps with a plant for making gas from coconut oil, which would supply fan burners through a pipe laid down one archway.* This proposal met with a dusty answer, although the plant would have cost only £160 and would have produced gas for less than half the bought-in cost. But as the shield bored on beneath the river, other gases made their presence felt.

'July 10th. The gaz was extremely offensive in the works below.' And the following day: 'Being in the works at the breakfast hour, found the air quite suffocating ... At eleven and twelve the atmosphere was quite putrified.' After spending the Sabbath in Rotherhithe's comparatively balmy atmosphere, the men were reluctant to return to the tunnel, and Monday's absentee rate went up.

The new legs were fitted in July, the tunnel grew another 40 feet, and 12 feet more were added during the first week of August; but Armstrong could not withstand the relentless pressure, the sickening atmosphere and the anxiety engendered by the deteriorating conditions. He left the works on 5 August, hoping to regain his strength—but the tunnel had broken him, although he returned several times for a day or two during the following six weeks.

The impossibility of recruiting an engineer with relevant experience made Isambard's assumption of control inevitable, but it would have been impolitic to have proposed him as Resident Engineer, so he remained a member of his father's staff, and enjoyed the responsibility although denied an official salary and status.

Even the directors were by this time convinced that no two men could control the labour force, so Brunel engaged two junior assistants as replacements for Armstrong. The first, Richard Beamish, began work on 7 August. He was followed, a week later, by William Gravatt, who was made responsible initially for the operation of the shield.

They were a dissimilar yet well-chosen pair. Beamish, a 28-year-old Irishman, had served with the Coldstream Guards, retiring two years previously after a

---

* Fifty-four triple jet burners (forty of them below ground) would have been required to light the completed tunnel, at a cost of 25s. per 1000 cubic feet as compared with £3 per 1000 cubic feet for bought-in gas.

period on the half-pay list. Although
he had seen Belgium with the army
of occupation and subsequently
became Sir Stamford Raffles's *aide-de-
camp,* the pleasures of an officer began
to vex his conscience, and he left
the service when his father forbade
marriage to the lady of his choice.
Bent on financial independence, he
returned to the family home in Cork
and studied books on engineering
before returning to London in search
of work. He had all the Guardsman's
qualities. He was tall and strong and
brave, sure in command, deliberate in
expression, cautious, unimaginative
and profoundly respectful to Brunel.

*A watercolour by Goodall of the Rotherhithe
shaft viewed from the end of the Eastern
Archway.*

Gravatt was a horse of a different colour. A contemporary of Isambard, he was a capable engineer whom Donkin had employed and warmly commended. He was an accomplished mathematician and a quick thinker who reached rapid and fearlessly expressed conclusions. Although not over-burdened with social graces, he was resourceful, and came to regard Isambard with immense admiration and affection.

Beamish was, above all, dependable; Gravatt had what might now be regarded as an 'Australian temperament'.

We may conclude from Brunel's Journal that the assistants arrived in the nick of time. 'August 10th. Found the lowest cell of No. 1 left by the workmen *without a single poling board against the ground.* This is indeed a most unjustifiable neglect.' But it is a measure of his confidence in the new team that he felt free to go to Liverpool with Sophie on 30 August.

The excursion resulted in Liverpool's first floating embarkation pier. Brunel watched the ferries, crammed with women carrying baskets of produce, grounding some distance from the quay. 'As soon as they could be boarded,' he noted, 'a great number of ragamuffins made their way [aboard] ... wrenching the baskets from their hands. The confusion is beyond power of description ... Upon the whole; nothing could be more inconvenient than the present mode of landing.'

While his father considered this little problem, Isambard guided the new assistants, rejected the odd bargeload of bricks from the Patent Brick Company (as was customary), dealt firmly with Wilkes and understandingly with Wilmot, who had contracted to carry spoil from the shaft to river barges, for a fixed sum for each foot of tunnel. He found time to conduct a series of borings across the Thames, which revealed yellow clay overlying the blue clay found earlier; and he directed his new assistants to force bricks into the sides of the face beyond the outermost poling boards, so as to keep the side staves running true, and the shield on its proper course.

All this Isambard accomplished, and on 7 September, three days after his return from Liverpool, Brunel was able to report that the tunnel extended 110 feet beneath the river. Its total length was 253 feet. Sixty feet had been added during the last five weeks.

It seemed a great achievement, but the headlong rush had played havoc with the shield. One side member of number 12 had fractured in two places, many of the new legs had jammed, and many heads had broken. Goaded by the bricklayers, the miners excavated the faces to a depth of 18 inches, and since the top poling boards in each cell were two feet higher than their shoulders, they were powerless to resist bursts of slush from the treacherous faces. Worked in this fashion, the shield afforded but scanty protection, it had become untrue to its name, and the cost of repairs exceeded the savings resulting from the faster working.

'To lay the greatest number of bricks in a week was all that was cared for by the bricklayers,' noted Beamish, 'and to urge on the miners was their constant effort.'

Brunel concurred: 'A work of this nature should not be hurried in this manner. Fewer hands, enough to produce nine feet per week, would be far better than the mode now pursued from necessity but not from inclination on my part ... The frames are in a very bad condition.' These measured words concealed a situation which, by the end of the first week of September, had become one of mortal danger. Beamish recalled an incident on the 1st which, in retrospect, seems a portent.

> The feed pipe of one of the boilers of the steam engine burst. To stop the pumps might have been attended with considerable inconvenience, if not danger. ... Isambard ... seizing some packing and a piece of quartering ... jumped upon the boiler, applied the packing to the fissure, and one end of the quartering upon that, jamming the other end against the slanting roof of the building; but finding that the roof was being raised, he clasped the quartering and there hung like the weight on the safety-valve, until I was able to procure sufficient weight to attach to the timber, and relieve him from his perilous situation. By this expedient time was gained, the other boiler was filled, and the steam engine continued its interrupted work.

They dared not stop the pumps; the influx at the face was increasing alarmingly.

Brunel spent the greater part of these days in the tunnel and missed nothing. On the 7th he found some faulty brickwork: '... the delinquent was immediately discharged.'

The following (Friday) morning Beamish was on duty and noted water dropping from behind the top staves or 'tails' of numbers 7 and 8.

> This [he recalled] was checked by a stuffing of oakum. In two hours diluted silt made its appearance, and during the night it burst in with considerable force, and at three o'clock in the morning [of Saturday], when I relieved Isambard Brunel in the superintendence, that force was so great, as to resist the united efforts of three men to retain the necessary stuffing in place. The contest was continued until six o'clock in the evening, when, the silt having been washed away, the clay settled down and checked the flow. ... It was now Saturday evening [9th], and the utmost vigilance was required during the whole night to retain the men at their posts, that the works might be secured against the usual suspension of the work on Sunday; not until eleven o'clock on Sunday morning, with the exception of a feverish doze of three hours, were we enabled to retire to rest.
>
> On Monday [11th] the contest had again to be renewed, water and silt occasionally bursting from the back of No. 6 frame when any attempt was made to move on, and Mr Brunel senior, who constantly supported our exertions with his presence, being unwilling to disturb the top staves, directed that they should be detached from the head. Timbers were introduced in front where the ground was more solid, and, capped with clay, were forced up by powerful screw-jacks. While this operation was going on in front, gravel and broken pieces of yellow mottled clay forced themselves in behind. Upon an effort being made to move forward the contiguous frames, water appeared in front in such abundance, as to threaten destruction to the faces.
>
> To relieve the ground, borings were made through the brickwork of the centre pier. ... At ten o'clock that night [Monday] the object was attained, and the water flowed with great velocity. ... All was now in full activity; the din of workmen and the plashing of the water, broken in its descent of 22 feet by the iron floor plates, was deafening, when suddenly the water ceased to flow. The workmen ceased their labour; not a sound relieved the intensity of the silence. We gazed on one another with a feeling not to be described. On every countenance astonishment, awe perhaps, was depicted, but not fear.
>
> I saw that each man, with his eyes upon Isambard Brunel, stood firmly prepared to execute the orders he should receive with resolution and intrepidity. In a few moments—moments like hours—a rumbling gurgling sound was heard above; the water resumed its course; the awful stillness was broken; life and activity once more prevailed; and the works proceeded without further material interruption.
>
> Shortly after the eventful pause, which I have endeavoured to describe, what was my amazement, upon visiting the bottom boxes, to find men fast asleep, with the water within a few inches of their heads.

These incidents involved Beamish in two unbroken spells of duty which lasted 53 and 20 hours. They were separated only by the short Sunday rest. Isambard's tasks were even more onerous. He remained in the works for five successive days of 24 hours, snatching brief naps on a wheeled stage behind the shield. The faces became perilously soft when mining was interrupted, and on 17 September Brunel was forced to extend the shifts from eight to 10 hours.

Such were the conditions, and the expedients to which the engineers were driven during September. They did not improve materially. It was the 23rd of the month before new top staves could be fitted to number 6 to replace those that had been bricked-in.

If William Smith and his friends thought that the August results justified piecework, then September must have provided them with a rude shock. Only 12 feet 8 inches had been added to the tunnel by the month's end. Young Pascoe, a master miner, and 14 other hands were away ill. The frames were out of level. The influx of river water * continued to increase.

During the summer, infiltration had been a minor problem, occasionally affecting the men in the bottom boxes. When there were stoppages, like the five-day suspension to move the shield sideways, it made the floor muddy, and hindered the bricklayers building the roadways. It was an inconvenience certainly, but a hand pumper in each archway kept the work clear. In September the trickle had become a stream. By the middle of October, the stream was in spate, its flow averaging 180 gallons per minute.

Country-born Irishmen, in shifts of 20, worked round the clock, seven days a week, pumping the water away from the face. Their hand pumps discharged into wooden chutes, which carried the water to the cistern beneath the shaft. To provide the necessary fall to the cistern, the ends of the timber channels had to be fixed half-way up the walls behind the shield. The hand pumps were at a corresponding level and, with their sweating operators, were mounted on the frames. Hand pumping cost £150 a week during October. The expenditure was mostly on wages, but repair costs were considerable because the silt-laden water destroyed the pumps' leather valves.

Water came in everywhere. Like a curtain behind the shield, it cascaded down past the tails of the top staves. It spurted through cracks between poling boards. It ruptured the faces and burst, heavy with debris, upon the miners when a board was removed. Sometimes these 'runs' threatened disaster.

In his weekly report of 3 October, Brunel told the Court of one such incident, when only the miners' coolness had averted an inundation.

---

* Whether water entering the tunnel came from the river or from land springs was established by comparing its temperature with that of the river.

River and tunnel: a section (looking south) through the river, its bed and the tunnel.

Smith reacted characteristically. Brunel had never 'given them any intimation of the circumstances'—he had deliberately concealed the true situation—only now had it been 'extorted from him'. He went on to recount a report from one Richardson—a 'friend' who had visited the works: 'twenty men ... surrounded him [Richardson] and asked him for money ... The men had nothing to do.' 'This' Brunel noted in his Journal, 'is a most barefaced falsehood which is too gross to be believed.'

Smith's behaviour, and his outbursts about the cost of repairs to the 'unnecessary shield', had become an embarrassment to his co-directors, so a small Committee of Works was set up with the twin objectives of controlling expenditure and restraining the Chairman.

The idea was timely. Brunel had trouble enough with the pumpers, to whom Beamish displayed an attitude of condescending superiority. 'A class of men were brought into close connection with the working,' he wrote,

> whose habits were foreign to such operations; and, however characteristic
> may be the daring of Irish labourers when under the happier influences

of an open sky and free air and the applauding voices of comrades, there was something, in the circumstances by which they were surrounded in the tunnel, so new and incomprehensible that their energies seemed entirely paralysed, except for flight.

New heads were fitted to the frames, which besides permitting the top staves to be jacked forward singly once again, also allowed them to tilt; and the brick roadways were laid on stout timbers, which were pressed into the floor of the excavation by jacks. But for Armstrong's weariness this would have been done months before. Slowly the silt-jammed frames were advanced, although turning the fleeting bars to extend an abutting screw often required the combined strength of 11 men. A blacksmith named Sheldon set up his forge near the shield, and effected speedy, if simple, repairs to the frames. Water still flooded in, but the work became more purposeful, and on 17 October eight-hour shifts were restored.

Towards the end of October Isambard was forced to take three weeks' rest, as was Beamish, whose sight was affected. Gravatt carried on, although suffering from a heavy cold. 'He is,' Brunel noted, 'a most interesting young man.'

Because of the absence of Isambard, Beamish and many of the *corps d'élite*, Brunel remained in the tunnel for nine consecutive days of over 20 hours' duration. 'I feel very seriously,' he wrote at this time,

> the fatigue of my present situation, in being without a Resident Engineer. With an unceasing duty, I have still more to think of to provide for our security; and to devise means for present exigencies. What an incessant labour of both mind and body! I should, however, feel perfectly comfortable under this heavy burden, was it not for the expenditure which I cannot reduce.

It was an inopportune moment to protest against the use of competitors' cement. 'Mr Wilkes came to bully me into the conviction that his cement was good ... that he was determined to compel us to come to his terms ... I declared to him that I could not suffer any of his cement to be used in the tunnel.'

Dispensing with the drain, doubling the shield's stride, piecework and the continuing use of condensed gas, had proved false economies. In opposing the Chairman's expedients, Brunel was seen to have been rational and prescient. Smith was hoist with his own petard; the Committee of Works stood by Brunel and he used his new authority to enforce uncompromising standards.

Piecework was abandoned early in November and thenceforth slipshod workmen received short thrift. Robert Greenshield was dismissed, and another miner, Nelson, who also clung to careless ways, was suspended for a week. The rest took heed.

A Sunday outing: William Hawes and Isambard in their 'funny boat'.

A shelter was built adjoining the boilerhouse, where clothing could be dried, and the men of incoming shifts mustered 'without the possibility of getting away' after the roll had been called.

Because of the cost of hand pumping, it seemed likely that the Company's coffers would be emptied before Wapping was reached, so the Court decided to admit visitors for a shilling a head and plans were made to decorate the western archway. The public could not be exposed to the dangerous gas lamps, so the oil-gas plant was sanctioned and work to install its pipe and burners began in December.

The closing weeks of 1826 were a busy time for the engineers. A secondhand railway was purchased, the track laid on the roadway of the eastern arch, and installation begun of an endless rope, which would harness the steam engine to the trucks, and draw them back and forth between the shield and the winding gear in the shaft. Weights were added to the engine's flywheel, to reduce vibration when running on one cylinder. (The power of one cylinder sufficed to operate the winding gear, the railway and three of the force pumps.) A hand capstan was rigged, so that the tunnel hands could work the force pumps in an emergency, and repairs were made to the brickfield roadway.

These tasks, supervising the men, and the search for better and cheaper bricks, involved Brunel's assistants in spells of duty which often exceeded 30 hours' duration. The faces were treacherous. Sometimes the supervision was inadequate. Sometimes, as Brunel noted on 20 December, the weary miners made mistakes.

> The poling screws of numbers 10 and 12 being on number 11, Moul, the miner in that frame, removed his butting screw; the consequences was that the frame started back, the polings and poling screws fell down with a tremendous crash, and the ground followed to a considerable extent. This is the most formidable accident that has yet occurred.

Reducing the burden carried by Isambard, Gravatt and Beamish became Brunel's chief concern. He arranged for Charles Butler, the Company Secretary, to move to Rotherhithe so as to free them from the chore of paying the men. He ordered a movable cabin to be built in the eastern archway in which they could work and rest. Yet more helpfully, he engaged a young man named Riley as a third assistant.

It is a measure of the change in the directors' attitude that these steps were possible in December. Two months earlier Brunel had reminded them that the shield alone made the tunnel possible. Its components were failing, not because the frames were 'lanky' as Smith had then alleged, but because the pieceworkers abused it. If the destruction did not cease, the Thames would swallow the shield, and the tunnel with it. Belatedly the warning had been heeded. Control had been re-established, and despite the inclement conditions seven feet a week had been added to the tunnel since Michaelmas,

Isambard had played a decisive part in the work of restoration and three days before Christmas Brunel submitted recommendations for a new chain of command. He proposed his son as Resident Engineer at a salary of £200 a year with Gravatt and Riley as assistants at salaries of £100 each. Beamish should continue at his lower salary and act in a responsible although less technical capacity.

The proposals were well received and although bad conditions at the face made it impossible to stop work on Christmas Day, Isambard welcomed the New Year with nine friends, who dined with him in the western archway beneath the Thames. As the bells of St Mary's tolled the midnight hour, the great blind bore extended northwards 355 feet from the shaft. Almost one-third of the tunnel had been built since work began in earnest at the beginning of March. Surely a sufficient reason for a celebration.

To Isambard the future looked hopeful. Pitt had been Prime Minister at twenty-two. He, Isambard, would accomplish much before he reached that ripe old age.

'After all, I may be said to have almost built this tunnel ... What castles!! ... What a field—yet I may miss it.

'... What will become of me?'

22

ISAMBARD AS RESIDENT
ENGINEER

Isambard assumed control on 3 January following an agreeable visit by two directors. 'Mr Marten came,' he noted, '... he expressed himself as usual in a most liberal and kind manner. Mr Hawes informed me that the Court had approved of my appointment as Resident Engineer.'

There was no honeymoon period. The directors' liberality did not extend to the miners and bricklayers, whose wages were reduced to 2s. 10d. a day, and three days later Isambard's diary told of a strike.

> When pay began this afternoon, the bricklayers refused to receive their wages. They came down to me in the tunnel. They surrounded me, remonstrating, by their spokesman [Mills] ... against the reduction ... and entreating for a continuation of their pay ... I thought it time to exercise some authority. I ordered the men [the labourers] to return to their work and the others to leave the shaft immediately. I was obeyed by both.
>
> When above ground they still persisted in refusing their wages, reiterating their request for the full wages; which could not, of course, be complied with.
>
> I have every reason to suspect that the miners are in the plot. They, however, have shown no disposition to follow the example. They have received their money, waiting for the end.

New bricklayers were engaged, but three days later the old hands returned chastened, and 12 of them were taken back.

Then there were accidents. On 8 January one of the portable gas lamps was dropped down the shaft and exploded. Isambard ran down, hearing

> a loud rustling sound, immediately followed by a mass of light aflame all over the bottom of the shaft. It lasted six or eight seconds. A number of men came running up all terrified, Nelson crying that he was burned all over. I gave him to the care of Gravatt. Robert Greenshield [who had been re-engaged] was dreadfully burned. Osborne, Bowling and Davies were also injured more or less ... Every attention was paid to the men by applying oil, which relieved them much. The surgeon was sent for.

Three days later the valve of a hand pump failed, and water filled the bottom boxes. The following day Beamish was injured by a fleeting bar. On the 23rd a leading miner, Collingwood, was discharged for drunkenness, and throughout the month an average of seven per cent of the men were absent sick—including Munday and Lane, and briefly Isambard and Gravatt. On the 31st Riley succumbed. 'Riley cannot survive,' Brunel noted seven days later, 'water on the brain.' He was buried on 13 February.

The foul air was taking its toll. Considering the conditions, adding 14 feet to the tunnel during the first half of January was not a bad performance; but Isambard spurred the men on, and during the next ten weeks weekly progress almost doubled.

Much of the credit for this acceleration belongs to Gravatt. Early in the New Year, while investigating the failure of some of the new stronger legs, he discovered that their mud-caked joints had been deformed when Maudslays chipped them out. When they were freed the shield became more manageable.

The fast progress was timely; Brunel was being pressed to complete the tunnel by contract and on 23 January reported to the Court on this proposal.

> We have been visited by almost all the tunnel makers of the country. I have made it a point on most occasions to put the question to such as were best qualified, whether they would undertake the tunnel by contract. No one has given me credit for being in earnest for making such a proposition ...
>
> ... I have no hesitation [he concluded] in giving it as my decided opinion that neither the excavation or the brickwork can be done by contract; and if my responsibility is an absolute condition, I must declare that I would take none upon myself if the work is done by contract.'

He was not going to be caught on the piecework hook again.

Completion of the railway at the end of January saved some hands, and when the new gas plant was commissioned, six weeks later, the engineers were able to give more of their attention to tunnelling. But, because of the need for economy, Riley was not replaced; instead, on 12 March, Beamish became an engineer officially—somewhat to Gravatt's chagrin—and was given an increased salary which was backdated to 1 January.

He had to keep his wits about him. The miners were frequently compelled to support the roof with sheet piling when frames were advanced and during February the tunnel floor became equally treacherous. 'On one occasion,' wrote Beamish, 'had not the eastern frame been slung to the contiguous frames, and long timbers laid under the shoes, the whole would have gone down, as a five-feet crowbar and a ten-feet rod disappeared from my hands one anxious night, when the hard crust of gravel which covered the sand had been broken through.' They were skating over the deep quicksand, which geologists called the 'forty-foot sand'.

The face changed ominously. As many as nine separate strata, many of them bands of shells, confronted a miner in his box—and each was separated by a filament of water which, Beamish noted, 'were found to be very sensibly acted upon by the movements of the tide'.

Isambard's reaction was to move the frames quickly—before the faces softened. Brunel concurred, but Beamish, an innately cautious man, thought operations should be conducted only when the tide was ebbing. He had little opportunity to press his views. On 14 February, while helping to prepare for the Sunday shutdown, he was reminded of the strange things the tunnel could do to a man. 'A haze rose before my eyes, and in the course of half-an-hour I lost the sight of my left eye.' Despite active treatment, his sight was never completely restored, and the Irishman was unable to resume his 'subfluvial duties' until 7 March.

Beamish was not the only sick man. Exhaustion and the polluted air affected miners, bricklayers and engineers alike—Isambard and Gravatt both suffered further bouts of sickness during February—but the tempo did not slacken.

By the end of the month the western arch had been decorated, and carpenters were busy erecting a barrier at its end—a few feet back from the shield—and placing bars across the connecting arches in the dividing wall. Others were building an entrance lodge and stairways in the shaft—in readiness for the visitors' arrival—and on 26 February Brunel took his family along for a preview. 'The *coup d'oeil* was splendid. Mrs Brunel, Emma, Sophia and her three little children, were the first. It gave me great pleasure to see the whole of my family in the new scene.'

The archway was opened on 21 March and the public thought it was splendid; as many as 700 visitors a day paid a shilling a piece to inspect it although, as Isambard observed, they were 'not all gentlemen'.

Their shillings were useful. Four hundred and sixteen men laboured in the archways during March, and Brunel's end-of-the-month report gives a glimpse of the conditions.

> We are obliged frequently to have two men in some of the lower cells, one to remove, with his hands, the shingly ground, which in those places is quite deliquescent, while another is ready behind to prepare clay to make a facing to lay the poling against ... We have ... a considerable influx of water, which at high water (and particularly at the last spring tide) has exceeded in quantity all the springs we have ever met before; it is evidently not from the river that it proceeds, but from land springs, oozing through the middle stratum of shells and the bed of gravel.

Each day a few men were carried off suffering from chest pains, dizziness or suppurating arms as a result of scooping the filth behind the poling boards with their bare hands. The sick numbered 30 by the third week of April.

The healthy men lived for the day, as Brunel observed on the 6th:

> Nothing was done yesterday at the night-shift; all the bricklayers came in sober, but not one eighth part of the miners made their appearance, and upon sending round to the public houses, the others were found drunk. Circumstanced as we now are we cannot turn out these men, because a stoppage would be very injurious, if not fatal.

Isambard celebrated his coming-of-age with a concert in the western archway on 11 April, and the directors spent an agreeable month, counting receipts from visitors and welcoming Dr Wollaston and a brewer named Perkins, who had joined the Board in March, but in the tunnel conditions deteriorated and progress slowed to eight feet a week.

The roof was breached on the 21st. The miners plugged the hole with no more difficulty than on a dozen former occasions, but instead of clay and silt, trash poured in from the bed of the river—gravel and brickbats—coal, butcher's bones and fragments of china. Where was the 'strong blue clay'?

An old waterman said that the river had been dredged for ballast at this spot, so Brunel borrowed a diving bell and barge from the West India Dock Company, and on 25 April Isambard and Gravatt descended in it and inspected the breach from above. They tapped the top staves with an iron rod, and Nelson, the miner in the upper box, heard every blow. 'Subsequently,' says Beamish, 'an iron pipe having been passed through the ground, a direct communication was held with the diving bell, and some gold pins supplied by Mr Benjamin Hawes, jun ... were passed up the tube to be presented to friends as a memento of this extraordinary communication.'

The next day Brunel descended, inspected the hole, and directed its filling with gravel. The shield was pushed forward again, but the Irishmen were uneasy and the following Sunday deserted their pumps and rushed away up the shaft, ringing the bell at its entrance.

Isambard was enjoying the day of rest.

> Having got up rather late, Gravatt and I were at breakfast when Cook came running with a face like death to say that 'All was over', the tunnel had fallen in, one man only escaped. Gravatt, being dressed, ran down immediately. I followed half-naked and ran down the east arch, astonished to hear—nothing. I ran on, found Gravatt in the middle boxes, the pumpers all gone, but not seeing their dead bodies concluded that they were safe.
>
> A long time discovering the cause of the alarm—at last perceived a slight run between two and three. The silt, having accumulated on the floor plate, at last fell—splash!!—away, away ...

Early in May the miners struck and picketed the tunnel, although 'earning', noted Beamish indignantly, 'from 3s. 3d. to 3s. 9d. a day'. They returned after eight days and were re-engaged—except for the ringleaders.

The face softened during the interruption and the abutting screws rusted and became difficult to turn. River debris, including the sheave of a block and an old shoe buckle, burst in more and more frequently and Brunel recommended closing the tunnel to visitors—but the directors would not hear of it.

Number 6 was advanced at high tide on the 12th. One of the miners had carelessly left some poling boards unsupported in front of its top box, and a vein of yellow clay began to swell ominously as Isambard arrived.

His Journal records what followed.

> Ball, coming immediately into the box, I directed him to cut away the ground—which he did to the proper depth—and replaced the two polings; but in vain did we attempt to replace the screws—which were too long—against the ... ground, which continued to swell very fast upon on us.

While Ball struggled in the top box of number 6, the poling boards in front of 4 and 5 started to slip down, and silt burst in between 3 and 4. Isambard directed two miners, Goodwin and Burt, to deal with these troubles while Ball again cut away his clay and tried again unsuccessfully to secure the poling boards.

Twice more the swelling clay filled the box, and twice more Ball, lying on his back, cleared it away—then 'the ground came in with a tremendous burst (being much more loose and wet than before), and roaring into the box, prevented all access to the polings; expelling us by force'.

All they could do was to board up the back and sides of the cell, but while this was being done, there was another run of silt and mud in the top faces of 7 and 8. Water followed, driving the miners from the bottom boxes and rising 15 inches above the floor.

After 12 hours' labour Isambard and Gravatt brought the situation under control, and the miners set to work to clear the shield, removing—along with clay and silt—the pin of a block, fragments of Italian pottery jars, and a shovel and a hammer, which had been dropped from the diving bell.

Brunel's diary reveals his anxiety.

> May 13th. Notwithstanding every prudence on our part, a disaster may still occur—may *it not be when the arch is full of visitors!* It is too awful to think of it. I have done my part by recommending to the directors to shut the tunnel. My solicitude is not lessened for that; I have ... no rest, I may say, I have had none for weeks.

Two days later, the influx of water reached 500 gallons a minute, but it was slowly checked, and on the 17th Brunel noted, 'There is no doubt of the ground having improved very materially since last Saturday. Very cheering indeed.'

Isambard's diary, however, contained less reassuring intelligence.

'A queue of colliers formed for the first time just over the present work—went afloat in the evening to examine the anchorage of these vessels. Found all clear above and below—the vessels, though, nine in number, right over the frames.'

After his reconnaissance, Isambard returned, late in the evening, to the river's soft under-belly. The tide was ebbing, but the top faces were tender and the miners worked with wary deliberation.

The Irishmen toiled at their pumps.

The tunnel was 549 feet long. Fifty feet more—75 feet at the most—to the halfway mark. If only they could creep on for one more month —making a yard a week until they reached better ground—they could finish it in a year. Twelve months like March would see them through. Wapping in June 1828? Well, why not?

The tide began to flow.

Shortly after Beamish had taken over from Isambard at five in the morning, there was a burst of liquid silt between 6 and 7. 'The ground seemed as though it were alive.'

At six the shifts changed. The new men were in no hurry, hanging back in the boilerhouse until the foremen urged them down none too civilly. Then the first shift departed.

Brunel visited the tunnel during the morning. The faces were too soft to be left, so some of the morning shift stayed on, and some of the night men came in early. There was nothing unusual in this, and the colliers had moved. At least the river bed would not be scoured by another tide ebbing beneath their keels.

In the afternoon, while Isambard and Gravatt supervised the work, Brunel and Beamish escorted Lady Raffles and a party of her friends around the western archway. They left at six, Brunel with them; Isambard and Gravatt went above ground to examine some prints, and Richard Beamish prepared for what he felt sure would be a trying night.

> My holiday coat was exchanged for a strong waterproof, the polished Wellingtons for greased mud boots, and the shining beaver for a large-brimmed south-wester.
>
> The tide was now rising fast. On entering the frames, Nos. 9 and 11 were about to be worked down. Already had the top polings of No. 11 been removed, when the miner, Goodwin, a powerful and experienced man, called for help. For him to have required help was sufficient to indicate danger. I immediately directed an equally powerful man, Rogers, in No. 9,

to go to Goodwin's assistance; but before he had time to obey the order, there poured in such an overwhelming flood of slush and water, that they were both driven out, and a bricklayer [Corps] who had also answered to the call for help, was literally rolled over on to the stage behind the frames, as though he had come through a mill sluice, and would have been hurled to the ground, if I had not fortunately arrested his progress.

I then made an effort to re-enter the frames, calling upon the miners to follow; but I was only answered by a roar of water, which long continued to resound in my ears. Finding that no gravel appeared, I saw that the case was hopeless. To get all the men out of the shield was now my anxiety. This accomplished, I stood for a moment on the stage, unwilling to fly, yet incapable to resist the torrent which momentarily increased in magnitude and velocity, till Rogers, who alone remained, kindly drew me by the arm, and, pointing to the rising water beneath, showed only too plainly the folly of delay. Then ordering Rogers to the ladder, I slowly followed.

As a singular coincidence, I may here remark that this man, Rogers, who showed such kindly feeling and devotion, had served with me in the Coldstream Guards.

While the old comrades, engulfed in the torrent and battered by flotsam, struggled away from the stage, through a connecting arch in the dividing wall, and into the less obstructed western or visitors' archway, Isambard fought his way down the shaft past fleeing labourers and pumpers. Gravatt followed him, but finding the stairs blocked, jumped a fence and rushed, past a fainting woman, down the visitors' stairs. The pair reached the bottom and found themselves standing on a dry floor surrounded by a throng of miners.

Meanwhile, as Beamish recalled, he and Rogers had struggled through the waist-high tide to the barrier which limited the visitors' approach.

Arrived at the barrier, four powerful hands seized me, and in a moment placed me on the other side. On we now sped. At the bottom of the shaft we met Isambard Brunel and Mr Gravatt. We turned. The spectacle which presented itself will not readily be forgotten. The water came on in a great wave, everything on its surface becoming the more distinctly visible as the light from the gas-lamps were more strongly reflected. Presently a loud crash was heard. A small office, which had been erected under the arch, about a hundred feet from the frames, had burst. The pent air rushed out; the lights were suddenly extinguished, and the noble work, which only a few short hours before had commanded the homage of an admiring public, was consigned to darkness and solitude.

Isambard ordered the men up the stairs. There was some confusion in the sudden blackness and, as Beamish realised, they were all in mortal danger.

For the first time I now felt something like fear, as I dreaded the recoil of the wave from the circular wall of the shaft, which, if it had caught us, would inevitably have swept us back under the arch. With the utmost difficulty, the lowest flight of steps was cleared, when, as I had apprehended, the recoil came, and the water surged just under our feet. The men now hurried up the stairs and, though nearly exhausted, I was enabled to reach the top.

But old Tillett, the engine man, had not got out. Gravatt peered down and saw him struggling in the water

> like a rat ... quite spent. I was looking about me how to get down, when I saw Brunel [Isambard] descending by a rope to his assistance. I got hold of one of the iron ties, and slid down into the water hand over hand with a small rope, and tried to make it fast round his middle, whilst Brunel was doing the same. Having done it, he called out, 'Haul up.' The man was hauled up. I swam about to see where to land. The shaft was full of casks. Brunel had been swimming too.

The roll was called; no one was missing and Beamish mounted a pony and rode to Bridge Street.

Brunel took the news calmly. 'Relieved as I have found myself,' he wrote, 'though by a terrible catastrophe, of the worst state of anxiety that I have been in for several weeks past, I had a most comfortable night.' But on Sunday, his diary betrayed a feeling of irritation: 'The Rotherhithe curate, in his sermon today, adverting to the accident, said that ... it was but a just judgment upon the presumptuous aspirations of mortal men, etc.! The poor man!'

And *The Times* was uneasy. 'Beside the workmen, there were two or three visitors, one of whom was a female, whose feet, in their retreat, were actually washed by the water.'

23

SALVAGE

———◦•◦◦•◦———

Brunel's first concern was to allay anxiety, and the day after the flood he sent a letter to Charles Butler, which was promptly published: 'I have adopted means to remedy the evil and remove the water, and feel confident that the work will, in a short time, be resumed and proceed as usual.' He added a tribute to the men's coolness with a special word of praise for Richard Beamish.

While he wrote these words, Isambard and Gravatt explored the river bed from the confines of the diving bell. They found a cavity, and when their air bubble was lowered into it, stood on the top staves of 10, 11 and 12. Brunel descended the following day and confirmed the staves' solidity; meanwhile careful soundings were taken, and from them a picture of the river bed emerged.

There was a saucer-shaped depression, 50 feet across, with an average depth of nine feet. In the middle of this hollow was a steep-sided pit, 10 feet long, seven feet wide, and where the easternmost top staves and the rim of roof brickwork were exposed, six feet deep. In the evening, when the crater had been mapped, a great bung was fashioned in a barge moored over the shield. It comprised a hundred or more clay-filled jute bags, all lashed together with stout ropes. This plug was lowered into the stream, and came to rest in the hole in its bed.

Night and day during the following week, bargeloads of clay-filled bags, through which hazel rods were driven—like knitting needles through balls of wool—were dumped into the pit, while Isambard and his helpers continued their aquatic explorations. On 24 May the pumps were started and a head of between 25 and 30 feet was maintained with the engine turning very slowly.

The struggle to regain the tunnel held the public in thrall. It was a favourite subject for letters to editors, and a magnet to armchair inventors. A spectacle was staged called 'The Thames Tunnel or Harlequin Excavator'; one scene depicted a 'Subaqueous Grotto Beneath the Source of the Thames', another 'The Interior of the Thames Tunnel with its Curious Machinery'. The cast included eels, fishes, jolly water sprites and gloomy watermen.

A chorus of melancholy shareholders would have provided a background of realism. It had been clear for some time that existing funds would not suffice to complete the work; but had low-water mark at Wapping been reached, the problem of borrowing more money would have not been unduly daunting. Now, even if all was not lost, the cost of salvage would curtail future progress, and the memory of the flood might induce a financial draught. The directors heard from the shareholders, and Brunel heard from the inventors. The latter's schemes were acknowledged and passed to the Court, receiving attention from Donkin and Smith, who eagerly examined any idea that might ingratiate them with subscribers at their chief engineer's expense.

One suggestion, which Brunel reluctantly agreed to try, was to sink a ballasted lid on top of the clay bags so as to compress the filling and seal it from the river. A raft measuring 35 feet by 15 feet was built, by spiking outer skins of four-inch-thick planks across a core of foot-square timber baulks. At the beginning of June, this unwieldy craft was moored over the shield and loaded with 250 tons of clay and gravel—the operation being supervised by Isambard.

'The tide came in in grand style! Heaving stuff overboard from the barge. After taking some elder wine, went to sleep on the raft.' At low water that evening the raft was sunk, and after several bargeloads of clay bags and gravel had followed it to the bottom, the pumps were worked at full speed. The water in the shaft dropped at once, and the following afternoon Isambard climbed inside it, waded some way along the western archway, and cleared some casks and loose timber. But in the evening the river broke in again, and in a few minutes the shaft, was full.

Early next morning, Isambard descended in the bell and examined the raft. He found that the ebbing tide had scoured away the river bed from under its northern side. The covering was therefore dredged away, and on 4 June, after the raft had surfaced, the bed of the Thames was surveyed once more. A new cavity was found which extended downwards to the roof brickwork and the top staves of the middle frames, numbers 6 and 7.

This setback was a great disappointment for Brunel. During the previous month, his hours of sleep had been few and irregular. He had descended many times in the diving bell—a pastime not much sought after by men of 57—and the safety of the divers was an unending anxiety since their barge was continually threatened by shipping and the small craft of sightseers. He had suffered the curiosity of the public, the fanciful schemes of inventors and the hostility of the chairman's entourage. Two months earlier he had sold his interest in the Battersea sawmill, but the burden of responsibility was greater than ever. He was nearly exhausted, and after directing Isambard to lay a lattice of iron rods in the new cavity and then to fill it with bags of clay and loose gravel, he retired to bed, taking his diary with him.

June 5th. There is much danger in getting out of the diving bell, the bags
are so loose in some places. One might sink and be swallowed, which very
nearly happened today. Isambard and Pinckney [a miner] being down, the
latter lost his hold. The footboard having been accidentally carried away, he
could not have recovered himself had not Isambard stretched out his leg to
his assistance .... Isambard and Gravatt went down a third time to examine
deeper into the frames by sinking themselves one after the other.

Not having begotten the tunnel, Isambard did not allow the directors to
oppress him unduly. He discharged 200 men and pressed on. When the new
hole had been plugged he started the pumps and slowly the water in the shaft
was lowered. Pumping had to be done cautiously. If the head was too great,
then the river might burst in again, and if, by some mischance, the water in
the shaft was higher than in the river at low tide, then the filling would be
forced upwards out of the hole.

By 11 June 722 cubic yards of clay and gravel had been strewn on the
river bed. The second hole had been filled. Water in the shaft rose and fell
in harmony with the tide, but each day a few more rungs of the workmen's
ladder-stairway were exposed. The clay bags were still sinking, but each new
depression was quickly mapped and filled.

On the 12th the head was 25 feet; within a week the crowns of the
archways were revealed, and five days later, when only a little water covered
the base of the shaft, some distinguished visitors, including the geologist Sir
Roderick Murchison and Charles Bonaparte arrived. Brunel had recovered,
but the party was entrusted to Isambard's tender care, and had a lively day,
as Murchison revealed.

The first operation we underwent (one which I never repeated) was to go
down in a diving bell upon the cavity by which the Thames had broken in.
Buckland and Featherstonehaugh, having been the first to volunteer, came
up with such red faces and such staring eyes, that I felt no great inclination
to follow their example, particularly as Charles Bonaparte was most anxious
to avoid the dilemma, excusing himself by saying that his family were very
short-necked and subject to apoplexy, etc; but it would not do to show the
white feather; I got in, and induced him to follow me. The effect was, as I
expected, most oppressive, and then on the bottom what did we see but
dirty gravel and mud, from which I brought up a fragment of one of Hunt's
blacking bottles. We soon pulled the string, and were delighted to breathe
fresh air.

The first folly was, however, quite overpowered by the next. We went
down the shaft on the south bank, and got, with young Brunel, into a punt
which he was to steer into the tunnel till we reached the repairing shield.
About eleven feet of water was still in the tunnel, leaving just space enough
above our heads for Brunel to stand up and claw the ceiling and sides to
impel us. As we were proceeding, he called out, 'Now, gentlemen, if by

accident there should be a rush of water, I shall turn the punt over and
prevent you being jammed under the roof, and we shall then be carried
out and up the shaft!' On this C. Bonaparte remarked, 'But I cannot swim!'
and, just as he had said the words, Brunel, swinging carelessly from right to
left, fell overboard, and out went the candles with which he was lighting up
the place. Taking this for the *sauve qui peut*, fat C.B., then the very image of
Napoleon at St Helena, was about to roll after him, when I held him fast,
and, by the glimmering light from the entrance, we found young Brunel,
who swam like a fish, coming up on the other side of the punt, and soon
got him on board. We, of course, called out for an immediate retreat, for
really there could not be a more foolhardy and ridiculous risk of our lives,
inasmuch as it was just the moment of trial as to whether the Thames would
make a further inroad or not.

Murchison's forebodings proved well-founded; that same evening water
again rose slowly up the shaft. A reconnaissance of the river bed revealed a
new depression over the centre frames, and when this had been filled, two
tarpaulins well weighted with chains were spread over the place and covered
with still more gravel.

By 25 June the hand pumpers had pumped 155 feet of the tunnel dry,
and at seven in the evening, Brunel ordered an expedition to the shield.

Isambard, mustering the men who had been the last to quit the frames,
told them that they would be the first to take possession of them again—a
precedence due, he said, to Rogers, Ball, Goodwin, Corps and Compton,
who were accordingly ordered to trim themselves for the expedition, provided
with a phosphorous box, and with light clothes to be fit for a swim.

They were ready at ten, and with Isambard and Beamish punted down
the western archway, broke through the visitors' barrier, and reached the
wheeled stage which, except for its crane, was buried in a great mound of
clay and silt that almost barred the way to the shield. 'Finding that they could
not get nearer, they gave three cheers, which were rapturously answered by
the men at the mouth of the Tunnel. Having placed candles on the ground

Regaining the shield.

... and upon the head of the crane, they returned ... This,' Brunel concluded, 'is a great day for our history.'

Two days later, having cleared some of the debris, Beamish and two miners, Woodward and Pamphilon, voyaged down the eastern archway, past the other wheeled stage, which had been swept halfway to the shaft, to within 120 feet of the shield, where their punt grounded on a mound of earth, like the one in the western archway. 'Leaving the men in the boat and supplied with a bull's-eye lantern,' Beamish scrambled into the frames and found them roughly in place. Bulging bags protruded menacingly in the eastern corner, where a stream of water flowed in. The western frames were full of mud, but those on the east side were clear.

Brunel decided to see for himself, but when he saw how much flotsam remained, he forbade further expeditions until it had been cleared. He had scarcely departed, however, when Robert Marten and Richard Harris arrived, and asked Gravatt to take them down the tunnel. Gravatt could not refuse his directors, so, taking two miners, Richardson and Dowling, as crew, they boarded a dinghy.

> Richardson [Beamish recorded] ... insisted in getting in at the stern of the boat when he had shoved it off ... The water came in; and though one of the gentlemen was requested to go forward that the boat might be balanced, neither was willing to stir, until Mr Marten, feeling the water inconvenient, and forgetting that the boat had made considerable progress down the archway, diminishing rapidly the headway, suddenly stood up, struck his head against the top of the arch and fell backwards upon the others.

The boat overturned, depositing the party in 12 feet of water. Dowling and Gravatt were the only swimmers, but the latter had to dive to release himself from a director's embrace. He swam back to the shaft, returned with the punt, and rescued Marten and Harris, who were clinging to the soffit of a connecting arch. Dowling had regained the shaft, but Richardson had disappeared. Isambard then appeared and dived several times in a vain search for him. At length the Humane Society's officials arrived and recovered the body with their drag. A newspaper report reveals the grief engendered by this needless tragedy.

> It [the body] was carried to Mr Gravatt's pilot house, and the usual remedies ... promptly resorted to, but without effect .... His poor wife, on hearing of the circumstance, went down to the works in the most frantic state, and it was with difficulty that she was torn away from the scene of death ...
>
> He was a man, though in a humble station of life, of such generally conciliating habits, and disposition, that he had drawn towards him the good wishes, and good feelings, of every man in the works, not excluding the officers themselves. Mr Brunel, junior, and Mr Gravatt observing the

prevalence of this sensation, and participating in it themselves, determined on stopping the works during the night.

By the month's end, a passage had been cut through the western mound of earth, and the shield inspected in detail. The inrush had displaced two rings of roof brickwork in the eastern archway, and as a result, some abutting screws had fallen down and their frames had started back. There were displaced poling boards, but the shield was intact, although many boxes were filled with mud.

There were no gas lamps. The hand pumpers toiled by the dim uncertain light of candles. Shadowy miners cut channels through the black mounds of earth, while their comrades pushed boats through to the shield, and there worked to secure the frames, nearly 200 dark, cluttered yards north from the Cow Court shaft. 'If we reflect,' wrote Brunel, 'that the only way to get to the frames is with a boat, it is truly awful to think how the men reconcile themselves with danger. The example set to them is the stimulus. What a man would shrink from when left to himself, he will face when acting before others.'

On 6 July a sudden torrent engulfed the miner in number 12. He fled in the boat, leaving his comrades marooned, Isambard, with some other men, hurried to the shield and tried in vain to board up the breach. Again, the tunnel was evacuated, and again Isambard dived in the bell. He was nearly killed. The lowering chain slipped through its stoppers, and had it not jammed providentially, he would have been trapped in a watery tomb.

Brunel was unhappy in bed. 'Can there be a more anxious situation ...? Not one moment of rest either of mind or of body. Mr Beamish always ready. Poor Isambard always at his post too, alternately below, in the barges, or in the diving bell.'

At low water next morning, a 40-foot-square tarpaulin was sunk over the spot, and covered with two bargeloads of gravel. This reduced the influx to 850 gallons a minute. Five days later an 80-foot-square sheet, whose edges were bound with nine tons of chain, was lowered under Isambard's direction. It was a tricky task. 'I cannot help observing, for my future guidance,' he noted, 'that being alone, and giving few but clear orders, and those always to the men who were to execute them, I succeeded in an operation not altogether mean, and which a very trifling want of precaution or order might have caused to be a total failure.'

More bargeloads of clay and gravel were flung on to the blanket, and then the men were able to return to their labours below. This time the Thames was beaten. There were alarms, however. A hand-powered waterwheel was rigged behind the frames, but the timber chute into which it discharged collapsed with a frightful clatter, and the men fled. They returned soon enough, but

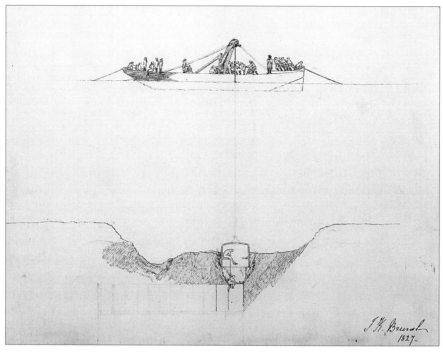

Isambard's sketch of a descent in the diving bell.

their hardly concealed fears were revealed by Fitzgerald, the Saturday night watchman at the shield. In the small hours of Sunday morning, Beamish heard him call out, 'Wedges, clay, oakum ... the whole of the faces coming in—coming in altogether!' More surprised than alarmed, he sent Rogers to the frames with the desired materials, 'but the only sounds that met his ear were the clang of the monotonous pumping and the gurgling of the water from No. 12 ... upon going up on a stage erected in the western arch, there lay the careful watch, comfortably ensconced on clean straw, sound asleep.'

By the end of July the roof brickwork had been restored, and the frames and the archways cleared of mud.

'28th. Turned on our own gaz in the first six arches—no ventilation, the consequence was that the smell from emptying the pipes very offensive—and the place altogether very foggy.' The ventilating shaft above the dividing wall had been irrevocably blocked with mud, and restoring the gas lights aggravated the pollution of the stagnant atmosphere. But although the men in the shield suffered giddiness and sickness, and a black deposit formed around their lips and nostrils, visitors were readmitted to the western archway. They were in some danger; their exhalations were unwelcome; but their shillings were needed.

A newspaper report confirms that these were not Brunel's only preoccupations.

> We understand that upwards of four hundred plans have been sent to Mr Brunel for mending the hole made by the river. ...
>
> Since the water has been stopped, several of these contributors have applied to Mr Brunel for pecuniary compensation, under the impression that there could be but one way of stopping the hole, and that way as pointed out by themselves. Some of the claimants, we understand, have been extremely troublesome.

Brunel, the writer explained, had classified the proposals. There were:

> Thirty-nine plans for a covering of sails or tarpaulins. Twenty-two plans for lids of cast or wrought iron, etc. Forty-two plans for rafts, etc. Forty plans for inverted vessels to act as diving bells. Four plans for coffer dams. Two plans for shafts. Five plans for plugs of suitable dimensions. Five plans for floodgates, etc. Six plans for sheet piling, etc. Three plans for a new tunnel. One plan for a new shield.

Many of the schemes could not be categorised, and 58 were secret although, of course, infallible.

On 11 August Brunel again succumbed to exhaustion, and for six weeks was unable to visit the tunnel. But another drama was being enacted at Walbrook Buildings from which he could not disengage.

Amongst the proposals that had come before the Court, there was one whose parentage was acceptable. Francis Giles, the engineer who had mapped the river bed in 1824, expressed interest in completing the work by contract. He may have agreed to lodge a surety with the Company, but whether he did this or not, his offer was subject to three conditions. First, a new geological survey must be undertaken; second, he must make the borings himself; and third, he must be paid for this work. Providing these conditions were accepted, and providing the borings revealed good ground, then he would finish the archways, in his own way, by contract. Giles took care not to commit himself too far, and some of the directors were sceptical. But Donkin and Smith swallowed the bait, and no doubt others found it tempting. A struggle for power followed. Marc Brunel and Isambard versus Smith, Donkin and Giles.

Smith and Donkin argued that, as the tunnel was costing twice as much as Brunel had predicted, and as the shield had not prevented an irruption of the river, the time had come to entrust the work to another engineer. Brunel replied that, although misled by Joliffe and Banks, he had built almost half a tunnel which, but for his shield, could never have been attempted. Despite the inundation, the works were intact, and soon, when all was ready, the shield would march again.

Some directors remembered that the Chairman's judgement was fallible, and realised that a break with Brunel might finish the Company. The tunnel was his creation, and no one had succeeded him in the public's esteem. No new shareholders would come forward if he left. No Exchequer loan was conceivable without him. Worse still, the present shareholders had not yet been called upon for all the money they had pledged; and since they had backed a Company formed to carry out Brunel's plan, under Brunel's direction—and many were Brunel's friends—their purses would be closed if he withdrew.

In view of his complaint about Joliffe and Banks's findings, Smith and Donkin knew that Brunel could not object to Giles's proposed survey— providing it was conducted to his satisfaction. No doubt a form of words could be devised. And if some mishap prevented the shield's advance, no one could then object to Giles's assumption of control. How, in that event, could Brunel deny the Company the use of his shield? If indeed the shield was really necessary.

The upshot was an agreement instructing Giles to probe the river bed, subject to certain rather ambiguous restraints. Isambard's Journal is warm on the subject of this document.

> September 6th ... Went to Dulwich by appointment to meet Benjamin [Hawes]. Ran over agreement, the most childish collection of absurd and contradictory clauses, grasping at petty rights which they know they can't make use of, and in fact, a humbug; it rather puts me in mind of the harmless though spiteful kicking and biting of a spoilt child—who wants to possess something but knows not what. Returned to tunnel ...

Giles was soon at work—despite Brunel's objections to his methods.

> July 24th .... If the Court will reflect that perhaps one hundred such holes are prepared to be made in the deep part of the river, at depths that could exceed the range of action of any dredging machine the Court will soon be convinced of the danger that would attend such operations.
>
> ... Mr Giles does not seem to be aware of the injury he might cause to the works. His foreman was preparing to drive six piles forty feet long on the middle of the tunnel, but as far as I can understand with no precautions not to drive so deep as the crown of the work .... I object most decidedly to the measures that are now in progress for obtaining borings.

Other broadsides followed, but Giles carried on. Downwards from a level 39 feet below Trinity high water, he found clay 'across the remainder of the river, which is to be tunnelled through—except immediately near the Wapping shore. The thickness of this clay I have ascertained in two places to be from fifteen to seventeen feet and that at such a level as to afford ample protection of the tunnel to any further irruption of the Thames water.' He expressed some reservations about the lower strata, which were very porous. 'Mr Giles', Brunel suggested, 'should be requested to give in his report the particulars of the state of the ground at *each of the borings.*' But the directors thought it would be better if Isambard made a boring alongside one of Mr Giles's holes. The instruction was received with no great enthusiasm. '... *a boring alongside* Mr Giles'—what consistency!!!' His temper was not improved when Donkin alleged that the Court had not been told of the planking beneath the tunnel floor, '... having known it all along ... —lies!!! Either Gravatt, I, or the directors are mad'.

Brunel had had enough. Isambard was sent to canvas friendly subscribers and subsequently presented the Court with several cheques—one for £8,358. With the cheques were letters empowering the Company to use the money *providing* Brunel remained at the helm. 'Cheque was received as a *matter of course,*' noted Isambard, 'yet some [directors] not wishing [to accept it] as the offer seemed to require that they should declare their disapprobation of my father's conduct.' William Smith had been checkmated, and Francis Giles slipped into limbo.

Down in the tunnel the bottom of the timber ventilating trunk was disconnected from the blocked duct in the dividing wall and extended a few yards down one archway, so as to draw stale air from the tunnel—although at a distance from the face. The struggle in the City had not distracted Isambard from the task of restoring the shield.

> September 17th .... I laid in bed to get a stock of rest for the remainder of the week. 8 a.m. Got up—breakfasted ... Mr G. [Gravatt] reported that the bolt holes did not appear to match in the new floorplates—very provoking!! ... Tunnel rather foggy. Ventilator throws down very little at the top of new trunk—could stop it easily with a handkerchief.

Brunel returned to the works at the end of September. 'How slow,' he wrote on the 30th,

> our progress must appear to others: but if it is considered how much we have to do for righting the frames, and for repairing them—what with timbering, shoring, drifting and refitting, all executed in a very confined situation—the water occasionally bursting upon us—the ground running in like slush—it is truly terrific to be in the midst of this scene. If to this we couple the actual danger—magnified by the re-echoing of the pumps, and sometimes by the report made by large pieces of cast iron breaking ... such has been the state of things. Nevertheless, my confidence in the shield is not only undiminished; it is, on the contrary, tried with its full effect.

Replacement frame castings—weighing more than a ton—were lifted into place. The air was putrid. Beamish succumbed to pleurisy and on 3 October Robert Greenshield died. Yet the work was done. In the first week of October the Shield stepped forward 18 inches, and Isambard found time to sit in the engineers' cabin and commit a few recollections to his private Journal.

> What a dream it now appears to be! Going down in the diving bell, finding and examining the hole! Standing on the corner of number twelve! The novelty of the thing, the excitement of the occasional risk attending our submarine ... excursions, the crowds of boats to witness our works, all amused—the anxious watching of the shaft—seeing it full of water, rising and falling with the tide with the most provoking regularity—at last, by dint of clay bags, clay and gravel—a perceptible difference ...
>
> I must make some little Indian ink sketches of our boat excursions to the frames; the low dark, gloomy, cold arch; the heap of earth almost up to the crown, hiding the frames and rendering it quite uncertain what state they were in and what might happen; the hollow rushing of water; the total darkness of all around rendered distinct by the glimmering light of a candle or two—carried by ourselves; crawling along the bank of earth, a dark recess at the end—quite dark —water rushing from it in such quantities as to render it uncertain whether the ground was secure; at last reaching the frames—choked up to the middle rail of the top box—frames evidently leaning back and sideways considerably—staves in curious directions, bags and chisel rods protruding in all directions; reaching number twelve, the bags apparently without support and swelling into the frames threaten every minute to close inside the brickwork. All bags—a cavern, *huge, mis-shapen* with water—a cataract coming from it—candles going out ...

24

RUN LEGS OR PERISH BODY!

————•◦₊•◦•————

Brunel had become a popular hero and journalists worked hard to satisfy the public's appetite for tunnel news. Their reports had an unwarranted aura of confidence. *The Times*'s story on 7 November 1827 is typical:

> The works at the Thames Tunnel are proceeding in the most satisfactory manner .... The measures adopted by the engineer to protect the works from any further irruption of the Thames have therefore answered all the expectations intended, and it may now be asserted with confidence that the completion of the undertaking is placed beyond doubt, provided adequate funds are raised to carry on the works to their termination ... The tunnel has now been extended beyond the middle of the river.

Hoping for a continuation of helpful despatches, Butler and Sweet began drafting a new parliamentary Bill, which would empower the Company to offer another quarter-of-a-million pounds' worth of shares. Brunel also sought to make progress more certain and more economical by ordering a dandy pump from Maudslay, which was to be installed at the base of the shaft and driven by the steam engine. It would draw water through a long pipe from a drainage well near the shield, and discharge it into the cistern. Unfortunately Maudslays were busy, so the pump was a long time arriving.

The made-up ground in front of the top boxes was almost fluid and often the miners were driven to using their poling screws as jacks to force the boards forward. Lower in the shield, the ground contrasted unfavourably with the strata beneath Cow Court. In the middle faces there were alternate veins of plastic clay and shells. The bottom faces were gravel, but this too was fissured by bands of shingle. Some of number 12's upper side staves provided an eloquent reminder of the ground's treachery when they were recovered from the lowest face of number 9.

With Beamish absent, Isambard and Gravatt suffered long and anxious spells of duty. Isambard succumbed to a fever during October's first week, and on the 22nd reported that, while walking near the engine house, 'I fell in the river tank and hurt my left leg and right side. Obliged to go home and

159

keep still in consequence. ... Being above, I did not like to take my boots off for fear I should not get them on again if anything should happen.'

At two the following morning Gravatt returned and unbooted him. 'I went to bed. My knee remains very swollen ... felt sick and shaken. Sent for Doctor Bardell, leeches, etc. etc.'

He returned to work at the end of October and found that 11 feet 4 inches had been added to the tunnel during the month—they were making less than a yard a week.

A fortnight earlier, when a boring tube had been withdrawn from the top box of number 12, gas had escaped from it and burned for several minutes. It was a visible sign of the pollution which seeped in and lay stagnant behind the shield in the deepest part of the tunnel. The men suffered spells of dizziness and sometimes strange hallucinations. Isambard's Journal reveals how jittery the pumpers were.

> October 17th 2 a.m. Having seen all right below, I retired as usual to supper; just as I had taken off my coat and boots, Kemble [the overground watchman] came in rather in a hurry to tell me in a trembling voice that the water was in again; I would not believe him—whilst hastily pulling on my boots I asked him how it happened—how he knew it. 'It was up to the shaft when I came, Sir'; ... I ran as fast as I could giving a double knock at Mr Gravatt's door on my way ... all the men were on top of the shaft, looking for, and anxiously calling to those they supposed had not had time to escape. Indeed, Miles had already, in his zeal for the safety of others, found a long rope, which swinging about, he called to the unfortunate sufferers to lay hold of, encouraging and cheering those who might be failing in their endeavours to swim. I ran, or rather threw myself, down the staircase. ... So quickly did I go, that before I was at all aware of it I found myself in the tunnel. I met one or two running out. I soon reached the frames in the eastern arch, and saw Pamphilon, who told me that *nothing was the matter, but a small run in number 1*; found Huggins and the *corpe d'élite* there, and a run of mud at the west top front corner—nothing serious. One of the bricklayers' labourers, hearing the man in number one call for assistance and straw, thrust in a whole truss of straw, and then, overcome with fear, jumped right off the stage crying, 'Run! run! murder! Put the lights out!', and his fellow labourers, following like sheep, repeated these extraordinary cries. Most of the men being at supper, and distant from the frames, the panic spread rapidly.

Displeased at having his supper disturbed, Isambard sought out Miles, who vouchsafed this explanation of his behaviour:

> I seed them Hirishers a'come a'tumblin' through one o' them small harches like mad bulls, as if the devil picked 'um—screech of 'Murther! Murther! Run for your lives! Out the lights!'... My ears got a singin', Sir—all the world like when you and me were down in that 'ere diving bell—till I thought as

Mapping the hole in the river bed after the first irruption. Good lungs were needed.

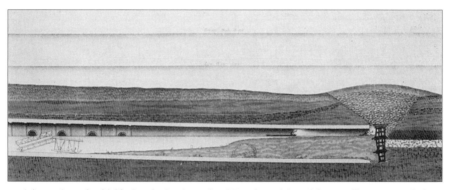

A boat trip to the shield after the first irruption. Note the position of the travelling stage and also the centring buried beneath the mound of earth.

the water was close upon me. Run legs or perish body! says I, when I seed Pascoe ahead o' them there miners coming along as if the devil was looking for 'im. 'Not the first, my lad', says I, and away with me—and never stopped till I got landed fair above ground.

On 1 November an east wind piled up a freakish tide, which inundated parts of Rotherhithe, and would have flooded the tunnel had not a rampart been built around the shaft. On this occasion there was no alarm; the great weight of water did not breach the face, and the shield crept onwards while it ebbed.

It was clear the Company would soon be out of funds. Another six months' expenditure, at the current rate, would empty the coffers, and Brunel made tentative plans to preserve the tunnel in case the work should be stopped. He reported this, without labouring the point. The directors knew the position, and in any event the ground might improve—already some clay was reappearing above the top staves—and then the shield would trot along, and their existing resources might carry them near to Wapping's shore. It would be possible to raise more money in that event.

Early in November, along with his weekly report, Brunel submitted an estimate for completing the tunnel. After mentioning that Giles's borings promised 'a considerable extent of good ground', he multiplied their average weekly progress with their average weekly expenditure, and arrived at a figure of £84,000 for completing the tunnel for foot passengers—including a shaft at Wapping. Another £56,000—evidently a contractor's estimate—would be needed for the Great Descents. £140,000, some of which was already in hand, should see them through.

This sounded distinctly encouraging—the more so because the cost of acquiring property was omitted—and during the evening of 10 November further goodwill was generated by a banquet in the archways at which Isambard presided.

The connecting arches in the dividing wall were hung with crimson drapes, and in the western archway a large table was covered with a crisp, white cloth and laid for 40 diners. Four decorative candelabra from the Portable Gas Company were mounted on plinths flanking this table, and bathed the magic cavern in brilliant light. In the eastern archway an even larger table was prepared more simply for 120 tunnel hands.

The Company men assembled early and at about eight in the evening Isambard's guests arrived, many of them in official regalia, and were welcomed by their young host while the uniformed band of the Coldstream Guards played an air from *Der Freischütz*. It was a proud moment for Beamish, who had recently returned to duty.

At length, when the banquet was under way, the artist Ramsey left the table and made sketches for a painting[*] to commemorate the scene. Then came the toasts. 'The King' (four times four) to the strains of the National Anthem; 'The Duke of Clarence and the Navy' (three times three), while the band played 'Rule Britannia'. This was followed by 'The Duke of Wellington

---

[*] The painting shows Isambard welcoming his father, an instance of artistic licence since Brunel was not present.

The bell barge in the river. A drawing by Clarkson Stanfield ARA, engraved by George Cooke.

[one of the noble proprietors] and the Army' (three times three) to a jubilant rendering of 'See the Conquering Hero Comes'. After drinking the health of the Royal Engineers, the civil engineers, and other good people, there was a moment of silence as Bandinel of the Foreign Office rose to propose a toast to Admiral Sir Edward Codrington,* who had succoured Brunel in prison and supported him ever since.

Flourishing a copy of that night's *Gazette Extraordinary*, Bandinel announced Codrington's victory over the Turkish fleet at Navarino. Byron had been avenged and, he declared,

> the Turkish power has received a severer cheek than it has ever suffered since Mahomet drew the sword. It may be said that the wine-abjuring Prophet conquered by water—upon that element his successors have now been signally defeated. My motto, therefore, on this occasion, when we meet to celebrate the expulsion of the river from this spot is—'Down with water and Mahomet—wine and Codrington for ever!'.

When the applause had subsided, the chairman of the miners and bricklayers came through and presented Isambard with a pickaxe and a shovel as symbols of their trades, calling for the traditional 'three times three and a bumper', which was cheerfully given, and the proceedings brought to an agreeably mellow conclusion.

---

* Shortly after his return from the war, Admiral Codrington became a director of the Thames Tunnel Company.

The celebration typified the Brunel flair for the great occasion, and by absenting himself Marc deliberately began to project Isambard as his successor. His son had been launched as the Company's Resident Engineer, and the event was proclaimed with champagne.

After the party there was the clearing up. 'Portable gaz man here to fetch away things,' noted Isambard on the 12th, 'although some were damaged, he was extremely civil.'

At a General Meeting ten days later, the mood of almost desperate enthusiasm is revealed by the principal resolutions. 'The difficulties which have arisen, and the effectual manner in which they have been overcome, prove to demonstration the entire practicability of the undertaking,' and the shareholders hoped 'that the work would be deemed by His Majesty's Government so far of a national character, that there would be found a disposition to afford such further assistance as could, with propriety, be granted.'

Expenditure rose as conditions worsened. The infiltration increased but the dandy pump had not yet arrived. The new clay ceiling was faulty, and water flowing through it eroded away sub-strata, causing the clay to sink and fracture, and making yet more passages for the water. Soundings were continually taken over the shield, and depressions were filled with clay and gravel, but this was a hit-and-miss procedure, and Brunel lamented the loss of the diving bell, which had been returned to John Rennie at the West India Docks.

During the second week of December, Brunel was busy with another engagement and delegated his weekly report to Isambard, who described how the tide affected conditions below.

> At the half-flood tide the pressure is greatest; dry-hard clay oozes with great force through openings hardly observable, the silt and water running by starts. At high-water the pressure and quantity of water begin to diminish, and on the ebb-tide the ground is hard and dry, and can be worked with ease. On the flood-tide there are as many as twelve and fifteen of the best hands, beside myself (or one of my assistants) and the foreman engaged entirely at one face—this includes six cool, steady men, who must also be tall and strong—two in front of each box; others cutting small struts, wedges, etc., to the exact size called for, making up bundles of straw and fascines of different sizes, and lumps of clay ... others handing in what is called for, and poling screws of all lengths, and any tools required. I have entered into these details to account for the number of men employed, which, as I have often stated, sometimes increases as our progress decreases. During this time the men alluded to are working excessively under great excitement, drenched completely with spring water, and frequently blinded with mud. Many of them are obliged to go up on the stage, to put on dry things and take drink

to enable them to resume their work. I mention this to account for the clothes and drink which I have stated it was necessary to give them.

At spring tides work had to be restricted to the ebb, when the frames were all advanced in rapid succession, so as to push the shield forward three times during the course of 37 hours. Thus the tides played havoc with shift working, and the cost of making four feet three inches a week in November was greater than the cost of twice that progress during the previous March.

Smith and Donkin, although more circumspect than formerly, continued to clutch at any straw that might carry them to Wapping's muddy foreshore.

There were engineers in plenty, who were pleased to be consulted. All the notable 'scientific gentlemen' visited the tunnel in turn, and were courteously escorted up to the shield; and one visitor, of whom more will be heard anon, was Charles Vignoles, whom John Rennie had employed to survey a line for a railway to Brighton.

The Oxford Canal Company had asked Brunel to report on the feasibility of straightening their waterway between Hawkesbury and Braunston, and since he wished to delegate some of the detailed work, Vignoles was just the man he needed. Arrangements between them were concluded during November, and on 19 December Isambard met Vignoles at his Southampton Row house and

A watercolour by Goodall of the tunnel showing the cross arches and railway trucks.

took him to Rotherhithe for a tour of the tunnel.

Three weeks later, on 8 January 1828, Dom Miguel, the Pretender to the throne of Portugal, visited the works, and once again Beamish donned his shining beaver and waited on the party.

> The east stage [he recalled] had been moved back from the frames, that the magnitude of the work might be at once presented to the eye. On this stage, and on planks, one above another, were seated the miners. Whether from their elevated position, or the tranquil dignity of their aspect, the contrast which they presented to the eager, restless crowd below formed in my mind the most striking part of the whole exhibition. To us all, the relief was great when the last act of it had terminated.

The following day Francis Giles arrived but, despising Beamish's and Isambard's too pressing hospitality, withdrew in haste when Gravatt prepared to advance a frame. His caution was understandable. Since the Christmas 'holy day' the bursts of silt and water had become more frequent, and there had been ominous runs of river-bed debris. However, the miners pushed forward six feet six inches during the first ten days of January to make the archways 605 feet long. They were not much more than 300 feet from the low water mark at Wapping. Isambard was on duty during the night of 11 January. There were a number of bursts of silt, but on the whole it was a quiet night. Conditions were better, if anything, than they had been since Christmas. He wondered whether at last the ground was beginning to improve—or whether it was just the ebb tide in their favour. Low water was at 5 a.m. They would see on the next shift.

Gravatt had fallen sick, but Beamish came on duty a little before six, and issued a punch made from gin and warm beer to the miners who had had the worst of it during the night. Isambard remained in the shield while the shifts changed—it was a good opportunity to check the level of the frames.

The west side was, if anything, the more tender, and when the new men arrived, he directed the two strongest miners, Ball and Collins, into number 1 and told them to work down the top face first, while the tide was still low. Fitzgerald was stationed handily on the stage, ready to pass in clay and straw, if any should be needed. Isambard stood in the back of the box and watched while the two top polings were cut back and replaced. Everything seemed all right, but Collins had difficulty with his second screw and called for a hammer. Fitzgerald passed one to Isambard.

Suddenly, clay followed by a torrent of water burst through the gap between the second and third boards. It started by the side staves, but spread at once across the face, brought down several polings and almost swept Ball and Collins from their cell.

Stepping across into number 2, Isambard saw that the breach was irreparable, and ordered all the men out of the tunnel. Then, half drowned by the deluge, he struggled down the ladder from the shield in the wake of the two miners.

Fitzgerald was better placed. He ran to the back of the stage and slid down into the water. Almost before his feet touched bottom, he felt a tremendous burst of wind; then the lights burned blue and went out. In the tumult and darkness he fought his way along the western archway and, by climbing into the water chute on the dividing wall, surmounted the visitors' barrier. He dropped to the ground and ran for his life to the shaft. Fumbling in the dark he found the visitors' doorway. The catch was unfamiliar, and by the time he opened the door, the flood had covered his feet. In the deep part near the shield it was 14 feet deep.

Back down the archway, Isambard, Ball and Collins had struggled away from the frames, waist-deep in water, with not a glimmer of light to guide them. They were feeling their way along the stage, when suddenly it tilted and pinned them beneath the surface.

'I struggled under water for some time,' Isambard wrote later,

and at length extricated myself from the stage, and by swimming and by being forced with the water, I gained the eastern arch where I got a better footing, and was enabled, by laying hold of the railway rope, to pause a little in the hope of encouraging the men who had been knocked down at the same time as myself. This I endeavoured to do by calling them. Before I had reached the shaft, the water had risen so rapidly that I was out of my depth, and therefore swam to the visitors' stairs, the stairs for the workmen being occupied by those who had so far escaped. My knee was so injured by the timber stage that I could scarcely swim.

The watchman rushed across the tunnel yard. 'The water is in—the Tunnel is full!' he cried to Beamish, who ran to the workmen's staircase only to find it blocked with men; so, seizing a crowbar, Beamish battered down the door at the top of the visitors' stairs. 'I had not taken many steps down,' he reported later, 'when I received Isambard Brunel in my arms. A great wave of water had thrown him to the surface ... "Ball! Ball—Collins! Collins!" were the only words he could for some time utter; but the well-known voices answered not.'

While Beamish carried away the hardly conscious Isambard, news of the disaster followed fast on the heels of the fleeing labourers. Women rushed to Cow Court. A press report reveals the stricken mining village atmosphere.

Wives and children in a state of nudity, the accident happening at such an early hour, were seen in the utmost state of distress, eagerly enquiring after their husbands and fathers.

In the midst of this distressing scene, out rushed a number of men in a state of great exhaustion, some carrying their fainting comrades, who were removed to the house of Mr Timothy, the Spreadeagle, where they were brought to by restoratives.

Some of the women became widows that morning. Thomas Ball drowned leaving a wife. John Collins drowned, leaving a wife and two children. Thomas Evans and William Seton drowned; both were single men. A wife mourned John Long. Six orphaned children wept for Jeptha Cook.

In the evening, much more ill than he knew, Isambard wrote up his diary. 'Saturday 12th January. Two-and-a-half a.m. Went below, little thinking how I should come up again.'

He had been lucky. It was fortunate that Fitzgerald had opened that door, and providential that Beamish had appeared at the instant the water bore him to the surface.

25

CONVALESCENCE

——•••——

Beamish saddled his pony again, and called at Barge House, and then at 30 Bridge Street.

'I don't like your early visit! The water is in!'

'Yes.'

'Anyone hurt?'

'Unfortunately so!'

'Is Isambard safe?'

'Yes!'

'Who and how many?'

Brunel received the news without visible emotion, and after breakfasting, returned with Beamish to Rotherhithe. It was a raw January morning; fog blanketed the river and made boat work impossible, but the diving bell and its barge were brought across to the Company's wharf.

Next morning, while the Rotherhithe curate damned man's sinful ambition, and Brunel wrote to the Court about the disaster and affirmed his confidence in restoring the tunnel (but undoubtedly knowing the Company must be broken), Isambard was laid on a mattress on the bell barge's deck and directed Gravatt's descents to the river bed.

The lowering chain was too short, and the best Gravatt could do was to probe the bottom with a rod. A longer chain could not be procured on the sabbath, but a cable was found, which fortunately Isambard forbade Gravatt to use, for it broke while the bell was being hauled up after an unmanned descent. The work continued all day, and in the evening, Isambard, in great pain, was carried into the barge's cabin but continued to give orders with his customary clarity.

Next morning he could not carry on, and Doctor Morris came and took him to Barge House in his carriage. 'Never felt so queer, could not bear the least shake, felt as if I should be broken to pieces; put to bed, was cut, I believe, that night, but don't remember.'

The *New Times* reporter found the Brunels unruffled.

It is gratifying to state that Mr Brunel junior is rapidly recovering from the effects of his recent accident; and it is much to the credit of the faculty, and highly praiseworthy to the individuals as men, to state that many physicians of eminence and popularity have spontaneously visited Mr Brunel for the purpose of offering any assistance which their talents might afford. The state of the weather and the nature of his complaint have imperatively constrained him to keep to his apartment the whole of yesterday; and Mrs Brunel ... has at present taken up her residence in the same house with her son, and exercises that maternal attention to him which the situation requires. The elder Mr Brunel, so far from giving way to that despondency, which some misdirected accounts have attributed to him, appears to possess additional fortitude and determination.

The directors' published sentiments were in keeping.

This Court, having learned with great admiration of the courage and presence of mind displayed by Mr Isambard Brunel, the Company's Resident Engineer, when the Thames broke into the tunnel on the morning of the 12th instant, are desirous to give their public testimony to his calm and energetic endeavours, and to that generous principle which induced him to put his own life in more imminent hazard to save the lives of the men under his immediate care.

While Doctor Morris ministered to Isambard, Brunel spent his days on the river or amongst the bones and blacking bottles on its bed; and when night came prepared plans for the Oxford Canal Company, plans for a floating pier at Blackwall,* and acknowledged plans from other men who knew, much better than he, how to expel the river.

January 14th. I was preparing to go down, but the air-pipe, which had been lengthened from an ordinary hose, not proving air-tight, was obliged to come up again before I could reach the bottom—the weather was all the time most tempestuous, cold and rainy, the tides very violent both up and down, and our barges were exposed ... to the shipping ... At 6 p.m .... I went down, Mr Gravatt with me, the sextant having fallen overboard, we were not very sure of our position: the signals not being well understood above, we were carried against the west side of the cavity and exposed to the danger of being upset; obliged to come up again.

They explored the hole, stood on the top staves of number 1, and found the side brickwork intact, although a ring or two of the brick roof had been swept away, and number 2 had started back.

Again a bung of clay-filled bags was lowered into the breach, and then more bags of clay, which were pierced, this time with iron rods. Gravel followed, and still more gravel as the river bed subsided. The pumps were started on the 21st.

---

*   This was not constructed.

While the water in the shaft was slowly lowered Isambard revived visibly, and on Sunday the 27th travelled to Brighton with Benjamin Hawes and put up at the *Albion* hotel. Benjamin returned the next evening, but Isambard found the atmosphere agreeable. He explored the town, visited the theatre, dined with new acquaintances, and went to a fancy dress ball.

> Monday 4th February. Very comfortable at the *Albion*—some pleasant company. ... Strolled on the pier smoking my Meerschaum before breakfast— breakfast at twelve. Rode about—visiting works [the new sea wall then building] ... dined at six or seven—very busy doing nothing all day.

Encouraged no doubt by the local bucks, he unwound a little too quickly, and on the 8th suffered a haemorrhage. A doctor was sent for, who put him to bed, but three days later he was up again although still inconvenienced by internal bleeding. Brighton was not perhaps the best place for Isambard's convalescence, so Beamish was sent down, and on 15 February brought him home to Bridge Street in a 'hired chariot'. The jolting journey induced another haemorrhage, and he lay in bed too ill to write his Journal until the end of the month, when he began making a tray for his compasses. Even this was too much and a third haemorrhage occurred the same evening.

Fortune smiled with equal fickleness on his father. At the end of January a 20-foot head of water had been gained, but on 3 February a new hole formed over numbers 11 and 12, and the shaft filled up. More clay and gravel, and then, cautiously, the pumps were restarted; but on 9 February, when the head was 27 feet, the river broke in again and Beamish had to dive in the bell and map the new hole. Meanwhile Brunel assured the Lord Mayor that as soon as the tunnel had been extended into better ground, the artificial mound which he proposed to make over the shield would be levelled off.

Gravatt, who needed Isambard's firm hand, thoughtlessly added to his chief's anxiety.

> February 18th. On hearing that Gravatt was gone to town, merely to take a lesson on the flute, I went immediately to Rotherhithe and gave ... directions for the bell to be ready as soon as the time would serve. Gravatt not coming, I requested Mr Beamish to go down, which he did .... This is quite inexcusable in Gravatt .... The tide passed without his coming.

It was clear that Isambard would be off duty for many weeks, and on the 21st the Thames gave warning that it would not easily be beaten, breaking in yet again, although on the previous day Beamish had attempted a boat trip to the shield and supervised the repacking of the pumps. Six days later Brunel was due in Leamington to report to the Oxford Canal Company. Obviously he would have to delegate his authority either to Beamish or to Gravatt and, not surprisingly, decided that the former was more responsible.

The two assistants were told of the decision in good time, but to Gravatt, the son of a colonel of the Royal Engineers, the notion of taking orders from a Guardsman with 'only twelve months' engineering experience' was hard to swallow. He wrote an aggrieved letter to Brunel on the 25th. Certainly he had been told to consider 'Mr Beamish in place of my son as Resident Engineer', but he had understood that Beamish would merely deal with money matters; however, in Beamish's Journal he had chanced to see 'Mr Brunel directed that I should be the organ of his wishes during the absence of his son God give me strength, etc.'. He, Gravatt, therefore requested the opportunity to 'shake hands and resign'.

Isambard rallied to his father's side and replied to Gravatt. Perhaps Beamish had sometimes unintentionally 'wielded his authority with a rather heavy hand' and so 'slighted your pride, which *entre-nous* is your great fault ... That same pride prevents you seeking early explanations of what might appear to you just cause for complaint. ... Having told you what I feared, let us see what really, according to your own account, has occurred.' After pouring quantities of oil, Isambard reproved Gravatt for harbouring spiteful feelings towards his father. 'You keep it all to yourself, and now you say you must resign.'

After a month and several letters, Gravatt recovered his composure. Meanwhile more clay and gravel was dumped into the river, Brunel journeyed to Leamington, agreed that Vignoles should execute his plans for the Oxford Canal, and whilst in the Midlands reported to the Tunnel Company regarding the 360 plans which he had received from well-wishers. Before he returned, the pumps were restarted and slowly the tunnel was drained.

'Sunday March the 10th. Head of water twenty-nine feet eight inches. Ball was picked up today, poor fellow! A brave one!'

Isambard improved during the second week of March, and enjoyed a boat trip to Chelsea with his mother on the 15th. But again the activity was premature, another haemorrhage followed, and two new doctors, Travers and Brown, were called in. Their treatment was rigorous. 'March 23rd. Mr Travers bled me, and he and Mr B. prescribed sugar of lead. Felt much better after bleeding.' And the following day, 'Much better. Bleeding, sugar of lead, and starvation for ever.'

Better or no, he was kept in bed for six weeks, passing his time letter-writing, sketching, studying German and algebra, and enjoying occasional visits from miners who recounted their adventures afloat in the barges.

By the end of March, when Brunel made a trip to Birmingham and Liverpool, the clay and gravel dumped into the river had grown into a mound which rose fourteen feet above the surrounding bed. The West India Docks had claimed back their diving bell, but the tunnel was being drained, and on 10 April Brunel returned to find hand pumpers on the stages.

'Beamish has been near the shield at the west arch,' he noted,

> it is quite full to the crown of the arch with soil. The water flows irregularly.
> Everything seems to do well, but the want of a diving bell is a very serious
> thing—we cannot examine the ground when it settles. More ground is ready
> to be thrown in. Mr Beamish very unwell. Mr Hammond [a temporary
> assistant] very useful.

Two days later Gravatt re-entered the shield in the eastern archway, but
in the evening the infiltration increased and more barges were hurriedly
emptied, lest the Thames should take possession once again,

Much to Gravatt's relief, Beamish left for Ireland six days later to visit his
sick father. By this time 4,500 tons of clay and gravel had been dumped into
the river, but at last the new ground was consolidating and the infiltration
had diminished to a comparative trickle. By early May the archways had been
cleared of flotsam, and Maudslay delivered the dandy pump and suction
pipe. This was soon installed, and on the 6th all hands began clearing the
great mound of earth which almost filled the shield and blocked the end of
the western archway.

Anxious perhaps to show what he could do without Beamish dragging at
his coat-tails, Gravatt pressed on with a will, and in little more than a fortnight
cleared the tunnel and redecorated the western arch ready for visitors, who
were re-admitted in great numbers on Whit Monday, 26 May, although the
ventilator was not restored for another seven weeks.

While the miners began the laborious task of restoring the shield, Isambard
enjoyed the sunshine and took gentle walks in Blackfriars. He had first got up
from his sick-bed on 4 May, and subsequently took tea with Vignoles when
the latter had visited Brunel. Now, with his strength slowly returning, he
made himself useful planning gaz experiments, and sketching improvements
to the triangle-frame engine.

On 12 July he embarked in *The Thames* for Plymouth, where he arrived
on the 17th, and spent an interesting 10 days inspecting the dockyard, the
breakwater, and places nearby, including Saltash. 1 August saw him back and
once again in charge of the work. He had recovered, and felt no qualms
about returning to the scene of the disaster—indeed, an earlier entry in his
private Journal makes it clear that the spectacle was something he would not
willingly have missed.

> I shan't forget that day in a hurry, very near finished my journey then; when
> the danger is over, it is rather amusing than otherwise—while it existed I
> can't say the feeling was at all uncomfortable. If I was to say the contrary
> I should be nearer the truth in this instance. While exertions could still be
> made and hope remained of stopping the ground it was an excitement which
> has always been a luxury to me. When we were obliged to run, I felt nothing

in particular; I was only thinking of the best way of getting us on and the probable state of the arches. When knocked down, I certainly gave myself up, but I took it very much as a matter of course, which I had expected the moment we quitted the frames, for I never expected we should get out. The instant I disengaged myself and got breath again—all dark—I bolted into the other arch. This saved me—by laying hold of the rail-rope—the engine *must* have stopped for a minute. I stood still nearly a minute. I was anxious for poor Ball and Collins, who I felt sure had never risen from the fall we had all had and were, as I thought, *crushed* under the great stage. I kept calling them by name to encourage them and make them also (if still able) come through the opening. While standing there the effect was—*grand*—the roar of the rushing water in a confined passage, and by its velocity rushing past the opening was grand, *very grand*, I cannot compare it to anything, cannon can be nothing to it. At last it came bursting through the opening. I was then obliged to be off—but up to that moment, as far as my sensations were concerned, and distinct from the idea of the loss of six poor fellows whose death I could not then foresee, kept there.

The sight and the whole affair was well worth the risk and I would willingly pay my share, fifty pounds about, of the expenses of such a 'spectacle'. Reaching the shaft, I was much too bothered with my knee and some other thumps to remember much.

If I had been kept under another minute when knocked down I should not have suffered more, and I trust I was tolerably fit to die. If, therefore, the occurrence itself was rather a gratification than otherwise and the consequence in no way unpleasant, I need not attempt to avoid such. My being in bed at present, tho' no doubt arising from the effects of my straining, was *immediately* caused by me returning too soon to a full diet at Brighton; had I been properly warned of this, I might now have been hard at work at the tunnel.

26

WELLINGTON TAKES AN INTEREST

In 1828 Brunel's personal position was stronger than it had been after the first irruption. It is true that two months before the earlier flood the directors had resolved that 'it would be contrary to the interest of the proprietors; dangerous to the ultimate success of the undertaking, and at variance with the duties of the Directors, to risk a change in the mode of proceeding to any other mode not fully sanctioned by Mr Brunel, and in which should not be preserved, intact, that responsibility under which the proprietors confided this important undertaking to his management,' but this had not prevented the flirtation with Francis Giles. One resolution can be superseded by another as easily as blonde hairs are dyed black. In 1828 it was not the resolution, but the memory of their humiliation, that muted Smith's and Donkin's voices. They had little appetite for a second encounter with their engineer.

A fortnight after the second disaster the shareholders assembled and learned that £21,000 was all 'that could fairly be relied upon for continuing the work. Your Directors,' the Chairman continued,

> have kept their attention fixed on the great object of the finances of the Company, and on the 24th of December issued a circular letter to enquire of each proprietor what sum he was disposed to lend to the Company at five per cent. per annum ... But the recent accident occurred previously to the period fixed for the reply, and the Directors have not received any offers.

Brunel spoke next and reiterated his confidence in repairing the breach and completing the work providing money was forthcoming. They had built 52 feet of tunnel since the first irruption and were 'within twenty-five feet of the middle of the channel of the river'. Another 300 feet would bring them to the low watermark, and 200 feet more to the line of the northern wharf.

The subscribers were chastened, but the meeting closed without recriminations, and a fortnight later Brunel submitted fresh estimates for completing the archways.

> Allowing ... a sum of ten thousand pounds for the present mischief, and two hundred pounds a foot for the next thirty feet, I still feel confident that the

174

remainder may be done at the rate I have estimated before, one hundred pounds per foot run, but if, for greater certainty, the Board were to propose one hundred-and-twenty pounds per foot to low-water mark ... it would, I should hope, be found to cover the expense of that part of the enterprise.

He then added this postscript: 'The sums I have mentioned are independent of the item which is to be provided for obtaining the means of security ... —a diving bell with a suitable apparatus.'

The subscribers assembled again on 4 March and heard Francis Giles offer to complete one of the twin archways. He did not say how, but declared that the toll revenue of Waterloo Bridge proved that a tunnel for pedestrians would be profitable.

Brunel spoke next. He 'had no doubt of the work being completed if he was furnished with the necessary funds, but if the meeting gentlemen were of the opinion that any experienced engineer could complete the work in a more satisfactory manner, he was willing to give it up into their hands'.

A newspaper report refers to several subsequent speeches from subscribers, some of whom

> had advanced £10,000 and £20,000 in the undertaking, and they spoke with confidence of it being completed. They strongly disapproved of the plan proposed by Mr Giles which, they said, would make that which was to be the most magnificent undertaking, and the pride of the Empire, into a mere gimblet-hole, and a disgrace to those who were concerned in the work.

A resolution was passed empowering the directors to receive voluntary contributions, and Francis Giles again retired into obscurity.

During April it became apparent that Brunel would wrest his tunnel from the Thames, and on 29 April *The Times* reported that the workmen clearing the tunnel 'have resumed their work with great spirit and alacrity'. The correspondent added that plans continued to come in

> even from distant parts of Europe and America, all equally infallible in the opinion of every one of the more than four hundred contributors, many of whom suggest, as may well be supposed, the same means, consisting chiefly in rafts, convex coverings, tarpaulins, coverings of various descriptions, and metals, gates, penstocks, etc. and amphibious men to work under water. Hardly one will allow the engineer to preserve his own plan, because it takes so much time to stop the hole, whereas theirs, it is hinted, would infallibly have succeeded in one tide or two, and at a very little expense.

But the Prime Minister believed in Brunel's plan—for, that same day, Isambard sat up in bed and wrote this in his Journal.

> My father, in returning from the House, met the Duke of Wellington. The Duke stopped him and asked how much money we wanted. Also as to its

eventually paying, and was astonished and pleased to hear of our being in
the frames. I think this augers well. He is not a man to stop my father in the
middle of the street ... still less to ask such questions, without a motive.

One barrier in the way of any help that the Duke might care to give
was removed on 23 May, when the Bill empowering the Company to raise a
further £250,000 and to open the tunnel to pedestrians before constructing
the Great Descents, received the Royal Assent.

The subscribers reassembled on 11 June. They heard Brunel reaffirm his
conviction that his shield would carry the excavation safely to Wapping, and
found the Chairman and directors confident that toll revenue from pedestrians
would cover interest on £200,000 worth of five per cent debentures, and
provide an income for existing subscribers as well. (The new Act of Parliament
empowered the Company to raise £200,000 initially and later, if needed, an
additional £50,000.)

Although it was proposed that interest on the debentures should take
priority over interest on the original shares, the Act's stipulation that existing
shareholders be given a first refusal on the new stock spiked the guns of
dissident subscribers who, in any event, could see no hope of profit unless
the tunnel was finished, and no hope of finishing it unless new funds were
secured. Resolutions were passed instructing the directors to proceed with
the new issue subject to two provisos: first that 'when a sum of £100,000 shall
have been agreed to be subscribed, the directors do proceed with the works
and commence making their calls on [the new] subscribers'. And secondly
that 'all persons who have voluntarily contributed to this undertaking and
who may be desirous of taking debentures ... shall be allowed the amount of
their donation in part payment'. (Some of Brunel's friends had organised a
'Tunnel Club' and collected donations exceeding £300.)

The i's were dotted and the t's crossed at a Board Meeting the following
day when a committee, which included Brunel, was set up to prepare for
the new issue. The fruits of their labours were a sales broadsheet for general
distribution, and a more elaborate booklet for important people. Both
stressed the Company's achievements, noted the traffic across London
Bridge, and dwelt on the richness of the tunnel's hinterland. The booklet also
drew attention to the funds available to pay interest to debenture holders.
Thus, if £100,000 were called in equal monthly instalments during the first
year the interest would amount to £2,500 ... '*To meet this the Directors are now
in possession of £2,500*, the amount of the visitors' money received up to this
time. So that, in fact, the Company *has now a fund from which to pay the first
year's dividends.*' If, during the second year, a further £100,000 were called
for in the same way, the interest on it would again be £2,500—add to this
£5,000—a full year's interest on the first £100,000—and the total interest

charge for the second year becomes £7,500. 'To meet this charge,' the booklet explained, 'the Directors will be in receipt of *two years' visitors' money* and also the *rent of their property for two years*, which is also appropriated to the holders of debentures.

> Now the Directors have stated that the sum they receive daily from visitors is at the rate of £3,000 per annum—and it is an increasing fund—and the rent received by the Company amounts to £300 per annum. Hence it is also clear that *the second year's dividends are also very nearly provided for.*
>
> We now come to the period when the tunnel will be opened to the public and tolls receivable; it is hardly possible for anyone, who knows anything of the local trade and population, and the existing traffic across the river in the neighbourhood of the tunnel, to doubt that sufficient income will be received to pay the interest on the debentures secured as it will be on all the property of the Company; *property which will be greatly enhanced in value, when the tunnel is completed.*
>
> Thus the holder of debentures can hardly fail of getting five per cent for his money ... The last very able report of the Directors ... contains every information requisite to form an opinion on this subject.

Brunel's diary covering the four days preceding the public appeal is filled with notes of committee meetings at the British Coffee House, and with journeys to Westminster to invite the support of Cabinet Ministers and all the Royal Dukes. At last, at half-past-twelve on 5 July, the concourse, which had gathered at the *Freemasons' Tavern*, rose to applaud the arrival of a distinguished party, which included the Dukes of Cambridge, Wellington and Somerset, the Earl of Aberdeen, Earl Powis, Sir John Sinclair, Sir Edward Owen, and Charles Nicholas Palmer, MP for Surrey.

At a signal from the Duke of Wellington, Palmer took the chair and, after opening the proceedings with a suitably brief speech, he called upon the Prime Minister. When the cheers had died down, Wellington spoke.

'I assure you, gentlemen,' he said,

> that I am exceedingly flattered by the honour which has been done to me by being called upon by certain members of this association to propose the resolutions which I shall presently have the honour of reading to you ... [Applause.] At the same time, gentlemen, I cannot but feel that there are many here present, who, although not more zealous in the cause than I am, and not more sensible than I am of the advantages which will result to this metropolis, to this country, and to the world, from the performance of this great work, are yet much more capable than I am of displaying to you all its advantages, and of exciting towards it your interest. [Cries of 'No'.]
>
> Gentlemen, there are in this country many works of extraordinary utility, beauty, and magnificence; but what is still more extraordinary is, that they are the works of individual enterprise. The sagacity of individuals has

suggested to them the utility, or their taste has suggested to them the beauty and magnificence of these works, and they have not been deterred from undertaking and completing them by the risk and expense to be incurred by carrying them into execution; but, gentlemen, I speak from my own knowledge, and I could appeal to others now present more capable than I am of stating what is the opinion abroad upon this subject—I speak from my own knowledge when I tell you that there is no work upon which the public interest of foreign nations has been more excited than it has been upon this tunnel. [Prolonged applause.] Every man feels not only the benefit which will result from it to the immediate neighbourhood, to the populous district in which it is established, to the counties of Surrey, Kent and Essex, between which it will establish a short and convenient communication, but likewise, men cannot but see the great political, military, as well as commercial profit that will be derived from the example of such a work, by the establishment of others in other places, and in other countries in which such works may be considered necessary. Under these circumstances, gentlemen, I cannot but congratulate you upon the enterprise which has induced you to undertake this work, notwithstanding its novelty and all the disadvantageous circumstances under which it is undertaken. ...

Gentlemen, at the risk of fatiguing you, I will now draw your attention to some of the financial details appending to this measure. The original estimate was for £200,000. Of this sum of £200,000, the sum of £193,000 was subscribed; of the sum of £193,000, subscribers failed to pay their deposits to the amount of £13,000; there remained, therefore, £180,000, and of that £180,000, £170,000 has been expended.

Gentlemen, it is not extraordinary that mistakes should be made in the formation of the estimates upon which this work was founded; the novelty of the work, the difficulties of ascertaining the nature of the bed of the river through which it was to be carried, or the accidents to which it was liable, which have occasioned a considerable expense, all tended to increase the expense of this great undertaking; but, gentlemen, I beg particularly to call your attention to this fact, that the work itself has cost only £120,000, the remainder has been the purchase of machinery and the purchase of premises, and of ground which is absolutely necessary upon one of the banks of the river in order to carry the work on, and I beg you to observe that in proportion that the expense, particularly the expense of the premises and of the ground, have been large, in the same proportion does the work promise to be useful, and promise to be profitable in case it should be completed. [Applause.]

Gentlemen, the sum now necessary in order to enable the directors to complete the work is still £200,000. Of this sum £96,000 will be required to complete the tunnel across the river; of the remainder, £45,000 will be required to purchase the ground and premises on the left bank of the river, together with the salaries of officers and other contingent expenses of the undertaking, and £50,000 to make the ways up to the tunnel on both sides of the river, making altogether the sum of £191,000 and leaving (if £200,000 should be subscribed) the sum of nearly £20,000 in hand, including the sum of £10,000 which now remains in hand ...

You must all see as well as I can detail it to you what the chances are of the success of the undertaking; this I will say, that if this money is found it is quite certain that the tunnel must be completed. [Applause.] The accidents which have occurred—and which appear to have occurred only to demonstrate the enterprise, the genius and the ability of the engineer who has conducted it—[applause] have proved to a certainty that it is absolutely impossible that the work should not be completed. They have also proved this, that the work itself is excellent, and that if once completed it will be durable in proportion as the honour of having completed it will be durable to this country. Gentlemen, under these circumstances I have only to conclude by moving these resolutions and by earnestly entreating you to give your assistance to carry on this great work. [Applause.]

The resolutions, asking the meeting to endorse the Duke's sentiments, and to approve the debenture scheme, were seconded by Sir Edward Owen and carried unanimously. The books were at once opened and those present hurried to subscribe.

No one could accuse the Iron Duke of leading from the rear, he, the Duke of Cambridge, C.N. Palmer, Henry Maudslay, and Francis & White, the Roman cement suppliers, each subscribed £500. There were no fewer than 26 subscribers, including Brunel and every director, who individually pledged £100 or more.

Everyone thought it was a splendid meeting. Brunel wrote in his diary that there could be 'nothing more gratifying'. Monday's *Times* referred to 'this great work' and quoted Wellington at length, and other journals were no less generous.

Alas, the labour of counting the money was not to prove unduly onerous. Three weeks later a 'non-subscriber' wrote to *The Times* and quoted a Company broadsheet which listed the new subscriptions. Their total was a paltry £9,660.

The Thames had been expelled again, the archways had been cleared, and the shield had been restored. 'The most distinguished character of the age' had rallied to the Company, and had spoken generously of past achievements and confidently of the future's promise. And the result? Not one-twentieth part of the sum solicited; not a tenth of the £100,000 which was to be raised before tunnelling should be resumed.

The bright vision of a grand uninterrupted communication, which still beckoned Brunel, the Wollastons, Ben Hawes, the good Admiral Codrington, and the Iron Duke, had faded from the public eye. It has been washed away by the Thames and by the yet more muddy stream of bickering and recrimination that had flowed from Walbrook Buildings.

The public did not subscribe. The public had grown cynical. A letter to *The Times* from 'Caution' exemplified the mood.

> This project was, from the first, in the very first class of desperate hazards, and two warnings have been given (the last attended by the loss of six lives) of the probable result of the scheme. Should it be completed, it will always be liable to disruption, and the consequent sudden annihilation of all within; and should it endure, it will be found, I am of opinion, an inconvenient mode of transit, and most likely end in affording a pretext for Government interference, and fix upon the public additional evils of patronage and taxation ...
>
> As to the estates of the Company as a security for the money subscribed ... it is by this time pretty well understood that the estates of Companies when sought for by subscribers are very difficult to find.

Beamish and the miners were 'released', and under Isambard's direction, Gravatt* supervised the few remaining bricklayers as they built stout piers between each frame's side members and the tunnel brickwork. As soon as these 'permanent abutting screws' had been completed, the ends of the archways were walled up.

'Saw the last of the frames!!!', Brunel wrote sadly on 9 August; and soon after, Gravatt and the bricklayers were paid off. Isambard was philosophical. 'The tunnel is now blocked up at the end ...' he wrote, 'a year ago I should have thought this intolerable ... now it is come—like all other events—only at a distance do they appear to be dreaded.'

He set the remaining hands to work decorating the end of the visitors' archway, adding to the gas lights and converting the plant to produce gas from coal instead of coconut oil.† A touch of splendour was provided by a large mirror on the new end wall, which created the illusion of an unending arcade.

Brunel secured the Lord Mayor's reluctant agreement to a raft which he anchored over the mid-river mound. Then he filled his days designing a new and better shield ready for the time when the great work would start again.

Earlier, some weeks after Francis Giles had been given the floor at the March meeting, Isambard had taken stock in his Bridge Street sickroom and had found the future clouded and uncertain. 'Here are these directors,' he then wrote,

> damning the tunnel as fast as they well can. If they go on at this rate, we must certainly stop. ... Where the devil money is to come from in that case, I know not. ... Where then will be all my fine castles?—bubbles! Well, if it was only

---

* Gravatt's subsequent career reveals his original mind. He carried out some excellent railway surveys, made a notable contribution to suspension bridge design and invented the surveyor's dumpy level. He remained outspoken and made no fortune.
† Coal gas was cheaper.

for myself I should not mind it. I fear if the tunnel stops I shall find all those flattering promises of my friends will prove friendly wishes.

The young Rennies, whatever their real merit, will have built London Bridge, the finest bridge in Europe, and have such a connection with government as to defy competition. Palmer has built new London Docks and thus without labour has established a connection which ensures his fortune, while I shall have been engaged on the Tunnel which failed, which was abandoned—a pretty recommendation.

I have nothing after all so very transcendent as to enable me to rise by my own merit without some such help as the Tunnel. It's a gloomy perspective and yet bad as it is I cannot with all my efforts work myself up to be *down* hearted. Well, its very fortunate I am so easily pleased. After all let the worst happen—unemployed, untalked of, *penniless* (that's damned awkward), I think I may depend upon a home at Benjamin's. My poor father would hardly survive the tunnel. My mother would follow him. I should be left alone—here my invention fails, what would follow I cannot guess. A war now, I would go and get my throat cut and yet that would be foolish enough—well 'vogue la galère', very annoying but so *it is*; I suppose a sort of middle path will be the most likely one—a mediocre success—an engineer sometimes employed, sometimes not—£200 or £300 a year and that uncertain; well, I shall then have plenty to wish for and that always constituted my happiness. May I always be of the same mind and then the less I have the happier I shall be.

I'll turn misanthrope, get a huge Meerschaum, as big as myself and smoke away melancholy—and yet that can't be done without money and that can't be got without working for it. Dear me, what a world this is where starvation itself is an expensive luxury. But damn all croaking, the Tunnel must go on, it shall go on. By the by, why should I not get some situation, surely I have friends enough for that. Q. Get a snug little berth and then a snug little wife with a little somewhat to assist in housekeeping? What an interesting situation!

No luxuries, none of your enjoyments of which I am tolerably fond? —Oh horrible—and all this owing to the dam'd directors who can't swallow when the food is put into their mouths. Here is the Duke of Wellington speaking as favourably as possible, offering unasked to take the lead in a public meeting and the devil knows what, and they let it all slip by as if the pig's tail was soaped.

Now that the shield was bricked up—immured in its natural element like a sailor's body on the ocean floor—Isambard busied himself with the day's tasks and devoted no more pages of his Journal to the directors. His father was equally philosophical. 'I feel it my duty,' he wrote to the Court on 19 August,

> to give up the salary attached to my office, whilst I shall be equally ready to discharge every duty that may be required of me.
>
> As, however, other avocations will occupy a large portion of my time, sometimes perhaps at a distance; I propose to leave the works in the charge

of my son who will continue to reside on the spot and direct every necessary measure for their preservation.

I may be permitted to add that I consider the tunnel as safe and durable as it can be rendered in an unfinished state, and I consider the resumption and the continuation of the works, from the present end, perfectly practicable and that in the mode I have adopted to close it, I have provided to that effect.

I exceedingly regret the unforeseen expenses that we have incurred; but I must assure the Court that nothing but the want of funds can prevent a completion of the undertaking.

And so it was left to Isambard to look after old Tillett, to see that the raft did not drag its anchors, to stop up the pipes in the end wall one by one, and to carry the visitors' shillings safely to the Company's bank.

At the end of October, Marc and Sophie set off for France, leaving Isambard to make the best of this useful but uninspiring sinecure. They were away for Christmas, but when they returned home on 2 January Brunel found the insignia of the Legion d'Honneur awaiting him. On the same day he went to the tunnel to meet a committee of the directors, reduced Tillett to 45 shillings a week, and wrote asking a Monsieur Allegre in Calais to forward some cases which he had characteristically forgotten. Then he returned to his drawing-board and this, if we may judge from his diary, gave him more satisfaction that his new French distinction.

'Engaged on shield!'

Soon after, Isambard thankfully crossed the Channel for his holiday. A caretaker's job was not to his liking and he was tired of being taunted; for the tunnel had become an object of ridicule, a butt for music-hall comedians, a 'great bore'. Thomas Hood's *Ode to Monsieur Brunel* caught the mood.

> I'll tell thee with thy tunnel what to do;
> Light up thy boxes, build a bin or two,
> The wine does better than such water trades,
> Stick up a sign, the sign of the Bore's Head—
> I've drawn it ready for thee in black lead,
> And make thy cellar subterranean—thy Shades!

27

SMITH RAMPANT

---•+•---

CHARLES MACFARLANE, in his *Reminiscences of a Literary Life,* has left us a glimpse of contemporary stage-coach travel and of companions on the road:.

> One cold raw February morning a little after daylight, in the year of grace 1829, I embarked at Paris for Calais in a big rambling *diligence.* I had taken my place in what they call *l'interieur,* thinking that would be warmest; and in I got, and was seated opposite an unmistakable John Bull, when two young men passed and clambered into what they call the coupé, that is, the front part of the machine ...

MacFarlane's companion 'was top-coated and cloaked to that degree that he looked like a bale of broad-cloth ... He had ruddy cheeks and a red nose which betokened the *bon vivant,* but his countenance was as clouded and gloomy as if there were no cakes and ale in the blessed world.'

Arrayed in a scarlet Turkish fez with a blue silk tassel, a waistcoat and undercoat from Naples, a top-coat from Smyrna and trousers and boots from Constantinople, it would not have been surprising if MacFarlane had excited his companion's interest but no, 'Broadcloth' maintained a sulky silence. However, at the first change of horses, a cheery voice in the coupé called out, 'Apportez-nous deux bottes de foin, je vous en prie!'

> The hay was brought and put in, and then from the same coupé I heard a good English voice saying, 'It is not enough to cover up the legs, let us have some more while we are about it ...'. So on we went, Broadcloth being as taciturn, and I as cold as ever. And all this stage, I was tantalised by hearing the sounds of merry voices and of frequent and loud laughs in the coupé

After another stage or two, MacFarlane gladly accepted an invitation to the 'front part' and found himself

> comfortably ensconced between two delightful young men, brimful of vivacity and fun. 'While we are stopping, and have the opportunity, I think we had better take in some more hay', said one of them, who then repeated the *mot d'ordre,* 'Mon ami, apportez-nous deux bottes de foin!' We did the same at each relay; until, by the time we got to Beauvais, we were buried

183

in hay nearly up to the chin, and looked like three stone Schiedam bottles packed and embedded in hay for safe carriage. This comparison, which I made, renewed the laughter that had scarcely ceased from the time I entered the coupé, and had got packed up and unfrozen. I could now say with as much pathos as Jean Jacques, 'Ah! on était jeune alors!'

MacFarlane, who was hailed as 'Pasha' or 'Asia Minor', christened one companion—'a fair and handsome man of nineteen or twenty'—'Juventus', and the other—'a little, nimble, dark-complexioned man, who did not look more than five or six-and-twenty'—'Mathematicus'.

> What a happy dinner was that we had in the homely roadside inn at Beauvais! We had a bottle or two of Bordeaux besides the *vin ordinaire,* but we did not need this stimulus, for we had been just as merry, on a cup or two of coffee and a slice or two of bread for breakfast, as we were during or after dinner. The *conducteur* was a good-natured, jolly fellow himself, and not very particular as to time, so we sat rather a long while talking and joking; and all this while there sat, at the farthest end of the table, old Broadcloth, as mum as ever, eating at a rare rate, drinking champagne, and then settling it with hot brandy and water. We cast side-glances at him now and then, but otherwise took no more notice of him than we should have done of a bale of cloth or any other merchandise.
>
> I forgot now whether we took in more hay at Beauvais, or were obliged to take some out. I know that at some halting-place on the road, during that stormy snowy night, we performed the latter operation, being so very warm when settled and fixed in so many *bottes de foin.*

Juventus's good nature, Mathematicus's ready wit, and Pasha's fund of anecdotes enlivened the night, and warmed by wine and the hay, the following day passed as quickly. But in the evening as they neared Boulogne, they got, says MacFarlane,

> upon the subject of the Thames Tunnel, about which I had heard very much on the Continent, and concerning which I felt great curiosity and interest. The elder of my companions gave a minute, clever and spirited account of that work, of its present state, and of the causes of the late accident and suspension of operations.
>
> 'You seem to know all about the tunnel,' said the younger man. 'I ought to know something about it,' said the elder, 'seeing that I am the only son and assistant to the engineer, and that my name, like his, is Isambard Brunel!'
>
> We gave him an extra shake of the hand on this announcement.
>
> 'I had been thinking for some time,' said the junior, 'that as we three fellows have met in the dilly, and are likely to meet again, it would be as well if each of us knew the names of his comrades. My name is Orlebar, my present condition is that of a cadet at Woolwich.' I followed by disclosing my Highland patronymic of which I was, and still am, rather proud ....
>
> We went on talking and laughing into Calais, rather late at night, and we continued the sport at supper at the *Hotel Bourbon.* The next day we had an

equally merry and delightful passage over to England, from which I had so long been absent.

After attending to the Dover customs, the friends dined heartily at the *Old Ship*, but when they paid the bill, found themselves nearly 'drained out'.

'I should have been uneasy before we got to Calais,' said Orlebar, 'but I thought it most likely that one or both of you would be well stocked.' 'That's what I thought of you, and still more of my senior The Pasha, who is evidently a very thoughtful, cautious man.' 'I had just the same hope in you, and in Juventus', said I.

They travelled cheaply in the dickey of the London night coach. The hay they bought blew away in the gale, but at midnight they reached Canterbury and stopped at an inn where there was still 'a barmaid at her post, and a good blazing coal fire in the taproom, where some half-dozen fellows, apparently connected with the Dover and London coaching, were drinking and disputing about the last season's yield of hops, a subject seldom long out of the mouth of a Canterburian'.

After warming drinks the journey was resumed; 'another pinching, biting drive across Gad's Hill, and another across Blackheath. There was a bright, rather full moon, but it was frequently obscured by drifting clouds, which resolved themselves into snowflakes, which froze as they fell, and cut our faces like miniature icicles, sharp as needlepoints.'

At six in the morning Isambard entrusted his frozen, but still merry friends to the night porters of the London coffee-house in Ludgate Hill, and after port and negus and hot baths, they retired gratefully to bed.

'But before I was well awake,' says MacFarlane,

at about the hour of noon, Brunel was at my bedside, with five sovereigns for me, and five for Orlebar. He pressingly invited us both to his father's house, and bade us go often. There would be dinner *en famille* at six, and knife and fork for us. He was in a great hurry, going down to the Tunnel.

A day or two later, MacFarlane called at 30 Bridge Street and

was ushered up to the drawing-room, where I found his mother, a very charming unaffected, warm-hearted, thorough English gentlewoman, who received me as if she had known me all my life. I returned the five sovereigns, at which she laughed rather heartily, as she did also at some of the stories about our journey which Isambard had related and embellished.

The following evening he returned for dinner and met Isambard's sisters and young Benjamin Hawes.

Best of all, I met the head of the house, dear old Brunel, to whom, in an instant, I flew and attached myself as a needle to a big lodestone. Not that old Isambard was big, on the contrary, he was a rather smaller man than his son. The dear old man had—with a great deal more warmth of heart than belonged to that school—the manner, bearing, address, and even dress, of a French gentleman of the *ançien régime*, for he had kept to a rather antiquated, but very becoming costume.

I was perfectly charmed with him at this our first meeting, and from many subsequent ones I can feel bold enough to say that he was a man of the kindest and most simple heart, and of the acutest and purest taste in Art, whether architecture, painting, sculpture, or medalling. Of his mathematics, which seemed to be at once profound and practical, I cannot venture to speak ... nor could I risk an opinion on his very numerous mechanical inventions, being by habit or nature, debarred from any clear notion of even the simple mechanism of a wheelbarrow. But what I loved in old Brunel was his expansive taste, and his love or ardent sympathy for things he did not understand, or had not had time to learn ... And what I most admired of all, was his thorough simplicity, and unworldliness of character, his indifference to mere lucre, and his genuine absent-mindedness ... He had lived as if there were no rogues in this nether world.

That MacFarlane found his host refreshing says something for Brunel's resilience. The business of refunding debenture subscriptions must have reminded him of past disappointments, and Charles Vignoles's frequent visits to the tunnel must have presaged storms to come, yet his diary records nothing but cheerful industry. He worked at the design of a better shield, he canvassed for support and, on 18 February, he petitioned Lord Althorp for government aid.

Although in opposition, Althorp, Lord Spencer's eldest son, remained the Duke of Wellington's confidant; and, as a recent chairman of the Finance Committee, was well equipped to unlock the Treasury chest. He readily agreed to help, and on 3 March accompanied Brunel and George Hyde Wollaston to the Prime Minister, who had gathered about him the Lord Mayor, Charles Nicholas Palmer, and a number of other MPs. Wellington welcomed Brunel's petition, which Althorp presented with Palmer's support. The Duke then asked for a technical memorandum so that he could familiarise himself with the details of the estimate and the probable return, before the petition was submitted to Parliament.

Brunel and Wollaston left the Duke and hurried to the Company's Annual General Meeting at the *City of London Tavern*. Smith was in the chair, and it soon became clear that he was more interested in producing a scapegoat than in completing the tunnel. 'The chairman,' Brunel wrote later, 'expressed his disapprobation of the plan and of the mode on which the works of the tunnel had been conducted, and concluded by assuring the proprietors that he knew very well that the Government would do nothing for the tunnel.'

On 7 April the technical memorandum was handed to Wellington together with a report from Lord Althorp which recommended a government loan to the Thames Tunnel Company of £300,000—£27,000 more than Brunel had asked for—against the security of the Company's premises and in anticipation of toll receipts averaging £25,000 per annum. But while Brunel sought government aid, Smith strove to convince his colleagues that none would be forthcoming unless the Company severed its connection with Brunel and treated with Vignoles, who had offered to complete the tunnel by contract without using a shield. News of this boardroom argument soon became public—no doubt it was intended to—and on 22 April Brunel sent Isambard to Lord Althorp with minutes of the meetings, and with a message that a government loan was solicited on the merits of his plan and not on grounds of friendship.

At another General Meeting six days later, Smith requested authority to seek alternative plans to complete the tunnel. He did not mention Vignoles by name and was strenuously opposed by other directors including, it seems, Bryan Donkin. His motion was adjourned *sine die* to the relief of Brunel who remained outside the room.

A diary entry of 7 May, referring to an encounter with Robert Marten, shows that Brunel thought the public wrangle untimely. Marten was evidently in favour of obtaining authority from the shareholders to treat with anyone who 'may submit them a plan'. '*Wait till you have the money!*' was Brunel's private comment, and it seems entirely reasonable. Dissension could only jeopardise the hoped-for loan, and until it was obtained the Court had nothing to offer a responsible engineer. Indeed, while the Company remained impoverished, any adventurer could safely offer to complete the tunnel by contract in the hope of gaining short-term employment making borings.

The chairman's colours were publicly revealed by an article in the May issue of the *Mechanics Magazine*, which dwelt on the 'doubled cost' of the work under Brunel's direction. This could

> only have arisen from the grossest negligence, or the grossest mismanagement; from an utter want of calculation, or an utter want of thrift. Mr Brunel may take his choice of either view of the case as he pleases. If he embarked on the undertaking, and led others to embark on it (the more serious matter) without previously making the necessary calculations, then he has obtained the confidence of the public on false grounds; if he did make the necessary calculations, but has conducted the business in so extravagant a way, that the actual cost of everything has been double the estimated cost, then he is a most unfit person to retain the confidence of the public any longer ...
>
> Mr Brunel is known to reckon much upon the support of the noble Duke at the head of the Government; he may justly hope much from His Grace's friendship, so also may the public hope much from His Grace's well-known

detestation of anything in the nature of a 'Job'. The Duke of Wellington will not, to befriend Mr Brunel or anyone else, open the public purse wider than is necessary. Well assured of this, we care not how much 'others' may forget that there is a point beyond which friendship changes into subservience, and the patron degenerates into the partisan.

At the end of May, Smith received a most unwelcome letter from the Duke of Wellington informing him that he thought it best 'to postpone laying the affairs of the Company before Parliament until the next session *when he hoped to have the benefit of His Lordship's* [Althorp's] *assistance in so doing'.* Subsequently members of the Cabinet congratulated Brunel for having gained the Government's support and a few days later he had an informal meeting with the Iron Duke.

Smith knew that Wellington's letter made it almost certain that an Exchequer Loan would be approved during the next session; jealousy of Brunel drove him to oppose this loan, so he called a General Meeting for 30 June for the purpose of spiking the engineer's guns, and he arranged for Vignoles to give the shareholders a preview of his plan at Walbrook Buildings. Isambard seized his opportunity.

> Gentlemen [he wrote to the Court], I availed myself of my character as a shareholder to inspect [the models and drawings] accompanied by two friends, also shareholders—we examined them and received explanations from Mr Vignoles himself. Having been thus acquainted with the plan and convinced that there are considerable objections to such a plan being carried into effect, I feel it my duty to trouble you with this letter and to say that if it is the wish of the directors that I should communicate to them such objections, I should have great pleasure in doing so.

Vignoles's plan was a duplicate of Vazie's. A miner's drift would be driven to Wapping from the end of the existing tunnel and, when completed, would serve as a drain for the tunnel proper which would be extended northwards without using a shield.

It would all be done by contract most economically; and before the General Meeting Smith 'waited on His Grace the Duke of Wellington and acquainted him with the ... proposition'. Wellington pointed out that if the Thames broke into the drift, the existing tunnel would be inundated. To which the chairman replied, that an iron door, 'fixed at the commencement of the drift ... would entirely cut off any irruption of water and ground into the tunnel'. After considering this innovation, the Duke observed that 'although the water might be shut out, the workmen and the engineer would be shut in'.

On 30 June Brunel waited in an anteroom at the *City of London Tavern* while the General Meeting proceeded. He found it 'excessively animated and

* My italics.

virulent'. The chairman, he later recalled, first paid tribute to 'His Grace's attention and politeness' when he visited him to outline Vignoles's plan. He went on to say 'that the object for which the meeting had been convened was to obtain from the proprietors power to deal with the proposer [and] that tunnels might be made without Mr Brunel's shield'. He observed that

> the Thames Tunnel must remain unfinished without some such a man as the proposer, Mr Vignoles ... [since] the accidents which had occurred at the tunnel ... [resulted] from the grossest neglect on the part of the engineer ... [who], by the most profuse expenditure, ... had grossly lavished the money of the Company ...
>
> The honour and glory of finishing the tunnel had passed by as to Mr Brunel. ... He had no claim on the Company ... the Duke of Wellington had given him [Smith] most positively to understand, that whether the Government should 'give anything to the tunnel or no would not depend upon whether Mr Brunel was the engineer'... The Duke of Wellington would not hesitate to give the preference to the cheapest plan provided it was approved by some qualified person.

A resolution was then moved 'that ... the directors be empowered ... to treat with, engage, and employ any party or parties who may be willing to carry on and contract for the [work] ... and who shall produce security for the performance of such contract or contracts.' In the ensuing debate, Smith attributed to Wellington an unfavourable opinion of Brunel and took care to conceal the existence of the Duke's May letter. The motion was carried.

The press reaction was a blend of sorrow and surprise. One report of the meeting included a summary of earlier vicissitudes, and the correspondent concluded that the tunnel was not

> an ordinary speculation, in which the capitalist advances his money in the expectation of its yielding a profitable return, neither has it a political character, nor one in which the religionists can take part. It is, if we may use the term, at present purely monumental—a stupendous work of art— evincing the daring genius of its author and showing what human skill and enterprise can accomplish when the convenience of civilised man directs their operations.

Within three days, Brunel was told of C.N. Palmer's surprise at the chairman's remarks, and on 9 July Wellington sent for him and denied the opinions with which he had been credited. Smith had overplayed his hand, but there was little that could be done about it.

During August, Charles Butler confirmed that only Vignoles's plan was receiving the Court's attention, and while that engineer prepared to make a further series of borings Brunel busied himself with lesser matters and visited Bedlam which he thought 'a splendid establishment indeed!'—although 'the outdoors is not what it should be'. It was not a very stimulating time, and at the end of the month Brunel and Sophie sailed for France, where they remained until the 18th of the following January.

When they returned, Brunel found that bridges rather than tunnels awaited his attention. There was an enquiry from Warsaw for a bridge across the Vistula to replace the existing 800-foot floating structure and, nearer home, a committee of Bristolians sought designs for a bridge to span the Avon gorge and so link Clifton with the northern shore. With the rather nebulous Polish enquiry (which came to nothing) he dealt personally, but the Clifton bridge he gave to Isambard.

There is little doubt that, if the tunnelling had continued without interruption, Brunel would have gradually relinquished his command in favour of his brilliant son. Events had turned out differently, so he secured the caretaker's sinecure for Isambard, who thereby gained a measure of security and freedom to seek other engagements.

The Clifton bridge was the most promising of these early forays, and how much of the design came from Brunel's anonymous hand may be gathered from his diary which, during the early part of the following year, records several months of almost uninterrupted labour on 'Isambard's bridge'.

Isambard at his desk.

Much else had happened during the winter. Wellington's Government had fallen and the succeeding Whig Government of Earl Grey grappled with parliamentary reform. Brunel no longer had a staunch old friend as Prime Minister, but he could turn hopefully to Lord Althorp, who became leader of the House of Commons in March and has been called 'the very best leader of the House of Commons that any party ever had'. Althorp, who in November 1830 also became Chancellor of the Exchequer, accepted office most reluctantly but he remained faithful to old causes, as Brunel's diary reveals.

> Wednesday February 17th. My dear Sophia's birthday. Went to Lord Althorp to enquire whether we could rely on the Government coming forward for the tunnel.

The Clifton bridge.

He assured me that he understood it to be so ... that the Government had the intention to do so and that he would write to me on the subject by way of an answer to an application from me. I accordingly wrote to him immediately.

Althorp's reply confirmed the Government's readiness to help, providing the directors would compose their differences. But would they? Ben Hawes and the Wollastons were for Brunel, whilst Smith, Brunton and Marten inclined, to say the least, towards Vignoles.

Towards the end of February Vignoles sent to the Court his offer to complete the tunnel. Pritchard and Hoof would contract for the work and deposit a security of £15,000 which they would be liable to forfeit in certain circumstances. We have only the barest outlines of this proposition, but it seems that Vignoles offered to construct the archways for £250 per yard—substantially less than Brunel's estimate. The plan was disclosed to the shareholders at the Annual General Meeting on 2 March, but no decision was taken to adopt it—perhaps because Vignoles wrote in too many safeguards for himself and for the contractors. Instead it was agreed to refer it to professional judges, and the shareholders passed a resolution requiring the directors to press for a government loan. But as the meeting was breaking up, Smith was heard to say that he would not go to the Government.

On 9 March Brunel wrote, 'I beg the Directors will have the goodness to inform me whether I am to prepare for the resumption of the application to

Government,' but he got no answer, and his patience was running out. Much
time had been wasted discussing a plan he believed to be unsound. The Duke
of Wellington's and Lord Althorp's readiness to help had been deliberately
concealed. His professional competence and integrity had been questioned,
and still no decision had been taken about how to finish the work. Instead
there was vague talk of referring Vignoles's plan to Augustus de Morgan, the
first professor of mathematics at London University, and to Tierney Clarke, a
protege of John Rennie, who had worked on the Thames and Medway canal.
Neither of these gentlemen had tunnelled beneath a river; it would be better,
Brunel insisted, to seek Richard Trevithick's opinion.

He sent the Court a lengthy memorandum stating the objections to the
driftway proposal. The old Archway Company had excavated 870 cubic yards
of spoil at a cost of £16 6s. a cubic yard, whereas each of the 22,574 cubic
yards which he had excavated had cost only £7 15s. 'We have a substantial
structure, the strength of which has been proved beyond doubt; whereas,
with regard to the driftway or heading of 1808, nothing remains but the
recollection of it.'

He reminded the directors of Dr Hutton and Mr Jessop, who had reported
that 'effecting a tunnel under the Thames by an underground excavation (in
the old mode) is impracticable, but,' he continued, 'it is to this old mode that
you are now called upon to return, under the promise of *economy, security and
despatch.*'

How, he asked, would the Company compel a contractor to finish a loss-
making job? And how would they ensure that the work was sound? 'There
must be no inducement held out to the workmen to conceal difficulties in
the vain hope of avoiding them, or to hide defects in their work in a situation
where inspection must be imperfect.'

On 15 March he had a further meeting with Althorp, but a diary entry
of the 23rd shows that the directors were not ready to lay a new petition
before Parliament.

'The Court came to the resolution of referring the offer of £15,000
security made by Vignoles with his plan to a committee consisting of Mr
Smith, Admiral Sir Edward Codrington, Mr Donkin and Bramah—for their
report—when? Next year!!!!'

'Things are getting worse and worse.'

A week later Brunel resigned, much to the consternation of his opponents,
who foresaw what a troublesome shareholder he could be. He added to
his letter a plea that the Court appeal for other plans, rather than reject
Government aid on his account. The resignation produced results. Vignoles's
proposals were promptly referred to three independent arbiters—Tierney
Clarke, James Walker (Robert Marten's old engineer at the Commercial

Docks) and Peter Barlow, the originator of compass adjustment, who had published a treatise on the strength of materials.

Somewhat diffidently the directors enquired if Brunel would help these gentlemen. 'Yes,' he replied, 'the referees should be requested to visit the works, *where I am ready to meet them, and in the production of any information, I am always ready to meet the wishes of the Directors even now! The Court may command me in that respect.*'

Brunel's old friend George Hyde Wollaston called on 21 April, and told him that the directors had *withdrawn* his resignation. It is a curious state of affairs when an unpaid engineer may not resign, and a week later he wrote, 'Felt an extraordinary stiffness all over me, and nervous irritability—I have not felt before', so when the 'referees' had been furnished with all the documents they needed, he took Sophie to Newington near Folkestone for a few weeks' holiday and change of air'.

On 22 June the Company's patient shareholders assembled once again at the *City of London Tavern* to hear the arbiters' report. It was quite conclusive. 'It would,' the three wise men averred, 'be a waste of time and of money to attempt to complete the tunnel on Mr Vignoles's plan,' and the discomfited chairman was forced to accept resolutions that 'no other plan than that of Mr Brunel be used to complete the tunnel,' and that 'the directors be instructed to apply to Parliament for a loan'.

Knowing the report's contents, Brunel stayed away, but he sent each shareholder a printed letter, which explained his reasons for resigning and expressed his readiness to complete the work 'according to existing arrangements, whenever circumstances favour its resumption'.

The shareholders had instructed Smith to seek a government loan; perhaps they thought that he would do their bidding—if so a shock awaited them. On 2 July Lord Durham rose in the House of Lords to enquire whether a loan, solicited by a Canadian Company, might be diverted to the Thames Tunnel Company. To this the Duke of Wellington replied that the Thames Tunnel Company had already been offered a loan (of £250,000) but had refused it.* There is little doubt that Smith had declined this loan before he faced the shareholders on 22 June, and it is entirely characteristic that he concealed his action. All the shareholders could do was to meet again on 28 October and resolve once more to seek government aid. On this occasion Smith was absent and George Hyde Wollaston took the chair.

For Isambard, too, 1830 was a year of hopes deferred. In January he had offered himself as engineer to the Newcastle and Carlisle Railway Committee,

---

* It later transpired that Smith had offered to accept the money on behalf of the Company, provided the Government made an outright grant. He knew, of course, that this was out of the question.

whose Act had secured the Royal Assent the previous May; but he had been passed over in favour of Francis Giles—of all people. The venerable and august Thomas Telford, acting on behalf of the Clifton Bridge committee, had rejected all the designs for the Avon Bridge, and was busy that summer preparing one of his own. True, Maudslays were making the hardware for two commissions—a pumped drainage scheme for Tollesbury in Essex, and a new observatory for Mr James South at Kensington; but they were not the grand works he longed to accomplish. *Hors d'oeuvres* perhaps, but would there be a main course to follow?

In November, fortified by a £50 loan from his father, he surveyed a line for a proposed railway between Bristol and Birmingham, but the scheme was dropped.

The frustration of his personal ambitions put paid for the time being to any thoughts of marriage. 'I have had,' he had written in his private Journal at the ripe old age of 21,

> ... numerous *attachments*, if they deserve that name. Each in its turn has appeared to be *the true one*. E.H.* is the oldest and most constant, now however gone by. During her reign (nearly seven years!!!) several inferior ones caught my attention. I need hardly remind myself of Mlles D.C., O.S, and numerous others.

Marriage was not Isambard's spur, and William Smith's machinations did not make him 'turn misanthrope'. Occasionally serious, he was always companionable, and though friendship and his sister's marriage bound him most closely to the Hawes household, the Horsley family was soon to be enlivened by his society.

William Horsley, an organist and composer, had married Elizabeth, the daughter of his Oxford tutor, John Wall Callcott—a well-known musician. Their house, No. 1 High Row, Kensington Gravel Pits,† had welcomed Felix Mendelssohn, Brahms, Bellini and Chopin, and their five children were a bright and charming reflection of their parents' artistic industry and good taste. The eldest, Mary, aged 19, was a dark and regal beauty; but the other four, who had arrived at two-year intervals, were less reserved. Fanny was a fountain of mirth and affection and an artist of talent, as was John, who later became a Royal Academician, and one of Isambard's closest friends. Sophy was a brilliant pianist, whose intellect and incisiveness would have been daunting but for her charity, and the youngest, Charles, later developed his musical talents with Mendelssohn at Leipzig.

There were many musical evenings and amateur theatrical productions at this house in Kensington. On less formal occasions, friends like Carl

---

*   Probably Ellen Hulme of Manchester.
†   Now 128 Church Street.

Klingemann, an attaché at the Hanoverian Legation, or Friedrich Rosen, Professor of Oriental Studies at University College, would call, and in summer walk in the walled garden with the girls, smelling the roses or 'Howard's hayrick' across the way, until the extinction of 'the domestic moon'—the lamp in Mama's room—signalled the time for departure.

Towards the end of 1830 Isambard's prospects brightened, thanks to Thomas Telford, who proposed a suspension bridge supported by two expensive and unlovely towers rising from the very floor of the Avon Gorge. Modesty did not prevent Isambard giving the bridge committee his views on this folly, and the members' early enthusiasm for Telford's design soon cooled, and a second competition was announced.

This encouraging news took Brunel back to his drawing board, and he spent the greater part of the first four months of 1831 designing details of four alternative bridges, each of which would cross the gorge in a single graceful span. He welcomed the task. The closing months of 1830 had been enlivened by nothing more challenging than a nostalgic dinner with Talleyrand and occasional visits to the Humane Society, the Royal Society, or to his club, the Athenaeum.

On 15 March, with £25 from his father in his wallet, Isambard set off for Bristol. His journey was timely. The following day, Davies Gilbert (formerly Davies Giddy) and John Seaward pronounced upon the entries, and had he not been present to disabuse them of certain ill-founded misgivings, another's design might have been chosen. All ended well; and on the 19th Brunel wrote: 'Isambard is appointed engineer to the Clifton Bridge—the more gratifying that ... I have not influenced any of the Bristol people on his behalf, either by letters or by interviews with any of them.'

There was not much else to cheer about during March. At the Annual General Meeting on the 1st the shareholders again resolved that a government loan be sought to enable Brunel to complete the tunnel. Smith had again concealed his blocking tactics, but in private made no bones about his hostility, and a few days later wrote to his fellow directors, declaring bluntly that he would warn Lord Althorp against advancing money. Later in the month the Government declined to sanction a tunnel lottery—although Brunel had canvassed this scheme and secured promises of French participation—and rejected a plan to apply revenue to the tunnel from a duty on coal.

That the chairman had a hand in all this was made clear on 1 August, when in conversation with Brunel at the opening of London Bridge, Althorp admitted that Smith had influenced him with tales of wasteful expenditure. However, the encounter ended on a hopeful note. Brunel enquired about a pending Bill, supported by C.N. Palmer, to create a million-pound fund with which the Exchequer Loan Commissioners could promote public works which Parliament approved. Althorp agreed to the insertion of a clause whereby a Company, like the Thames Tunnel Company, whose funds had been exhausted, might benefit from this resource.

The Bill received the Royal Assent during September, and on 12 October the shareholders met again at the *City of London Tavern*. Smith had earlier received a letter from Brunel, which charged him with failing to implement resolutions, and his fellow directors, now weary of his obstruction, insisted that he should stand aside and allow G.H. Wollaston to chair the meeting. Resolutions were moved instructing the Court to apply to the Exchequer Loan Commissioners, and although Smith at last revealed his true colours and warned the meeting that 'he could not do otherwise than oppose such an application or its object before the House ... and that two irruptions ... had proved that the attempt *was a complete failure*', they were carried unanimously.

During the remainder of October and November, Brunel busied himself preparing documents to support the Company's application. But the strain of the long struggle with Smith had affected his health, and on 23 November, shortly after the formal request had been submitted, he suffered what was evidently a heart attack.

> I experienced this morning, just before breakfast, a very extraordinary sensation, like something breaking in my chest, rather on the left side. I was going to put my foot on the stairs, without any effort or quickness. It almost knocked me down like an electric shock. It was instantaneous—effect the whole day has been a sharp pain such as I have experienced before just under the shoulder bone.

He carried on without bothering his doctor, and a week later the pain had gone. However, another shock was in store. Five days before Christmas the Loan Commissioners rejected the Company's application, and almost immediately his good old friend Wollaston suffered a stroke.

How much longer could he go on? He was 62, and twice during the year had been reminded of the inexorable passage of time. On 15 February Maudslay had died, and on 8 June, on learning of Lady Spencer's death, he had written sadly, 'A great friend is no more.'

Now Isambard wrote this obituary in his Journal, dignifying the entry with a black border:

> Tunnel is now, I think, *dead*. The Commissioners have refused on the ground of want of security. This is the first time I have felt able to cry at least for these ten years. Some further attempts may be made—but—it will never be finished now in my father's lifetime, I fear ...

28

MARKING TIME

◆━◆◆◆━

There was little for the Brunels to celebrate as 1832 crept in. Their hopes of a Government loan for the tunnel had been extinguished and there was no prospect of money being subscribed for the Clifton bridge. This was their darkest hour. But Marc bestirred himself that chilly January, when most old men preferred to sit before their fires, and in the company of Sir Anthony Carlisle and other surgeons watched Baron Heweteloup perform an operation. The Barons' dexterity, 'he was not above three-and-a-half minutes', impressed him and he returned to the gaz engine refreshed.

The sky brightened a little on the 17th and he noted, 'Isambard has been authorised to proceed with the work of the Woolwich Dockyard'. This was another of the previous year's enquiries, but there were no further chinks in the clouds, and as the Tunnel Company's Annual General Meeting drew near, the struggle with Smith once more dominated his thoughts.

Four directors, Sir Edward Codrington, Perkins, Brunton and Smith, were due to retire; but all, save the Admiral, hoped to be re-elected. Brunel had no quarrel with Perkins and Brunton, but the Chairman's candidature was another matter. 'Mr S. seems to make sure of his re-election,' he wrote on 3 March, 'he appears very comfortable about it.' In view of Codrington's withdrawal, it would be necessary to elect two new directors if Smith were to be ousted. A merchant named Sylvester had already offered to stand, and on 6 March, just before the meeting, Brunel enlisted the eminent physician, Sir Alexander Crichton.

The shareholders were expecting a showdown. Brunel had sent to each of them a printed letter describing Smith's surreptitious sabotage of all the attempts to secure a loan.

> If at this period [he had written in conclusion] the tunnel is not across the river, and the hopes of the shareholders are not near being realised, it is conclusive that no reproach can be imputed to the Government, nor to public opinion, but solely to the unsuspected rejection of the aid of the Government. The letter of His Grace, the Duke of Wellington, withheld from the knowledge of the proprietors at the meeting of the 30th of June,

1829, was unquestionably a proof of His Grace's solicitude towards the proprietors, to reconcile them with the unavoidable delay of a few months, in obtaining the means that were contemplated for their assistance.

Now, though there are no hopes of any assistance being obtained, it is not the less urgent that the proprietors should select some persons who would co-operate with the other members of the Court of Directors in such measures as may tend to the relief of the Company.

Smith was forewarned, for Brunel had told him of the letter's contents, but his time was up. Crichton and Sylvester were elected and the 75-year-old chairman spent his remaining three years in retirement. At a Board Meeting the following week, G.H. Wollaston was elected chairman and Ben Hawes became his deputy. At last the Company's affairs were in trusted hands, so Brunel set off on three weeks' travelling.

Birmingham was his first port of call.

Went immediately to the rail-way. A magnificent establishment in every respect at the starting station. Some of the directors ... ordered one of their engines to give me a run ... Some part was performed at the rate of one mile in a minute.

I returned and took my place on one of the trains starting for Liverpool, which place I reached in two hours including frequent stoppages.

After some time in the north, he travelled to Worcester—finding its cathedral 'a magnificent structure'—and on the 17th reached Gloucester, where he admired the canal and the docks.

Bristol was an unhappy contrast. 'No shipping in the harbour except for the coasting service ... the streets are wretched, the houses equally sad. ... Is that Bristol, whose name was uppermost in the West Indies forty years ago? ... I have not witnessed in this country any depression like that at Bristol.'

He contacted the members of the Clifton bridge committee.

The trustees ... are disposed to give their money gratis; I augur but indifferently for such liberality; they have resolved to draw a prospectus and to go round with it to invite the public to subscribe. ... I pronounce at once and unhesitatingly that the scheme of the Clifton bridge is gone by.

From Bristol to Bath, evidently with thoughts of retirement: 'Went round to inspect houses, found many that would suit and very moderate in rent, a splendid town Bath is.'

Back in London on 4 May he noted: 'The experiments on the gaz, after the most persevering exertions on the part of Isambard, have elicited a difficulty.' But there was a new gleam in his eye, and four days later he wrote to the Court asking permission 'to raise at my own cost, on the Company's premises at Rotherhithe, an experimental structure as represented in the outline design.

The object of this experiment is to demonstrate the practicability of forming arches with cheap materials and by very economical means.'

The 'outline design' showed a single bridge pier supporting two semi-arches. The arches were flat—the rise of the crown was to be only 10 feet 6 inches—and, if completed, the clear span between piers would have been one hundred feet. The sketch could be mistaken for one of the present Waterloo Bridge.

A week later he borrowed £100 from Isambard, who was earning some useful fees, and set to work. Hammond, who had earlier assisted briefly in the tunnel, was made responsible for building the structure, which was made of bricks laid in Roman cement and reinforced with hoop iron. The semi-arches were completed in October, and the following month a nine-ton load was hung from the extremity of the 50-foot-long eastern cantilever. Although it supported this burden for a year, the pier remained perfectly stable and the brickwork did not crack.

Early in the building Brunel approached Charles Francis of Francis & White, who readily agreed to pay for the experiment (which cost £164); so Isambard was repaid—indeed he profited greatly, for there is little doubt that these brick semi-arches were the inspiration for his splendid railway bridge across the Thames at Maidenhead.

This was a stimulating if unprofitable time. Besides the arch and the perennial gaz engine, Brunel experimented with bronze plates for ship sheathing, and the Navy Board provided the brig *Frolic* as a test vessel. He designed improvements to the triangle-frame engine, and it seems that Isambard incorporated two of them—an improved steam valve and a more efficient furnace—into the tunnel engine, which still worked gently an hour or two a day removing infiltration. Other men's ideas were no less interesting, and the diary is full of notes regarding Mr Bates' hydrometer, Lord Dundonald's steam engine (on which he reported to the Admiralty), Lord Cochrane's patent for tunnelling under pressure, and Babbage's calculating machine, which he thought 'truly admirable, it went to the cube root of numbers not exceeding however 99,999—it is as yet but a small section of the great machine as originally contemplated'.

Honours arrived in plenty. Besides the Legion d'Honneur, he received distinctions from Caen, Stockholm and Rouen, and was elected in November to the Council of the Royal Society.

December saw him at 'the polling common in Kensington', at the side of his son-in-law, Benjamin Hawes, who was contesting the new Borough of Lambeth.

'Engaged the whole day for Hawes ... on the electioneering concern,' he wrote on the 10th, 'the mob excessively excited against Hawes.' And two days later, 'Engaged the whole day in the election business—Benjamin was proclaimed Member of Parliament at four o'clock in the afternoon—the business went off exceedingly well considering particularly the excitement occasioned by the adverse feeling of interested antagonists.'

Isambard was less philosophical. 'January 30th 1833. Gaz,' he wrote in his diary,

> After a number of experiments I fear we must come to the conclusion. All the time and expense, both *enormous*, devoted to this thing for nearly ten years are therefore *wasted*. ... It must therefore die, and with it all my fine hopes—crash—gone—well, well, it can't be helped.

In December Wollaston had suffered another more serious stroke, and on the 14th Marc Brunel hastened to his bedside:

> Went to Mr Wollaston!! What a sad view. This excellent man's affliction is an irreparable loss to the concern of the Thames Tunnel. He never will be able to attend again as an efficient member of the Court.
>
> He still clings to the tunnel; he showed me a letter from the Treasury, sanctioning the clauses inserted in the ... Act of Parliament ... hoping, he said, with abundant flow of tears, still to see the tunnel finished.

Wollaston recovered, and in February Brunel found him 'rather thinner, but his intellectual power quite sound. His remarks on my paper were very judicious and his expectations of the T.T. affair were very well grounded.' The paper referred to was a petition to Parliament, which the House approved on 15 February. Alas, the Loan Commissioners had only £130,000 in their coffers, and once again the supplicant Company returned from Westminster empty-handed.

Would the tunnel ever be finished in Brunel's lifetime? The death of his brother at Hacqueville in April was a reminder of the passing years. So was the death of the chairman's brother, who bequeathed his considerable shareholding in the Company to Anna, his sister. But she did not want the shares, and Wollaston wrote to Brunel: 'She desired me to present them to you, in testimony of her regard, as well as in remembrance of our brother's admiration for your various works.'

Happily the news was not all of the death of old friends. The nation looked hopefully to its first reformed Parliament, and nowhere more hopefully than in Bristol, where men's thoughts turned away from the tragic riots, and Isambard's old plans were re-examined. Not plans of the Clifton bridge, but plans to modernise the city's docks, and on 7 February he left London to confer with the Dock Committee. A few days later he received instructions to carry out the work. Isambard was fortunate to secure this commission; not because the dock scheme was in itself one on which to found a reputation, but because it brought him to Bristol at a time when such a scheme—a railway to London—was being considered.

He soon scented the opportunity. 'B.R. [Bristol Railway]' he wrote in his diary on 21 February, 'how will this end? We are undertaking a survey at a sum by which I shall be considerably a loser, but succeeding in being appointed engineer—nous verrons.' He did not have long to wait. On 6 March, after making a local reconnaissance, he was appointed engineer; and with W.H. Townsend, a local surveyor engaged on the Bristol and Gloucestershire railway (a modest ten-mile tramway), was instructed to make a preliminary survey for the line. The job could not be profitable. Some of the £500 fee would go to Townsend, and some to assistants, who must needs be employed since the committee wanted the work finished in two months.

The survey was a fearful labour, but the railway was a vision. A year later he christened it 'Great Western'.

The promising overture to 'dear Isambard's' career was a relief to his mother, who remembered the King's Bench Prison, and very gratifying to his father. But Brunel père had some unfinished business of his own. In January he conducted a party around the tunnel which included members of the Royal Society and Clot Bey of Egypt, who observed, so *The Times* reported, 'that the work excited great interest ... in his own country, and surprise that at the same time so extraordinary an undertaking should not have been taken up and completed by the Government'.

The public was not allowed to forget. The King's Ministers were reminded. Even the ageing King was lobbied—for on 24 May Brunel attended St James's Palace with a carefully illustrated presentation booklet.

> At about half-after-twelve, introduced to His Majesty,* and having addressed me in French, continued in that language, which he speaks very fluently.
>
> I proceeded in explaining the progress of the tunnel, beginning with an exposition of the attempt made before—a preface which has invariably produced a good effect—coupling it with a comparison to the House of Commons, as an object illustrative of the magnitude of the undertaking.

At the beginning of July Brunel transferred his papers to a new office at 53 Parliament Street, which he shared with Isambard, and soon after designed a charming stone bridge to cross the southern arm of the River Lee. The enquiry for this little bridge, 'Cork Jail Bridge', came from Richard Beamish, who had been appointed engineer to the County. Brunel visited Cork City in August, and the bridge was built with local limestone soon after. It has a single flat arch of 500 feet span, and leads to the Physics Department of University College, Cork, which has been built behind the old County Jail's Doric portico.

---

* King William IV, the 'sailor king'.

With Sophie he welcomed another, more hopeful New Year at Ramsgate, whence on 7 January, after a 'very agreeable navigation considering the lateness of the season', they returned to London.

By this time the mound over the shield had been dredged away, and the mid-river raft dispensed with to save the wages of its attendants. There were, however, minor matters which required routine attention. The pumps and the steam engine had to be maintained—as did the gas plant and the timber roof of the boiler house—and in January the Company's wharf suffered damage, so Brunel gave directions for its repair and informed Isambard. Soon after, he met Lord Althorp and secured his agreement to a new petition being laid before Parliament.

The Annual General Meeting early in March was all sweetness and light. The shareholders and directors were united in seeking government aid, and high hopes were entertained that their petition would be approved on the 18th, but the ballot went against it and, as the next parliamentary opportunity would not occur until 29 April, Brunel busied himself designing a four-mile-long viaduct to carry 'Isambard's rail-way' through north-west London to a terminus near Vauxhall Bridge. (This viaduct was abandoned when the Paddington site was chosen for the terminus.)

Although the public had been gripped by railway fever, the Government remained faithful to the tunnel, and Brunel's undoubted high spirits received a fillip on 25 April, when members of the Royal Society gave a dinner at the *Crown and Anchor* to celebrate his 65th birthday; but bad news followed swiftly.

'April 29th: The tunnel petition was to have been presented this day by Major Beauclerk, but how it happened I know not, the petition was mislaid, and all our hopes frustrated again notwithstanding the assurances we have had from every quarter of support.'

Sweet prepared a duplicate, but another opportunity had gone by, and Brunel lobbied MPs relentlessly lest their good intentions be forgotten. On 16 June, in the middle of his campaign, Beauclerk unexpectedly presented the petition. It was seconded by Admiral Codrington, and approved by the House; but the Treasury mills grind slowly and a long wait ensued.

Brunel spent another fortnight with Sophie in Ramsgate, returning home in a packet named *City of London* on 21 July. This vessel interested him greatly because she was fitted with Samuel Hall's steam condensers. He filled a page of his diary with closely written calculations, and it is clear that her engineer had little time to himself.

Brunel had decided to live in Isambard's old house at Rotherhithe when tunnelling recommenced, so at the end of July, when Benjamin Hawes told him that Treasury approval of the loan was assured, he arranged for the house to be repaired, and set off on a sight-seeing tour. Sophie wanted to renew old French acquaintances, so Brunel escorted her to France and left her at the *Hôtel L'Angleterre* in Rouen before commencing his travels.

September 3rd. Left Rouen alone to return to England. Went to Dieppe by one of the great diligences.

September 4th. Crossed from Dieppe to Brighton in ten hours half. Calm all the way.

September 5th. Journey from Brighton to London in five-and-half.

September 6th. Set off for Edinburgh by the steamer *Soho*. Started eleven o'clock at night. ...

September 17th (From Edinburgh). Went to Glasgow—the place and the labouring class have the character peculiar to a manufacturing town. One might say the population likewise.

September 18th. Returned to Edinburgh.

September 19th. Went to the canal boat, and ran over four miles at the rate of ten miles an hour with two horses driven by a boy ... At two o'clock got into a public conveyance for Newcastle ...

September 20th. Reached Newcastle at six a.m. Started at eight for Sunderland where I arrived at half-past-nine. Put up at the *Wheatsheaf*. Went to the works at Wearmouth ...

September 27th. Reached Northampton late in the morning and set off at about ten o'clock to go to Lord Spencer.

The following night at eleven he left Lord Spencer and reached London at half past six in the morning of the 29th. Half an hour later he was in his office.

Meetings of the Court, clearing the eastern archway, and effecting minor repairs kept him busy during October, but on the 27th he crossed from Brighton to Dieppe, and two days later the 'great diligence' bore him back to Rouen. The next ten days were spent with Sophie revisiting boyhood haunts. Hacqueville, where they called on 8 November, seemed a little strange—La Ferme Brunel having passed into other hands—but Pinchon, the worthy wheelwright, now rising 72, was still in his shop, and surprised too when a strange old man jumped in through the window.

The boy Brunel!

'He called his good wife, it is fifty years—but yesterday—since I saw him.'

Marc and Sophie crossed to Dover on 14 November, and travelled to Sittingbourne where they put up for the night. The following day, en route for London, they visited Bacon at the Chatham woodmills and found all well.

Back in Bridge Street Sophie got ready to move, and Brunel stayed at his drawing board working on the new shield. It would not be long now.

'December 5th. On this day the first instalment has been made over to the Thames Tunnel Company to the amount of £30,000.

At last!'

29

THE TREASURY EDICT

uring the summer of 1834 it was Isambard's turn to see his hopes founder on parliamentary rocks. Despite his testimony, the House of Lords threw out the Great Western Railway Bill on 25 July, and for a few days afterwards he evidently relaxed. One of Sophy Horsley's letters to her favourite and youthful aunt Lucy Calcott, who was governess to a landed Reading family, describes with relish an August dance which the sisters did not leave until three in the morning. 'Isambard Brunel was there,' she noted, 'and he and Mary were of course a good deal together.'

Sensing that their Lordships could not command the tide, the Railway Company prepared a bold new Bill for the next parliamentary session while Isambard busied himself with a more comprehensive survey and brought his powers of persuasion to bear on refractory landowners. He had little time for dances, and since Mendelssohn did not come to England, the Horsley girls had to be content with the society of Carl Klingemann and Friedrich Rosen, whom Fanny and Sophy found perfectly delightful; but their older sister was a little disconsolate.

'We were handed off to bed by Mary,' wrote Sophy plaintively to Lucy Calcott in October, 'I most fully agree with you in wishing that she may shortly have a house to manage of her own, for she fulfils the duties of housekeeping admirably but ... no prospect of establishing herself offers, nor does it at present appear probable that any will.'

Greatly pleased that Isambard was at last well paid, Brunel completed

Mary Horsley.

his plans to finish the tunnel. The shield had stumbled over many obstacles during its earlier march, but essentially the lessons of its journey were three: first that progress depended on removing great quantities of water from the face; second that the air became more vitiated as the tunnel lengthened; and third that, whatever the surveyors might say, the ceiling of 'strong blue clay' was not reliable.

To provide both drainage and ventilation, Brunel proposed sinking a pumping well on the Wapping shore from the base of which a driftway would be driven below the proposed line of the northern half of the tunnel. This drift would be excavated by means of a small shield and would carry air to, and water from, the face of the tunnel proper, which would subsequently be extended northwards with a new shield.

To lessen the risk of an irruption, Brunel proposed to survey the river bed regularly, using a company diving bell, and to carpet it with clay bags and gravel when the slightest depression appeared. Lastly, the new shield would be fitted with extended top and side staves, which would overlap the tunnel brickwork (as had been proposed originally in the patent) and support the roof when a frame was advanced.

These were the refinements with which he hoped to perfect his proven plan. Unfortunately, save for the improvements to the shield, they were forbidden.

There had been changes at the Court. Ben Hawes had succeeded G.H. Wollaston as chairman, although the old physicist remained a director. Thomas Brandram, Thomas Brunton, Timothy Bramah, Bryan Donkin, Hugh Gray and Robert Marten had all departed and in their places were William Allen, John Buckle, a London shipowner, J.A. De Riemer, a friend of Brunel, John Brown, a geographer who had made a fortune from diamonds, two new representatives from long-serving families—F.L. Wollaston and Brunel's son-in-law Benjamin Hawes—and John Barker, probably a Treasury nominee, who became deputy chairman. Charles Butler was also superseded as company clerk by one Joseph Charlier.

There were many new faces, but it was a government directive, not the hostility of some would-be Smith, which thwarted the engineer's plans. Parliament had sanctioned a loan of £270,000, but the Treasury stipulated that the money should be 'solely applied for carrying on the tunnel itself, and that no advance should be applied to defray any other expense until that part of the undertaking which is most hazardous shall be secured'.

Brunel discussed the implication of this edict with Sweet on 16 January 1835. 'I strongly insisted on carrying on the driftway ...' he noted, '[but] it being objected that we ran the risk of losing the support of the Government in so doing, I found myself compelled to yield to the injunctions, as so interpreted, of the Lords of the Treasury.'

Marc Isambard Brunel: an early photograph.

For several months Brunel and the directors sought to persuade the Loan Commissioners that at least a pumping well should be sunk at Wapping, so that the local water-table could be lowered for the benefit of the miners at the face. An iron curb on which to sink this shaft, and a site on the northern bank were even purchased, but eventually this too was disallowed. Meanwhile, plans for the new shield were sent to Maudslays, Rennies and Galloways, and in due course Rennies' price of £7,400 was accepted and they were given the order.*

The refusal of the drainage drift and the Company diving bell and barge was a bitter disappointment, but the dandy pump had proved reasonably efficient in draining the face, and Brunel hoped that with two of these pumps he could keep the work clear, although he knew that they were not entirely reliable. His report of 2 March certainly betrays no doubts about the outcome. 'I cannot conclude,' he wrote, 'without reiterating the expression of my entire confidence in the power and efficiency of the means I have devised for the successful termination of our enterprise.' Had he foreseen the bitter fruits of the Treasury's penny-pinching, he would have expressed himself differently.

The previous December Brunel had offered Beamish the post of Resident Engineer, which he promptly accepted—naming a salary of £500 a year. To this the Company agreed, so he crossed from Ireland with his wife † and son, moved into a Company house and, on 13 January, resumed his duties. He was soon joined by two new assistants, Louis Gordon and Joseph Coulthurst— who took charge of a shift apiece—and by some of the old hands, amongst them Huggins, Fitzgerald and the draughtsman Pinchback, who added a leaven of experience to the Company's growing work force.

The Resident Engineer's new spell of duty began ominously. On 2 March Brunel received 'an intimation of Mr Beamish being too unwell to attend proceeding from an inflammation of the eye—the only good eye he has'. Mrs Beamish, a formidable lady, would allow no one to see her husband for several days, but fortunately Brunel and Sophie had moved to Rotherhithe, and a fortnight later Beamish returned to work.

The seven-year shutdown had played havoc with the services. The timber trunking surrounding the hoist had rotted and was replaced by an iron trunk; the chute and the water wheel were also repaired—since they might be needed in an emergency; the railway was given a new rope; the trucks were attended to; the steam engine and pumps were overhauled, and the

---

* Maudslays quoted £9,400, and Galloways only £6,200, but Brunel did not consider Galloways competent to manufacture the shield.
† Not the lady who first claimed Beamish's affections—she had died some months previously.

decrepit coal-gas plant was again converted to produce more expensive gas from coconut oil.*

When these jobs had been done, carpenters turned their attention to the stairways and stagings while millwrights installed the second dandy pump at the bottom of the shaft. They next laid an iron suction pipe down the eastern archway to connect this pump with a new drainage well built some twenty feet back from the tunnel's end wall. These services duplicated those installed earlier in the western archway, but Brunel connected the two mid-river drainage wells—so that one dandy could empty both—and from each well a drain was run forward to the end of the tunnel.

The work of resurrection and improvement left Brunel little time for other engagements. In the spring of 1835, after making a preliminary geographical study, he declined responsibility for a projected barrage across the Nile. The following January he turned down work on a proposed railway between Paris and Le Havre, and a month later refused involvement in the Brighton line. In the early summer of 1836 he did accept a retainer from the Margate and Ramsgate Railway Company, but the survey proper he delegated. The tunnel was enough.

Nor was Isambard looking for work. He completed the prodigious labour of surveying the line from London to Bristol and then, in August 1835, suffered an 11-day cross-examination before a House of Commons committee considering the Great Western Railway Bill. Thanks largely to his eloquence, it received the Royal Assent on the 31st.

'Only fancy how charming it will be when you can get to Reading in an hour-and-a-quarter,' wrote Fanny Horsley to Lucy Calcott the following month.

> If I understand it rightly, there will be a branch road passing very close to Swallowfield, which is still better. Certainly, if I live so long, and you live so long, and are still with the Russells, I shall pay you a morning visit some two years hence, taking care to be home for dinner not to displease Papa. Papa is going to take us for a long walk one day to Wormwood Scrubs to see the beginning of it, and the steam engine, which is at work digging and delving, to the infinite comfort and happiness, did they but know it, of sundry, lean, miserable 'ossifers', as John calls them.

Much had been done in the tunnel by the time Fanny wrote these lines. The end wall had been demolished, and the brick buttresses exposed to view. One by one the old polings had been removed, and the faces cut back two feet—to make room for Rennie's frames, which would be deeper than the old ones. The faces had been stabilised with iron pins—driven forwards

---

* Brunel mistakenly considered oil gas less liable than coal gas to explode accidentally; however, changing to the cleaner oil gas reduced the contamination of the tunnel's atmosphere.

horizontally—and clothed with new poling boards which were held in place by timber struts. A new enlarged air trunk had been connected to the boiler's furnace, and extended to the farthest end of the dividing wall. They were ready to dismantle the old shield, and at the end of August the hands were reorganised into three eight-hour shifts—Joseph Coulthurst supervised the first, Louis Gordon the second, and a new assistant, Thomas Page, the third.

Page had proved resourceful during three months' work in the tunnel, and there is little doubt that Brunel found his qualifications attractive. He was 32—young enough to be strong but old enough for authority—and he had a good background. After being educated for the sea, he had turned to engineering at Thomas Tredgold's suggestion, gaining useful experience first as a mechanical draughtsman and subsequently with the architect Edward Blore. He was an Associate of the Institution of Civil Engineers and quickly earned the men's respect.

After the buttresses had been demolished, the top staves were jacked up some 12 inches and then the millwrights began dismantling the centre frames. Theirs was a fearful labour. They sweated over seized fastenings. They strained at tackles to lift out the iron floors and side members—and reeled from the echoing explosions when they cracked. They grew faint from lack of oxygen—even the gaslights burned dim—for the ventilator was a feeble thing and no match for the gases which the infiltration released. Illness forced Coulthurst to resign on 18 October. Six days later Beamish fell sick again, and Page grew visibly weaker. But despite a reversion to two-shift working, the middle of November saw the last frame removed and the sides of the excavation lined with timber.

Only a lattice of props filled the great cavern where the shield had been and some directors, whom Beamish conducted to the face, 'became so much alarmed that after one look they turned and made the best of their way to the top of the shaft'.

Boxing Day, which had been declared a national holiday, provided an opportunity to take stock.

Isambard sorted his papers in the Parliament Street office, ready for his secretary to take to 18 Duke Street—the splendid house overlooking St James's Park which he had just bought. Then, while his four-horse carriage waited in the street, he took down his long neglected Journal, settled himself for the last time in his familiar chair, and listed the works entrusted to him. They were worth more than £5 million.

> Everything at this moment is sunshine. I don't like it—it can't last —bad weather must surely come. Let me see the storm in time to gather in my sails.

Mrs B.—I foresee one thing—this time twelve months I shall be a married man. How will that be? Will it make me happier?

Down in the tunnel Brunel and Beamish surveyed their handiwork and made plans for completing it. The place had an atmosphere of unreality. The clanking trucks which had carried timber props and iron frame members lay still upon their track in the eastern archway. The shouting workmen had gone. The millwrights' hammers were stilled. The visitors, who promenaded as far as the barrier in the western archway, seemed oppressed by the silence, which was emphasised by the slow beat of the pumps, just as the emptiness of a deserted house is heightened by the hollow tick-tocking of a clock. There was something strange, too, about the scene at the end of the archways. New top staves propped in place beneath the old ones. Below them nothing but timbers and some new, half-completed bottom boxes, each standing on two shoes.

There was much to do, but the old shield had been removed, and the diary reveals Brunel's relief.

'We have done wonders,' he wrote as the year closed, 'in having accomplished so much without any accident or faux pas—may we be as fortunately circumstanced at the end of the year 1836. Thanks be to God!'

But the New Year opened sombrely.

January 1st. On this day one of the labourers (John Griffiths) being on top of the shaft on the side where things are lowered down, his attention was distracted by the flat rope, and in the act of examining it, he fell down and was killed, without any limb broken but the back of his skull.

30

'THE COMFORTS AND ELEGANCES OF LIFE'

————◆·❀·◆————

Rennie's shield had important new features.
Its top staves were stronger and could be retracted or tilted and they (like the side staves) were fitted with tails which would hold up the roof at all times. Its side members had more wrought-iron reinforcement, and neighbouring frames were coupled with slings—to prevent them sinking when they stepped forward. There were quadrants below the floor plates to ease the frames' steps and limit them to six inches precisely. The new legs had longer shins, and each frame had two jacks which would thrust downwards through the cloven forepart of its shoes, and force boards like poling boards into the ground beneath their soles.

It was a wonderful shield, but it weighed fifty tons more than the old one, and its complexity and the too-numerous manufacturing errors made its assembly tedious and slow.

At last, on 24 March—just a year after Fitzgerald had hammered his chisel through the end wall of the tunnel—Brunel pronounced it complete, and in the evening Beamish was elected a Fellow of the Royal Society. No doubt Brunel proposed him; no doubt the Irishman was delighted, and no doubt Brunel still thought the honour well deserved a month later when he informed the Loan Commissioners that 15 feet of tunnel had been built, and that the cost of progress had fallen to £101 per foot 'which sum already closely approaches the original estimate ... though under the disadvantage attending all mechanical labour when operating with inexperienced hands'.

However, the Resident Engineer had not been left alone very long. Indeed, save for a note about the annual Tunnel Club anniversary dinner, and a reference to a letter, which warned Isambard that the piers of his Maidenhead bridge would be 'exposed to the overwhelming effect of ice or to the attack of barges', there is little apart from tunnel entries in Brunel's diary during April. He had scarcely left the works.

In May he was absent more often. There was a visit to Ramsgate on railway business, and on the 20th he had to hurry to Kensington with Sophie; but

212

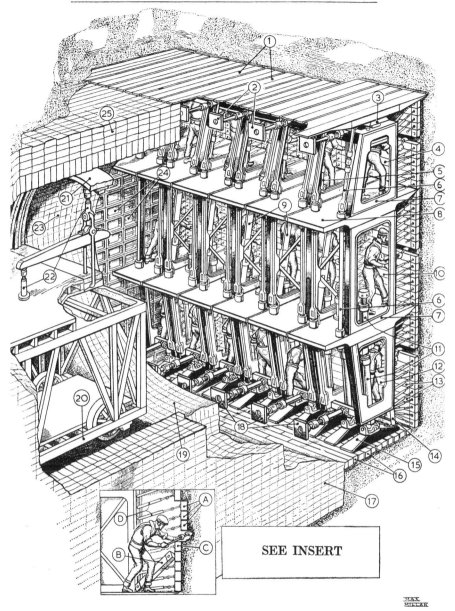

SEE INSERT

MAX
MILLAR

1	Top staves	12 Bottom box of Frame no. 6
2	Abutting screws	13 Poling boards
3	Head	14 Jack forcing down floor boards
4	Top box of Frame no. 6	15 Shoe
5	Tail jack	16 Floor boards on which brick

1 Top staves
2 Abutting screws
3 Head
4 Top box of Frame no. 6
5 Tail jack
6 Wrought-iron reinforcing
    chamber
7 Cast-iron side frame member
8 Upper floor plate of Frame no.
    6
9 Sling
10 Middle box of frame no. 6
11 Leg

12 Bottom box of Frame no. 6
13 Poling boards
14 Jack forcing down floor boards
15 Shoe
16 Floor boards on which brick
    roadways rest
17 Brickwork of dividing wall
18 Bottom abutting screws
19 Brick roadway
20 Travelling stage
21 Roof centring
22 Jacks for adjusting roof
    centring

23 Western sidewall
24 Side staves
25 Roof brickwork

INSERT

A Poling board moved forward
B Poling board removed so that
    miner can excavate
C Poling board that has not
    been moved forward
D Poling screws

the events surrounding this domestic excursion are best described by Fanny
Horsley's letter to another of her aunts.

> At seven o'clock [of 15 May] Mr Klingemann and Dr Rosen came to tea,
> and Isambard expressed a great wish to see Lord Holland's Lanes so, by way
> of doing a very genteel thing, we all agreed to go. Isambard offered Mary
> his arm—Mama went with John, I with Mr Klingemann, and Sophy with
> Dr Rosen. We walked all through the lanes to the house and then back. Mr
> Brunel and Mary walked all the way very slowly, and when, on our return, we
> were quite at the bottom of Bedford Place, they were only just visible, and
> Mama got quite vexed and annoyed, never thinking of the real reason. They
> were some minutes after us in finding their way up to the drawing-room, and
> when they did enter, Mama said, 'Upon my word, Mr Brunel, I never knew
> anyone walk so slowly in my life.
>
> 'Why indeed,' he said, 'I walk so seldom that when I do, I like to make
> the best of my time.' ... He almost immediately took leave. ... Mr Klingemann
> staid late, and directly he had gone, Sophy and I went up to bed. In about
> half-an-hour we heard Mary come up and called her in.
>
> 'Well, what could you be doing lagging behind in that way?' said Sophy.
>
> 'Indeed, Mary,' I said—but quite in fun, without any idea of the truth—
> 'one would think he had been making you an offer.'
>
> 'And what would you say if he really had?' said Mary in an awful hollow
> voice. ...
>
> He came every day till Friday, and on Friday, melancholy to relate, he
> was obliged to go to the country, and does not return till Sunday. I think
> Mary has borne it very well with the constant aid of pen, ink and post, and
> sundry double letters. You know I must have a little laugh, but really, *love* is
> such a very new character in our family, not to speak of *marriage*, that I only
> wonder at my good behaviour on the occasion. ...
>
> On Friday Mr and Mrs Brunel and Emma came over and staid some time,
> and were most affectionate and pleasant. I and Sophy were out so we did not
> see them. On Monday, Mama, I and Mary set off at half-past-ten to town in
> a fly. I took a book and well it was I did, for the hours they spent at Turner's
> making endless substantial purchases would have been unbearable. We got
> about four to Rotherhithe and found the family at home. What a perfect old
> man Mr Brunel is! I leave Mary to adore the son, but I really must be allowed
> to adore the father.
>
> Mama and Mrs Brunel retired to a private conference after some time,
> and then Miss Brunel and Mary, so he proposed taking me to see the tunnel,
> which is only six or seven yards from their house. It was the first time I had
> seen it, and I cannot tell you how much I was impressed with wonder and
> admiration at it and at the mind of the man who could conceive it. There are
> numbers of men at work at it now, and it is going on most briskly. I believe
> it will be finished in about two years.

In truth, progress was becoming less than brisk. Whereas four feet
six inches had been gained each week during the latter part of April, the

rate fell to two feet six inches during each of the six weeks of Isambard's engagement.

Of course the shield was under the deepest part of the river and the men faced difficulties. Twice during June the infiltration shot up to over 500 gallons a minute—more than the dandy pumps could remove—and the Company's newly acquired hoy *Ganges* had to heave overboard a lint of clay bags and gravel while Brunel searched for hire barges which could apply a more substantial bandage to the river's bleeding belly. There were also teething troubles with the shield —some of them seemingly unaccountable—but the infiltration *averaged* less than 100 gallons a minute, and the conditions did not account for this snail's progress of 30 inches a week—or for the undercurrent of discontent which the diary reveals—especially among the bricklayers.

It is true that, unlike the miners, the bricklayers had not been reared in darkness and weaned on foul air; it is also true that there was work in plenty for them above ground in the sunshine; but they were highly paid by the standards of the day. Why then were they often found in the local pubs too drunk to work? How did they contrive to leave the tunnel and steal away before their shift had ended?

A spur and an example were needed, and although Brunel wrote nothing that could be construed as criticism of Beamish, it is clear that the men disliked his parade-ground manner and that he expected, but did not earn, the same deferential admiration from his assistants that he quite naturally accorded to his chief. In truth, he was giving the tunnel no more than half his attention. When the new shield had been made ready for its march, he had written asking Brunel for an increased salary. It is probable that his letter suffered much diligent rephrasing. It certainly reveals the man.

After a somewhat flowery paragraph about the anxious business of removing the old shield and inserting the new one, Beamish had expressed the hope that the 'long-felt duty to you, Sir, has been ... faithfully discharged', for he had allowed no 'personal ambition, interest, or inconvenience' to deter him from the path of duty 'even to the sacrifice of all other professional connections (which in my own country were not small) and to the declining of a place in the Legislature, though pressed on me free of expense. I now naturally give way,' he had continued,

> to the contemplation of the circumstances in which—shall I call it—my devotion to the cause of the tunnel has placed my family. My wife, nourished amid the comforts and elegances of life, has cheerfully borne the separation from her home and her friends, and has, without repining—though not without sorrow—witnessed the bloom fade from the cheek of our only child, and her own health fail in fulfilling my wishes.
>
> My duty to them will not permit of this continued sacrifice from a

prolonged residence in a vitiated atmosphere. But the change of air which medical opinion has declared necessary (while the conveniences for exercise to which they have been accustomed are retained) so far increases expense, as to render the outlay of my own private funds as great, if not greater, than it was previously to my connection with the works.

So long as any doubt existed as to the introduction of your wonderfully arranged instrument—the shield—so long as you and your protection remained unvindicated, I willingly met all the discomforts and expenses ... but ...

he had continued, casting a cool westward glance in the general direction of William Gravatt, who was working for Isambard surveying the Bristol and Exeter line,

I find that those who but a few years since were capable only of acting as my assistants are now in the receipt of a larger salary, in the superintendence of *ordinary* works, than is granted to me in that of the most *extraordinary* ... I believe that I do not go beyond the engineering market price when I name £800 per annum as the sum to which the individual filling the deeply anxious and responsible situation of Resident Engineer of the Thames Tunnel may fairly deem himself entitled.

Jane Trevithick had not liked Rotherhithe. Sophie Brunel might not, of her own free will, have chosen a residence at Cow Court, but neither lady dwelt too much on fading cheeks, or left her swain for a change of air.

Beamish got an extra £100 a year and probably Brunel hoped that he would stay; but no doubt, after a trying day, he wished that Isambard was there to take the reins and finish off his grand design. But Isambard's stock of work had grown half as big again by the middle of 1836, and on 5 July he married his Mary and took her to Capel Curig for the first part of their fortnight's honeymoon. There was a dance at the Horsleys' house that evening which Fanny described with exquisite detail in a letter to her elder sister.

'The band played extremely well, and very pretty Quadrilles, but the pianoforte man came so late that Mama had actually got off one glove preparatory to performing the first Quadrille with the harp man when he arrived. I really almost fell into kicking hysterics with horror.'

And again in another letter: 'Pray tell Isambard that we liked all his friends extremely except Mr Gravatt, who I think partakes of the Wild Beast. Sophy and I, however, paid him every attention, so don't frighten yourself about it, and from what Papa says, I think he must have half-emptied his snuff box.'

On 18 July Beamish was called to Ireland for jury service, and did not return for three weeks. Page was again ill during the last fortnight of the month, and Gordon was also off duty, although only for a few days. Fortunately another young Scot, Andrew Crawford, had been engaged as a trainee a few weeks earlier, but although the infiltration increased and Brunel again resorted to the time-consuming horizontal pins to stabilise the worst of the faces, progress improved a little.

Two days after his return, Beamish tendered a letter of resignation. Knowing that he could hardly have done so at a less auspicious time, Isambard came to his father's assistance and offered to release William Glennie, who was in charge of work at the great Box Tunnel, between Chippenham and Bath. Since it is doubtful whether Brunel considered Gravatt temperamentally suitable, there was no one, Company employees apart, better fitted for the job than Glennie; but on 20 August, while visiting Ben Hawes at his new home at Mortlake, Brunel learned that his host had heard that Page and Gordon 'would not serve under another if Mr Beamish withdrew'.

That the assistants did not feel free to communicate direct with Brunel indicates that Beamish still 'wielded his authority with a rather heavy hand', and on the 23rd Brunel asked them to state their position. The assistants replied jointly the next day. They desired to express their loyalty, but considered that

> the introduction of a stranger ... [would be] so strikingly anomalous, that to act under him would be to admit our incompetency ... and we should have the additional mortification of finding the result of our exertions transferred to the credit of one whose direction during this most important period was purely nominal.

The sentiments were almost certain Gordon's, but the reaction was understandable, and on 31 August Page was appointed Acting Engineer 'pro tempera', given a salary of £300 a year, Beamish's old house, and an allowance for coals and candles. Despite an increase in pay, Gordon left a month later, and was succeeded by Crawford, whose salary was raised to £50 a quarter.

The diary reveals Brunel's concern at the shield's deteriorating condition, and the men's indiscipline.

'September 21st. Mr Murdoch has reported to me that the chief cause of the illness amongst the men is the ardent spirits—they are, or many are, found sleeping in the public houses after having retired from their work—their day shift.' Again typically on 6 October: 'Had indeed the shield been maintained in good order everything would be right ... Minall reported to me that the frame number three which is now so deteriorated by fracture, has been left without the slings being keyed' (locked).

The mention of Murdoch and Minall, although in anxious contexts, is evidence of remedial steps. The former had been appointed Company Medical Officer, probably on the strength of his experience in a Paris cholera hospital, and the millwright Minall was made responsible for the blacksmiths and grandly designated, 'Master of the Frames'. He was a craftsman who diligently restored and cherished the shield, and Brunel in turn cherished him.

Page made mistakes but, being endowed with a keen brain, and having acquired the habit of industry, he soon found his feet. He eschewed giving orders from the Cow Court office, and earned the men's respect by spending long hours in the shield. That he disciplined his undoubted ambition and made himself constantly accessible were signs of intelligence, and in all his efforts during the early anxious months he was supported by his tireless chief.

> September 23rd—Went down at two a.m. ... Visited at four p.m.
>
> Visited again at half-past-seven, found things right. (Crawford on duty).
>
> October 22nd—Up at three after a sound rest of five hours.

Pages are filled with entries like these; and even the few grudging hours Brunel spent sleeping were punctuated by regular descents to the ground-floor office to read the reports which the duty assistant had left in his box.

The cause of the shield's failures came to light soon after Page's appointment. The assistants had taken to introducing timber props between side members of the frames and the end of the brickwork in order to 'relieve the abutting screws' after a frame had been advanced.

The side members were not designed to withstand this treatment—the abutting screws bore against the frames' stout heads and bottom floor plates—and by the time Brunel discovered and forbade the practice, many of them had fractured.

No wonder he wrote in the diary, 'None but mechanical heads can conduct these works'. Neither Isambard nor Gravatt would have tolerated such abuse—but the troubles did not end with fractured side members. Quadrants broke; then some frames fell inches below their proper level and, because it was impossible to raise them before they were repaired, the others had to be allowed to sink in line, and the tunnel's ascent was delayed. Because of this the upward-sloping culverts ceased to drain the bottom boxes, so another well had to be built a hundred feet further along the western archway and the old dandy pump's pipe had to be extended to draw water from it. Yet more trouble followed; the pipe's joints proved imperfect, and had to be laboriously repacked. All this, because abutting screws were 'relieved'.

By 7 December Minall's men had restored the shield and installed a fan to speed the airflow through the ventilator. Page had reorganised the shifts, giving one to Crawford and one to each of two new assistants—Francis and Richardson. The new Resident Engineer had inherited a legacy of difficulties and had triumphed over them. Progress since his appointment had averaged four feet a week. The tunnel was 720 feet long.

Brunel might well have hoped for a peaceful Christmas. Emma had married the Reverend Frank Harrison on 31 October and had gone to live at Longdon near Tewkesbury; so once again he was alone with Sophie. But the rains had come, and the diary tells an anxious story.

> Five in the morning [Christmas Day, 1836],* apprehensive that they should omit applying the planking against the frames, I got up and went to read the night report.
>
> I saw then that my apprehensions had been well grounded; but that *Mr Page had been down at four o'clock with the same notion*, and had applied the planking, that is, ordered it to be done.
>
> Thus, it is but too true, that we cannot rely upon our agents although instructions have been left yesterday for securing everything in the faces.

The infiltration increased as the water table rose, and with the water came silt—30 cubic yards were washed in and trucked away during one shift on 19 December. It clogged the culverts, jammed the legs of the frames and damaged the pumps; and the men toiled and sweated just to stay where they were. By the following May the silt removed from the tunnel equalled in volume all the spoil taken up during the excavation of the first hundred feet of the archways; but during the first five months of 1837 progress amounted to a mere ten feet.

The water brought in gas as well.

'January 4th. Eighteen men including the foreman absent from one shift of miners through sickness.'

The engineers suffered no less.

'March 10th. Mr Page had a bad night. Mr Mason complains much likewise—Mr Francis will not, I apprehend, stand long to this service.'

The poison's effects lingered.

'June 26th. Fitzgerald and Huggins affected in the hands ... Thomas Cotsworth, a bricklayer who left us in November last, and is now employed at Maidenhead, has not yet recovered of the affliction extending from his eye to his ear.'

Slowly the infiltration increased. By February it had risen to an average of 230 gallons a minute. During May it reached 350, and the engineers were driven to all sorts of expedients to pump it away. After repeated failures of the dandy pumps during January, Brunel ordered tall 'vats' to be erected in the archways. These were filled by hand pumpers and emptied by the dandies, whose suction pipes kept full because the water in the vats was higher than the pumps themselves.

'Hand pumping answers,' he noted on 31 January, '*but it is too barbarous for us.*'

---

* The shield was blocked up over the holiday.

Although the infiltration did not diminish sensibly during the summer, the water became largely silt-free in June, and the vats and hand pumps were dispensed with. Unfortunately its gas content increased. The miners were continually vomiting—and occasionally losing consciousness—so a sample of tunnel water was sent to Professor Taylor at Guy's Hospital.

The Professor's report was lengthy and conclusive. 'Sulphurated gas [hydrogen sulphide],' he wrote, 'gives to it [the water] its peculiar offensive smell. This gas, I find, constitutes about 1.61 per cent by volume; but, doubtless, when the water first escapes, it contains more than double this quantity.

> Now Sulphurated Hydrogen is one of the most deleterious gases with which we are acquainted ... it is certain from numerous observations made in emptying the drains of Paris, that when it forms not more than two, three or four per cent by volume of the air ... it gives rise in the course of time to alarming symptoms—nausea, loss of appetite, great feebleness, tremor of the limbs, and general wasting of the body ... the air of the tunnel must be contaminated with at least two or three per cent of this noxious gas.
>
> ... The most effectual means of purifying the air would be ... a communication with the northern shore, so that there might be a continual current through the tunnel.

'It cannot be expected,' reported Brunel on 7 June,

> that the miners who receive the deleterious water from the issue itself can be protected from those cutaneous diseases and from the debilitating effluvia that have affected them so powerfully as to disable them; nor can any ventilation free the bricklayers from the diseases, from which several of them have lost the use of their hands.

On 16 June he found the atmosphere 'intolerable'. On the 20th he wrote, 'Gas ignited in the frames under the east arch presenting a blue flame—very harmful'—and the following day, 'The gas, collected under the tails of number 8, exploded on the approach of a light.'

By the end of the month the fireworks had become routine.

> June 28th. The gas—evidently the *fire-damp* which is so fatal in collieries—ignites frequently, that is at every tide—sometimes with violence. One man was burnt—singed.

> July 4th. The explosions have been more violent than before, and the ignition excessively heating—work could not proceed.

Again, 14 days later: 'While number 2 was blowing out torrents of water, number 12 was vomiting flames of fire, which burned with a roaring noise—in less than three minutes it melted the side of a pint pot partly filled with water.'

£72,000, more than a quarter of the sum sanctioned, had been spent by the end of 1836. Silt removal and carpeting the river consumed more treasure during 1837. Money was poured away, and by June the directors were in a terror that the Treasury Lords might weary of their folly.

Every item of expenditure was scrutinised. Page had to justify the consumption of candles (more than 500 lb weekly), and the labour force was pared down. Despite Brunel's repeated protests, the lamps were converted to consume coal gas produced by a local company, and his year-old estimate of £116,000 for the two Great Descents was quietly pigeon-holed. (Higher wages resulting from the railway boom probably account for the virtual doubling of his earlier estimate.)

The directors need not have worried. Mr Spring Rice, Lord Althorp's successor as Chancellor of the Exchequer, had instructed James Walker to furnish the Government with progress reports on the tunnel. Walker's selection as engineering watchdog was not surprising—he had succeeded Telford as President of the Institution of Civil Engineers on the latter's death in 1834—but it was certainly fortunate, for although Walker was himself no innovator, he esteemed Brunel greatly, and the Loan Commissioners continued their subventions.

The Government did not lack critics. On 18 July, 'A Friend to Consistency and Fair Play' addressed a letter to *The Times* which complained that although Mr Spring Rice had earlier opposed a Bill to improve the Constabulary Force in his native Ireland, he had been pleased, upon assuming office, to give his powerful support to the English Constabulary Force Bill. He had become a Minister of the Crown and might welcome friends to a share in the patronage at the disposal of the Government ... .'

The editor was inclined to agree.

> As an appropriate accompaniment to this letter we add the report of the Thames Tunnel Committee, begging the attention of our readers ... to the abominable job which Mr Rice has humbugged the Committee into sanctioning. The hands of the Whigs are never out of the pockets of the people except to transfer the contents of them to their own pockets or to those of their hangers-on.

'The Thunderer' merely echoed the views of its proprietor, John Walter the second, who, as the Member for Berkshire, lost no opportunity to assail the rascally Whigs—and especially the Member for Lambeth—for diverting public money to a private venture.

As soon as the Government had renewed its pledge, Brunel made yet another request for freedom to use the money rationally. He despatched Page to the Kilsby railway tunnel works, which were being effectively drained by pumping from local wells and, armed with his report and with observations of his own regarding similar operations at Shadwell Docks, he drafted a memorandum which the Court received on 9 August.

First he proposed sinking the Wapping foot passengers' shaft and equipping it with a steam engine and pumps which would intercept the land spring water on its way to the face. Next he sought agreement either to the ventilating driftway, or to the installation of another shield at Wapping, which would march southwards to meet the existing frames. This second proposal would enable the miners to work whichever face was sound at a given time. 'I think I may say,' he concluded,

> that after two irruptions of the river and the progress of 190 feet beyond the point where the first of these two accidents occurred, and by our continuing progress, however slowly ... through greater difficulties than those encountered before; the practicability of the completion of the tunnel cannot any longer be doubted; it is in fact resolved simply into a question of expense.

He appended detailed estimates to prove that the cost of the additional shield would be recouped many times over by savings in wages and salaries which had to be paid even when the frames were halted. The Court endorsed this memorandum, and sent it to the Treasury.

Meanwhile the men struggled on despite foul air, despite water and despite bursts of gravel through the ruptured ground at the top of the face.

> July 18th. On removing a piece of four-inch quartering from the west top stave of number three, the water and gravel flew out in two or three bursts— and immediately an attempt was made to forward the frame. There came a sudden rush of mud, water and gravel, terrific in the extreme, filling the box and overflowing the shoots and tanks in a very short time. It was by the greatest perseverance and exertion that the quartering was again replaced. Tom Hannon was in the face bareheaded (the force of the water having washed his cap off his head) doing all in his power to replace the piece of quartering during which time the gravel beat with fearful violence against his uncovered head. He left the face perfectly exhausted, declaring that never before had he seen such a 'mess' whilst in the works. Blockings were put in, and the face filled with straw, after which the frame was put forward the full fleet [distance].

A raised timber walkway was built along the deep part of the eastern archway, so that the men might escape in the event of an irruption; also, at Faraday's suggestion, trays of chlorate of lime and pails of ammonia were placed near the shield, but these did nothing to improve the atmosphere and were soon removed. But during August the need for better ventilation became still more pressing.

'Gas being ignited, Harrison was slightly burned at the nose,' wrote Brunel on the 7th, 'it continued burning three-and-three-quarter hours. The gas seems to be of a more inflammable nature than before.' And again, four days later. 'In inspecting the frames it is hardly possible to distinguish any particular object—if you apply a candle, it is immediately dimmed or put out. At best it is a very difficult thing to mark one object—the surface being so besmeared with a slimy deposit.'

Men half-suffocated, men burnt, men battered by bursts of ground, men carried away sick; and at the end of the month a yard, even two yards. But on 23 August, the men came out of the gloomy tunnel for a spell of fresh air. Page has left us this account of the events preceding their liberation.

Mr Francis having relieved Mr Crawford at noon, I wrote a note requesting him to inform me of what state the water was previously to my following Mr Brunel to the meeting of directors. I received an answer that it was coming in rapidly at numbers eleven and twelve, and I went down having first directed Webb to take soundings ...

Having sent for my tunnel clothes, I made my way to the shield. I found Huggins, foreman of the second shift, with his top men engaged in blocking up numbers eleven and twelve, the water running from both these frames in a powerful stream—both from between the blocking-up planks, and also under the swivel pieces below the top staves—and with the same force, which characterised it on 20 June 1836.

The remaining frames, number ten to number one, were undisturbed, but calculating on the run extending itself across the entire face of the excavation as it has generally done since December last, I directed Huggins to block up the whole of the top frames in front with clay, straw and bricks, backed by three-inch planks, and then to put a second blocking of clay and bricks behind the first, filling the frames up to the back rails. ...

This operation being in progress, I returned to the visitors' arch, and wrote a note to Mr Brunel stating my impression that the tunnel would be filled, then sent up directions to stop the further admission of visitors, and set the carpenters to construct a raft in each arch for the purpose of conveying bricks, clay, etc. to the shield.

On returning to the shield, I found the influx had decreased, and we were in hope that it would gradually subside as it had done on previous occasions, but in a few minutes it burst out again with increased violence, and continued running without any diminution.

When the first shift came on, at two o'clock, to relieve the second, I directed Williams, the foreman, to continue the blocking-up of the west frames, and retained Huggins and his men in the east frames, where the rush of water was, they having been present at the commencement, and therefore less likely to be alarmed than the others.

The bottom and middle men were stationed along the platform which Mr Brunel had most judiciously and providentially caused to be constructed in the east arch some weeks ago, and Williams employed himself in directing the conveyance of materials along this platform to the shield. Twelve men were also put to the water-wheel, the bricklayers and labourers under Fitzgerald were actively employed with Miles and others in clearing the arches of floating timbers, and the work in hand went on regularly.

The water having risen breast high on the invert opposite to the cabin, and the raft not being able to contain many materials, I sent for the hoy's boat for the conveyance of the bricks to block up the frames.

Mr Brunel having arrived from the Board, I gave him an account of all that had been done in the shield, at which he expressed his satisfaction.

Notwithstanding the efforts of the men at the water-wheel,* and the steady action of the pumps, the water gradually rose in the arches, although the influx was confined to numbers eleven and twelve, but it was accompanied by a hollow roar as though it fell through a cavity.

The men continued their work of blocking-up the frames with the same steadiness and coolness that they had always manifested during runs of silt, etc., and all the top frames having been blocked-up in front ... and being satisfied that everything had been done ... I directed that the men should retire.

With Page, Francis and Huggins bringing up the rear, the men filed along the raised walkway and when they reached its end scrambled into the water chute on the dividing wall, and continued their orderly retreat. Brunel awaited them some two hundred feet from the shaft, where the tunnel's roadways broke surface. He ordered them down, and told them to carry as much timber as they could from the eastern archway.

Eventually [Page continued], when the water had risen to within fifty feet of the entrance of the tunnel, it came forward in a wave, and Mr Francis and Mr Mason, Williams and Fitzgerald and I, who were at the bottom of the visitors' stairs, ran up to the second landing whence we saw it fill the bottom of the shaft, and from there came up to the top.

The engine was then stopped, the dandy pump rope cut, and the gas turned off.

The following evening's edition of the *True Sun* carried a lengthy report of the inundation. After noting the orderly manner in which the works had been evacuated without loss of life, the correspondent considered earlier difficulties. He had evidently been well primed.

The horizontal suction pipe now in full operation extends to a length of 750 feet, exceeding anything of the kind in existence. Hitherto the influx has, since the last great breach, solely arisen from the Middlesex springs and land-drains, generally characterised by very ill odours, and it has become a great desideratum to get at these directly, by sinking a shaft at the Wapping

---

* This discharged into a chute which ran right back to the reservoir in the Rotherhithe shaft.

side. The operations on the Rotherhithe shore have been productive of much valuable experience respecting the permeable nature of the soil, and the commanding effect of the tunnel pumps on the neighbouring wells but the enterprising plans of the engineer and directors in this respect are as yet counteracted by the cautious monetary policy of the Government, which has determined that the funds advanced for the continuance of the work shall only be afforded to the tunnel at one end—whatever delays, difficulties and dangers may be incurred in the pursuance of operations in this limited manner. The directors believe they could complete the tunnel much more quickly and economically if not bound by this one-sided policy; but no—'it is so nominated in the bond'...

We are happy to hear that Mr Brunel treats the accident as a mere incident in the course of tunnelling, for which he was not at all unprepared. A few days since some of his friends were kindly enquiring 'if he expected further inroads on the part of the river?' 'Why, yes,' replied he; 'I have been honoured with two visitations from Father Thames during the first part of the work, and I cannot hope to escape without one at least in the other.'

But while Brunel was anxiously shepherding the men up the shaft, an official was handing the Court the Treasury's reply to his memorandum of 9 August.

Their Lordships ... cannot give their authority in proceeding in any other manner with the work than that which has already been sanctioned, until it shall be seen that, by the further progress of the tunnel towards the Middlesex shore, the final satisfactory termination of the work is absolutely certain.

31

MRS BRUNEL'S INVENTION

Observed *The Times*,

> The tunnel has had another irruption, and while the playhouses are ruined by emptiness Mr Brunel's enterprise is upset by an overflow. Of the tunnel where it is, we retain but one opinion—if practicable, it will be useless because the distance into the City over London Bridge is insignificantly different relative to the saving to be made by this dark and also precarious grubbery.

That the Thames was expelled in eight days says much for Page's resourcefulness during the flood. It is also a tribute to the manner he, Crawford, Francis and a new assistant, Osborne Mason* (who had replaced Richardson), had restored morale. But the most significant factor was mechanical; the tails fastened to the top staves preserved the ceiling, and the influx was confined to the face. Because the roof was not breached, the brickwork was not damaged and none of the frames started back. The divers on this occasion found a comparatively small pit directly over the face, which was quickly plugged.

The archways were cleared of 591 cubic yards of mud during the first ten days of September, and on the 4th, when the job was half done, the works were visited by Monsieur Marey, the grandson of Gaspard Monge, in whose cabriolet Brunel had travelled to Le Havre, 45 years earlier.

Tunnelling was resumed on the 11th, but the work was hampered by clay bags, which had sunk halfway down the fluid face, and the men's strength was sapped by gases. There were explosions—a violent one on 18 October—but at other times the gas burned steadily, and Brunel found the heat 'so intense as to render the ironworks and the cells exceedingly inconvenient'. Mason and 12 miners fell ill, amongst them Williams and Samuel Nettleship, who was admitted to Guy's Hospital with small hope of recovery.

Twice during October Brunel renewed his plea for the Wapping well, and twice the Treasury refused. Instead, Page was given £500 a year, and the assistants, by stages, £200 a year each. A fourth assistant, Richard Fletcher, was engaged on the 24th.

* Initially Mason was made responsible for the steam engine and the ancillary services.

The Thames showed scant respect for salaries and, at high tide on 3 November, rolled in again. Francis was on duty in the small hours that morning, and punctually reported to Brunel at one and again at three. Returning to the shield after the second visit he noticed 'sand and shells mixed with a portion of black gravel running from a hole cut in the second poling from the top floor plate of number one frame'. Giving instructions to keep a close watch, and to have straw and boards in readiness, he retired to a connecting arch and wrote a report. At a little before four, he recalled:

> Williams, the foreman of the shift, came to me and stated that the run of sand was very much increased, and wanted to know if he had better continue to block up the faces of numbers one, two and three, which he had commenced a few minutes previously. I went with him into the box and found the sand running with considerable force from all parts of that face—I then ordered the blocking-up to be continued with the greatest expedition possible.
>
> Williams went to the lower stage for the purpose of ascertaining the state of the middle and bottom faces, when he discerned parts of the polings from numbers one, two, three and four middle boxes being driven out and the water rushing in. He immediately gave the alarm for all hands to run. From that time to the filling of the tunnel did not occupy more than about five minutes.
>
> We all ran with the greatest speed to the shaft. It then lulled for a time, and I, again in company with Williams, Collins and Cook, went down the arch about two hundred feet and saw the water rolling up the archway in terrific grandeur. We then ran to the staircase and watched it there for a very short time, and finally ascended to the top of the shaft where the water arrived a very few seconds afterwards.
>
> When on top I met Mr Brunel. I had all the names called over and found only one missing. Garland, an old man, a miner. It was a most providential thing that the gangway at the crown of the west arch had been extended and finished, for had that not been there, many of us must inevitably have perished.

Garland's body was recovered in the east archway on the 12th, and 10 days later Mason and a party of miners re-entered the shield. This irruption was more sudden and violent than the August flood—twice as much mud was swept into the tunnel—but the shield and the brickwork remained intact.

'When it is considered,' Brunel reported to the Court,

> that this loose ground was impelled with an impetuosity that carried it not only to nearly the top of the shaft, but that it overflowed the street, *my street*, leaving there a thick deposit of the same substance, it must be a matter of surprise that the structure, or the portion just made, should not have been disturbed beyond a few bricks.

The tunnel was solid certainly, but the waste and suffering involved in building no more than six feet six inches since the previous disaster appalled him. The face was 754 feet distant from the Rotherhithe shaft. Given a sufficient expenditure of life and treasure it could be carried to Wapping, but to squander these resources without need was inexcusable. Certain directors seemed increasingly unwilling to embarrass the authorities, and he wrote tartly to Charlier: 'I propose, and have given directions accordingly, to preserve a tub of the mud and some bottles of the water for our gentlemen.'

Save for fitting three replacement side staves, the tunnel was cleared and the shield and services restored by 21 December. During the work of salvage, contaminated land-spring water continued to flow in at the face, and through pipes piercing the crowns of the arches behind the shield, at the rate of 200 gallons a minute. Both Page and Minall suffered bouts of sickness but, although James Walker warned that the frames might be halted because the ground had been made fluid by winter rains, the Treasury again refused permission for the Wapping well.

Confronted by such ignorant and negative obduracy, most engineers would have retired from the struggle amid expressions of sympathy; but Brunel was not the retiring sort. He made careful plans to prevent further inundations, without pumps at Wapping, and without a diving bell and a hopper barge. First he arranged for a new shipping channel to be dredged near the Rotherhithe bank and, when this had been done, began laying a much thicker carpet of clay bags and gravel in front of the shield.

Next he attended to the poling boards. They had been designed to support a solid face—not to contain fluid mud—so he fitted them with hook-and-eye latches which secured each board to the two beneath it, and transformed each panel into a rigid barrier, although at some cost in extra work for the miners.

During the last two weeks of December, while these measures and the restoration of the archways were being completed, the miners resumed their labours and pressed the shield forward. The artificial ground had consolidated satisfactorily, indeed it proved less treacherous than the river's natural bed, and by the year's end ten feet had been added to the tunnel.

This progress did little to compensate for earlier setbacks. 1837 had been a year of disappointments, and Brunel closed his diary sadly: 'Progress for the twelve months,' he wrote, averages just the breadth of a halfpenny per day.'

Andrew Crawford left on New Year's Eve, and Richard Fletcher was appointed Page's first assistant in his place. He found the service hard, for the winter was bitter, especially for the men in the *Ganges*, who spent their days tempering clay, filling bags and strewing their handiwork on the river bed. Four thousand bags were heaved overboard during the first week of

January, but the cold was numbing, and the easterly squalls made collisions frequent and more than usually dangerous. On the 12th, the Admiralty agreed to anchor a vessel upstream and another downstream of the hoy so as to protect her; but the Thames froze from bank to bank, and river work had to be suspended, before they arrived.

Under the hoy's keel, the shield bored slowly northwards, and by the middle of January only 150 feet separated it from the northern low-water mark. Conditions below had improved a little; there were no reports of explosions or of the faces spitting fire; the infiltration had dropped to 150 gallons a minute; and although the faces were still terribly treacherous, the latches on the polings were proving their worth. Thanks to a specially made model of the shield, the men had learned to handle the frames more intelligently, and although bent legs and broken staves continued to keep Minall's men busy, at least the millwrights were holding their own, which was encouraging, because the disturbed ground subjected the frames to exceptional stresses. Each week the horseshoe archways lengthened eighteen inches, and hope germinated in the directors' breasts and quickly grew into impatience.

Brunel wanted to halt the shield while Webb and his river gang completed their work, which had been interrupted by the freeze; but the directors had different anxieties. They feared that the Government might refuse further advances unless the House of Commons committee could be told of substantial progress by July. Political considerations were decisive, and the shield's slow march continued, the work being restricted to two shifts and the wages bill to £200 each week.

Page spent a few days at Mortlake with the chairman during the third week of March. In his absence Mason supervised the morning shift and Fletcher the night shift, while Francis helped his more senior colleagues as the occasion demanded. Despite a deterioration of the upper faces, the tempo was maintained, and the excavation extended 775 feet when Huggins and his men left the shield at six on the morning of the 20th.

Fletcher had been on duty during the night, and Mason should have relieved him just before the morning shift arrived. However, Mason overslept, so after Huggin's men had departed, Fletcher busied himself measuring the inclination of the top staves of number 8. This done, he inspected the upper faces and noticed water oozing from 11 and 12, but found the others drier than usual. There were only a few bricklayers and labourers near the frames, but as he descended the ladder from the shield, he noticed the morning shift coming down the eastern archway. The men seemed strangely quiet. Suddenly, there was 'a rumbling noise—unusually loud ... and a stream of water rushed out of the faces in number 11.'

The men panicked.

They rushed [said Fletcher] to the west stage, and the word 'Run' was heard from many voices, which had the effect of putting all in motion over the gangways towards the shaft. Wood, a bricklayer, and myself were, I conceive, the last who left that part of the shield. During this short interval the rush of water increased in the shield, and was distinctly heard falling into the bottom.

From this time until I arrived at the top [of the shaft] did not occupy more than three minutes, as the men who had thus left the shield were in the yard at twenty-five past six.

Unknown to Fletcher, Williams, the foreman of the morning shift, and two of his miners, Maund and Taylor, had already taken possession of number 12. Finding mud oozing between the polings of their top box, they began packing the cracks with pieces of sacking, and were considerably startled by the sudden burst of clay and water in the neighbouring frame, which blew their candles out. By the time they reached the bottom of their ladder, everyone had fled up the western archway and the tunnel was deserted. Maund and Taylor made off up the eastern arch, and since he could do nothing by himself, the hard-bitten Williams followed at a speed befitting a foreman.

When he reached the bottom of the shaft, he was met by his overseer Hannon, and by Mason—now wide awake—and Francis. The quartet were immediately joined by Short, foreman of the bricklayers, and four miners from the first shift who had been drinking coffee in the yard. If the breach were pluggable, here were enough men to do it, so, ordering Francis to clear the men off the stairs, Mason led the party back to the shield.

As soon as he had driven the curious into the yard, Francis descended again and hurried down the eastern archway after Mason's platoon. He did not get far. After 300 feet he found them beating a rapid retreat. 'The roaring noise and rush of air was very great,' he recalled,

and we ran up the arch. I saw the water and timber following very fast. The lights were much agitated—at one time flaring up to a great height—at another scarcely perceptible. When on the staircase I saw many of them go out entirely. The water entered the shaft with a dreadful rush and with a noise far louder than either of the two late irruptions.

The staircase being cleared, every person went up very orderly. The names were called over, and happily none were missing.

Webb and his men soon sealed the river bed, and 10 days later the shield was reoccupied. 'It was quite undisturbed from the state it was left in,' Brunel noted, 'I addressed 15 letters from it.'

Although the shield was intact, the stages and raised walkways were devastated, and the tunnel's roadways were covered with 900 cubic yards of mud. Brunel also found fractured latch-bolts on several poling boards, and subsequently attributed the irruption to their failure.

'April the 10th. Went down to see the starting of number twelve, it was easy enough—I had on the finishing of it the *cheers of the men*. I returned to them their greeting, which was acknowledged by a second burst of acclamation from them. *Most gratifying indeed*.'

It is remarkable how expert at salvage work the engineers and the miners had become. This inundation interrupted work for only three weeks, and after the flood the shield resumed its slow 18-inches-a-week pace as though nothing had happened.

In some respects the irruption was beneficial. Four months later Brunel at last secured permission to buy a hopper barge, and a 580-ton flat-bottomed ship, the *Brevig*. The ballast-laden *Brevig* was grounded over the shield at each low tide and effectively consolidated the thick covering of clay and gravel.

No doubt James Walker's mid-year report to the House of Commons committee also helped to pave the way for this concession. He visited the works regularly, and was greatly surprised by the shield's continuing progress. 'It is now my duty,' he wrote,

> to recommend Mr Brunel's proposals to be adopted as the economical and creditable way of executing the works ... I would even advise more effectual works in front of the shield than Mr Brunel's description and estimate of £1,800* contemplates; for if the work is to be considered a national or Government work, a repetition of the danger of the late irruption ... would be discreditable. ... As the Thames Tunnel is Mr Brunel's work as respects design and responsibility, any measure that may be proposed for executing the work should in my judgment have his approval. If that approval is refused, unless the Lords of the Treasury will consent to work which exceeds the amount they have yet thought proper to agree to, almost any course would be better than letting the complaint be repeated that the engineer had been deprived of the proper means of completing the work at the estimated cost.

A fourth assistant, George Dixon, was engaged on 16 April, at a time when the tunnel's atmosphere became terribly polluted. The diary provides an eloquent record of the gases' deadly effect.

> May 4th. The effluvia was so offensive that some men were sick on the stage.

> May 9th. Gas is particularly offensive as reported by Mr Page just at high water. ... Mr Mason ill—he made his report to me of sickness, headache and weakness. Three assistants are ill, Fletcher only capable to attend.

> May 14th. The gas had been extremely offensive this morning and ever since.

---

* The sum attributable to the formation of the artificial bed.

... Master Law,* 14 years old, is indentured from this day.

May 16th. Much gas ... the inflammable gas. Men complaining very much, viz. Williams and Huggins, Short and Wyatt and others, besides the assistants. Mason who is returned, is in good spirits, but Francis is very bad.

May 17th. It appears that there is a greater number of disabled men than at any time before. I feel very much weakened by the inspection I made at the shield.

May 23rd. Minall is reported to be very ill—I gave directions accordingly for his successor.†

May 24th. ... During the night, Mr Francis said that the gas burned fiercely and with a roaring like distant thunder.

May 26th. Heywood died this morning [of typhus]. Two men on the sick list. Page is evidently sinking very fast. ... It affects the eyes. I feel much debility after having been some time below. My sight is rather dim today. All complain of pain in the eyes. Dixon has reported that twice in one shift he was completely deprived of sight for some time.

May 28th. Wood, a bricklayer, fell senseless on the top floor. The assistants complain of being affected in different ways.

May 29th. Short came to the office and reported himself unable to work. Afflicted like Huggins and all the others—*a most efficient and intrepid man.* ... Bowyer died today or yesterday, a good man. Singular to relate the men went to take his body, but he was still alive ...

May 30th. This night, viz. about ten o'clock, walking as I did up and down the arches, which are lighted enough to give an extensive view of the work, I could not refrain from the reflection that the brave men, who are the agents of the execution of a work like this, are so many men sacrificed—and my assistants likewise—that in a few weeks most probably, they will be lingering under the influence of a slow and insidious poison.

June 4th. Sullivan—sent him to hospital, he being almost blind. Williams, the foreman of the first shift, gone. The men, the best men, are very much affected .... On my return from the G.W.R., on going to the office, I was just in time to support poor Page who had just fainted. Doctor Murdoch was sent for. He is in a very bad way—*all over with him*—I am persuaded.

Page reported for duty the following day, but on the 6th Brunel noted, 'Page went off to his friend Goodall very unwell, yet very reluctantly—he is indeed, in my opinion, *past recovery*—not a more zealous and persevering friend—whom shall I appoint now as a successor?'

* Henry Law, author of *Memoir of the Thames Tunnel*, 1857.
† Minall recovered.

On the 8th, Maund lost consciousness in the shield, and two days later
Brunel wrote this:

> DISTRESSING CASE. Richard Williams*—today we had to conduct this
> man to a lunatic asylum as being dangerous to be left out of doors. Cause—
> Several of our men say that since the irruption of the 3rd of November,
> he was not as he had been before. He admitted it, Mr Page had heard him
> too.

A long September holiday in Rouen restored Page's health, but although
the atmosphere improved the faces did not and Brunel succumbed to anxiety
and the strain of sleeping in two-hour snatches. He retired to bed for three
weeks at the end of November, and brooded on the Treasury's folly.

The tunnel would be no use without a shaft on the northern bank. The
shaft could not be sunk without a steam engine and pumps. Why delay building
it? No extra expense would be incurred. Indeed, the men could work on the
shaft instead of loitering in the archways when the face was unworkable. Did
the Treasury still believe that the tunnel might not be completed?

Again and again he pressed for the Wapping shaft but the Lords of the
Treasury would not relent.

Brunel and Sophie spent Christmas with Isambard and Mary at Duke
Street. Doubtless the day was a happy one, and doubtless the two engineers
pondered what the future held in store for little Isambard, their 18-month-
old namesake, whom Mary proudly dandled. There would have been much
talk. Good talk of ships and of railways and of bridges. Less agreeable talk
perhaps of directors and Government officials. And talk of the tunnel. The
obsessional, unending, 830-feet-long tunnel which the Treasury decreed
must be finished from one end.

What did the ladies discuss? What did Sophie think of her proud daughter-
in-law, who promenaded in the Park followed by a footman in fine livery?
The holiday soon passed. Isambard set off again on his travels, and Brunel
returned to his tunnel. He dealt with a millwrights' strike on New Year's
Day, rebuilt the drying loft which burned down in February, and pickled
an intrusive eel after a near irruption on 26 March. He celebrated his 70th
birthday 30 days later, and entertained the Grand Duke Alexander of Russia
on 7 May.

The tunnel air was foul, the miners fell sick, and the faces were bad, but
the directors sanctioned increased weekly expenditure, and the archways
lengthened a yard each week.

While lonely Mary slumbered splendidly between silken sheets at Duke
Street, Sophie slept in short watches by her husband's side at Rotherhithe,

---

*   Not the foreman of the miners.

and when the clock struck the even hours, lit his lamp and wrapped his coat about him so that he might go down to the office box to learn how his miners were faring. But one night in June, Brunel found a bell and a rope by the bedside window. 'When the bell rings, pull up the rope,' said Mrs Brunel, and when he did, up came a basket filled with samples of new-mined soil and the duty assistant's report. After consigning his instructions to the basket, Marc lowered away and retired to sleep.

This was Sophie's invention.

32

THE NORTHERN SHORE

O n 22 August 1839 the frames were halted beneath the spring tide low-water mark.

Brunel marked the place with four Admiralty buoys, grounded the *Brevig* over the ends of the 910-feet-long archways, and brought her crew, with the men from the barge and the *Ganges,* into the tunnel to prepare for the last lap.

The shield was overhauled, the rope railway extended, and the steam engine's second cylinder reinstated to enable it to cope with the additional load. The drainage culverts were cleared, but so foul was the muck in the mid-river wells that Fletcher and Dixon had to promise the men a whisky apiece to get them cleaned out. Unfortunately the combination of whisky and fresh air proved too powerful, and in the small hours the maddened miners erupted into the tunnel yard. News of the commotion soon reached the directors, and the luckless assistants were suspended. (A subsequent diary reference to Charlier's 'spies' is the only clue to the informer's identity.) Six months later, when the assistants were pardoned, Dixon resigned. His disenchantment is understandable.

Tunnelling was resumed during the second week of September, and thanks to the return of the river gang—which made a resumption of three-shift working possible—the shield set off at a cracking pace. During October a blower fan and an additional ventilating duct were installed, and progress immediately improved to nine feet a week—a rate which involved moving more than 30 frames a day—although there were still occasions when the miners were prostrated by gases, and they frequently worked knee-deep in water.

'When,' asked Brunel on 6 November, 'might work begin on the Wapping shaft?' The matter was urgent. An earlier decision to build the shaft nearer to the wharf than originally planned would shorten the tunnel by 50 feet. He broached the subject again on 11 December, pointing out that another six months would see the shield under the northern wharf. Of the tunnel's 1,030 feet, 88 feet 6 inches had been built during the last quarter, but the Treasury edict remained immutable.

The 1840 diary opens agreeably: 'Began the year with the cheerings of the men—and their expressions of respect and regard for me.' Soon after, the Institution of Civil Engineers acknowledged the invention of the tunnelling shield with a Silver Telford Medal; but the satisfaction engendered by these tokens of esteem was damped by exceptionally copious winter rains. Spring water flooded into the tunnel. The greater part poured in through pipes piercing the new brickwork, and then flowed down chutes to the mid-river cistern; but inevitably some spurted through the shield's staves and poling boards, and every gallon carried its quota of gas and silt. The influx climbed to over 400 gallons a minute, and it is remarkable that progress still averaged nine feet a week during January and February. A halt had to be called in March so that the choked drainage culverts could be cleaned again and the pumps overhauled. The ground seemed better when work was resumed, but on 3 April the influx reached 500 gallons a minute, and at eight the next morning a partly unlatched board in number 12 canted over, and there was a noise which the duty assistant described as 'like the roaring of thunder', followed by a rush of air which extinguished the lights; 125 cubic yards of gravel, slush and boulders roared into the tunnel, driving the men out of the frame. The labourers fled, but the *corps d'élite* stood their ground in the darkness, and eventually staunched this 'irruption of earth'.

While the miners contended with the avalanche, the citizens of Wapping saw their foreshore subside without evident cause. It sank, as if by some Act of God, to a depth of 13 feet, leaving a roughly cylindrical pit eight yards across. Had the tide been in, the tunnel would have suffered a sixth inundation.

The shield stood still until the end of May, when a further subvention was received from the Treasury. Brunel and Sophie spent a fortnight at Duke Street, but many of the Company's employees found the pause disagreeable. Most of the miners and bricklayers were stood off. Mason and Francis were given notice—and then re-engaged—but the greatest sufferer was the contractor Jackson, who carted away spoil from Cow Court. Brunel wrote of him in June:

> Amongst the many losses he has suffered, I may mention that nine of his horses have died since last September, principally occasioned by the nature of the labour, and the necessity of working them by night during a severe season in order to keep the yard clear, and had he failed in doing this extra service, the progress of the shield must inevitably have been interrupted, until efficient means of removing the ground could have been procured.
>
> Mr Jackson has of late, chiefly since the month of March, been without proportionate employment, and lately his horses and carts have been seized for the payment of his debts ... The ready manner in which he has come

under all circumstances, as Mr Page himself can confirm, had induced me to lay his case before the Board.

The directors were not philanthropically inclined, and no doubt Jackson and his family suffered a spell in Marshalsea, or King's Bench Prison. But some miners were re-engaged at the beginning of June, the shield moved slowly forward, and on the 11th Brunel at last took possession of the site for the northern shaft.

The plot was bounded on the southern side by a timber wharf, and covered with flimsy dwellings and warehouses, which were cleared during the summer while those near by were shored up to protect them from subsidence. Piles had to be driven into the foreshore, and the site enlarged, before there was room for the iron curb, which Rennie delivered in September. By the end of the month it had been married to a timber curb—ready for loading with bricks.

Brunel was determined to sink this shaft to its full depth of 70 feet without recourse to underpinning; he therefore decided to give the tower a taper; whereas the curb had a diameter of 55 feet, the top of the tower would be only 50 feet across.

Of the £270,000 sanctioned by Parliament, £190,000 had already been expended, and when Brunel presented a somewhat pessimistic estimate of £60,000 for the shaft, the directors were driven into a frenzy of anxiety. They sacked Francis and Fletcher, so that only Mason—himself under notice—remained to help Page in the tunnel. They sought a contractor to build the tower, but none came forward, for excavation within the curb had revealed an ancient timber floor resting on piles, and it was impossible to estimate by how long its descent might be delayed. Then masts, iron ties and the remains of ships' timbers were uncovered. An archaeologist would have found this ancient shipyard fascinating, but the directors did not.

They dismissed Huggins—the only man left who had worked on the southern shaft—but when Brunel vowed that he would pay his wages, they shamefacedly relented, and told their engineer to build the first 20 feet with Company hands. This was accomplished by the middle of November, when the shield was halted 45 feet from its journey's end—lest further tunnelling should disturb the ground and endanger the tower's descent.

'I am truly happy,' wrote Brunel to his friend James Howard,

> to be able to say that my arduous enterprise is drawing to a conclusion. It has been one of inconceivable labours, difficulties, and dangers. ... In fact, the four Elements were at one time particularly against us; *Fire* from the explosive gases, the same that are fatal in mines; *Air* of a mephitic nature, by the influence of which the men most exposed were sometimes removed quite senseless; *Earth* from the most terrific disruptions of the ground; *Water*

Street entrance to the Thames Tunnel.

from five irruptions of the river, three of which since the resumption of the work in 1836!

What had been the cost in lives? The records of Guy's Hospital are not revealing, but a sort of balance sheet, covering the last two years, survives. Originally there had been five small funds from which payments were made to disabled men. There was a fund for the riggers, another for the bricklayers, and one for each shift of miners—each being supported by fines imposed for bad work or unpunctuality. There was also a more substantial fund to which charitable visitors subscribed. At the end of June 1838 those five funds had been amalgamated into a consolidated fund, of which the ledger survives, and by the time the shield was halted its receipts totalled £1,089 11s. 4d., and its disbursements £869 11s. Eleven funerals accounted for £53 5s. of the disbursements. One of these funerals was Heywood's and one was Bowyer's—these men can be identified because payments were made to their widows; but another nine unnamed men died during these 28½ months: perhaps more than nine, for it is unlikely that the trustees would have sanctioned payments to widows of casually employed labourers.

The arrival above ground of Page and Mason was a help because building the rest of the shaft by contract put a premium on competent supervision; however, the directors dismissed Mason at the end of the month and told Page and Brunel that they could not be responsible for their salaries beyond the following Lady Day.

The work went slowly. Rennies delivered the steam engine late, and this delayed the installation of the bucket elevator. A deeper, and therefore older, set of shipyard timbers was uncovered, and nothing was done during January because ice closed the river and prevented the spoil being barged away. It was the end of February 1841 before the first 20 feet were sunk—after much alarming tilting—into the treacherous soil of Wapping. Thereafter tempers improved; Brunel and Page were reprieved; Mason was re-engaged; and during March the tower was built to its full height and the engine and excavator were erected on top of it.

March was a memorable month. '24th. *Levee of the Queen!* Today Her Majesty was pleased to confer upon me the honour of knighthood as Sir Isambart Brunel.'*

He was delighted that Sophie had become Lady Brunel, but queens cannot always please commoners, and Lady Noble tells us that during the investiture Isambard's old nurse and Ellen, the faithful (but alas no longer pretty) housemaid, prayed on their knees 'that the Lord would make him a Baronet', and were greatly disappointed at the outcome.

At the end of May, when almost half the tower had vanished, Mason and a small gang of miners set to work in the eastern archway extending the drainage culvert beyond the shield on a line which would carry it beneath the centre of the sinking shaft. They built 17 feet of driftway in three weeks and earned a paragraph in their chief's diary: 'Though [it is] so near the visitors' arch,' he wrote, 'no one can perceive that this operation is going on ... day and night without intermission. The service (a very arduous one for all) is however very cheerfully performed. Mr Mason has had the night duty of twelve successive hours for three nights.'

The following day Page reported sad news from Rotherhithe.

> Yesterday at four p.m. one of the boys (Knight), who assisted Tillett as a stoker, was caught by the strap of the ventilator and killed outright. Sir Isambard, coming upstairs, found the ventilator stopped, and on enquiring the cause Tillett went to the ventilator and found the man quite dead. The strap having pressed his ribs in.
>
> It appears *now* that he was in the habit of placing his foot on the shaft and making a part of it bright with his shoe, and is supposed to have slipped while so engaged and have been caught by the strap.

The driftway was completed during the first week of July, and iron pipes were driven downwards from the shaft's pit until they pierced its roof. As soon as these drains were in place, a few miners were reengaged and the shield marched forward once again. The frames' joints had grown stiff, but

---

* Isambart is a French spelling.

Projected view of the south side tunnel entrance by Brunel.

the men worked with a will and built six feet of tunnel by the end of July. At last all was going smoothly, so leaving Page in charge, Brunel and Sophie entrained on Isambard's railway for a fortnight's change of air in the West Country.

Nearby buildings sagged and cracked, but the shaft sank slowly downwards. Down in the tunnel some frames cracked too, but the miners pushed them forward. Six weeks after Brunel's return the top of the tower reached the prescribed three feet above Trinity High Water, and a month later its domed base had been completed. The shield was not far away.

'November the 16th. On this day Mr Page brought to me the first fragments taken out from the shaft cut out by himself.

'Alors! Sans toi, ma chère Sophie, point de tonnelle.'

They were through.

33

ROYAL WAPPING

The shield is now out of service, in an attitude, however, to demonstrate that it has been the chief agent in the accomplishing of a subaqueous structure, twelve hundred feet in length, after numberless difficulties of the most formidable character.

Any day you may please to come with a friend, *let me know* that I may be in the way.

When Brunel wrote these words to his old friend Charles Babbage on 12 January 1842 the 12 frames had marched through the brickwork of the shaft and were lined up, like battle-scarred veterans of some long campaign. Brunel wanted them preserved for posterity, but the Company needed money, and Rennie's shield, like Maudslay's, was sold for scrap.

By this time the brick archways and the shaft had been united, and the men were busy making the tunnel ready for the foot passengers who would walk between 'the bankside friends of Rotherhithe and Wapping', as Thomas Hood had called them.

The ventilators, the hoist and the rope railway were dismantled, and the tunnel's roadways paved. Every damp spot in the archways and the drainage culverts was pointed by Mason and his men, and then the eastern archway and the new shaft were rendered and whitewashed. The Company's premises on either bank were fenced, the Wapping wharf was finished off, and neighbouring landowners had their cracked property made good or were given compensation.

None of this was very exacting, but there were a lot of jobs to do, and the engineers suffered a deal of meddling from distraught directors. There was a feeling of anticlimax. They were clearing up after a party which had been much too expensive. Page, quite naturally, looked out for other engagements, but he was none too punctilious in seeking leave of absence and Brunel came to rely increasingly on Mason. But Page was a good 'Company man' and retained the confidence of the directors.

The new shaft was roofed over, and in August, while the contractors* built a new superstructure on the Rotherhithe shaft, sightseers were admitted

---

* Messrs Grissell and Peto, who built the Houses of Parliament.

241

from the northern end—much to the chagrin of Rotherhithe's innkeepers.

Brunel found the times trying, too. The shafts had to be equipped with spacious stairways and landings on which weary pedestrians could pause for breath. New, unobtrusive pumps had to be installed, for although the salt-laden water was slowly sealing the porous brickwork, the infiltration still amounted to 75 gallons per minute[*]—enough to overflow the culverts and the mid-river reservoir in three hours. Lastly, the Rotherhithe steam engine had to be moved to a new building alongside the shaft. The problems were not difficult, but the directors argued over every detail, and on 7 November their 73-year-old engineer suffered a stroke which temporarily paralysed his right side.

Isambard was called in, and bluntly told the Court that, unless there were a standby pump and boiler, routine maintenance, or some trifling fault, could cause a flood in the deep part of the tunnel's roadways. His advice was rejected. The Wapping engine was moved to Rotherhithe and connected to a single pump; then the old pumps and Brunel's triangle-frame engine were scrapped, and the directors occupied themselves with arrangements for the ceremonial opening. Nor surprisingly, their deliberations were interrupted by the very failures that had been predicted, and the opening was postponed *sine die* while Isambard installed duplicate machinery. Then there were teething troubles, which provoked expressions of concern of a rather more forceful character than Brunel junior felt inclined to suffer.

'I trust,' he wrote, 'that in a day or two I shall be able to make a more satisfactory report, and I must be allowed to express a hope also that if I again feel it my duty to suggest any precautions, my advice will meet with a better reception than it hitherto has from several gentlemen.'

By March 1843 Brunel had recovered, and the tunnel was ready.

> 15th. Attended at the Board, the chief question has been the *public opening*, which is fixed ... for the 25th, a Saturday, the most objectionable day.
>   All the drunkards and most outrageous part of the population will be collected in the most unsettled place that can be conceived. Page was absent the whole day.

Nor did he applaud the arrangements for controlling the throng. 'About twenty of our old hands would be of more service than double that number of policemen.'

He was overruled, and his old stalwarts drew no pay for showing off their handiwork.

The shareholders remembered him though, and at the Annual General

---

[*] A negligible amount, bearing in mind the surface area of the tunnel and the shafts. Only ten per cent of the infiltration seeped in through the older southern half of the tunnel.

Meeting, which preceded the opening ceremony, they recorded their appreciation of

> the distinguished talent, energy and perseverance evinced by him in the design, construction and completion of the Thames Tunnel, a work unprecedented in the annals of Science and Ingenuity and exhibiting a triumph of genius over physical difficulties declared by some of the most enlightened men of the time to be insurmountable.

Then the gates were opened. And what scenes of rejoicing there were! *The Times* was filled with it.

THE THAMES TUNNEL

> The ceremony of throwing open this 'great bore' to the public was performed on Saturday last under favour of good-natured old Father Thames. The grand rendezvous was the Rotherhithe shaft on the Surrey side of the river, where two marquees had been erected, one for the accommodation of the directors and proprietors with their friends, and the other for the reception of visitors. The hoisting of flags and the ringing of bells naturally drew a great crowd of idlers to the spot at an early hour of the day, but it was not until four o'clock in the afternoon that the entrances to the tunnel—*Wide open stood.*
>
> Before the procession started we had sufficient opportunity to reconnoitre the works, the appearance of which was not very pleasant. The area of the shaft is too small to give effect to the frontage of the tunnel, while its depth, when viewed from the top of the circular staircase by which passengers descend, looks frightful. The sensation excited by a first glance was by no means soothed on observing that the staircase was attempted to be propped up by sundry long poles, not very skilfully nor effectively applied, the mortices or notches intended to receive the projections of the several landing places being for the most part misfits, and slightly tied to the railings by small ends of rope. This was observed and commented upon by many of the visitors who were admitted into the shaft early, and who, *pour passer le temps*, very minutely inspected all that was to be inspected in so confined a place, which they soon discovered to be uncomfortable, in consequence of there being no opening or ventilator whatever, from the bottom to the very top of the walls by which they were encircled, except the small staircase door from the public street. This unpleasant feeling increased with increasing numbers, until the accumulation of breaths, the dampness of the ground, which was perceptible notwithstanding the loads of sawdust thrown about, and the walls, which the whitewash could not conceal, and the flaring of upwards of one hundred-and-thirty gas lights, combined to create an atmosphere at once disgustingly heated and fetid. ...
>
> At four o'clock ... the procession started from the grand marquee down the staircase in the following order: First came a very effective band belonging, we believe, to the Fusilier Guards, headed by a policeman wearing a Waterloo medal, who seemed highly delighted because they played 'See the

Conquering Hero Comes'. Then followed the standard-bearer and persons carrying various flags and banners, the clerk, the solicitor, the acting engineer, and surveyor, the chief engineer, the Chairman of the Board of Directors, the Directors, the treasurer, the auditors, the proprietors, and lastly, the visitors, an immense number of persons, including ladies. The route taken was along the western archway of the tunnel, and, on arriving at the shaft at Wapping, that was ascended and paraded, and then the procession returned by the eastern archway to Rotherhithe. The majority of the visitors went the whole distance, one-thousand-two-hundred feet; many, however, proceeded only a little way, pausing and looking about with an air of suspicion every four or five yards, while some did not venture into the tunnel at all, but remained in the shaft or on the staircase. Yet among the majority there was a perceptible anxiety, and notwithstanding the brilliance of the lights, the singular reverberation of the music, the shouting of the admirers of the undertaking, and all the means that were taken to give éclat to the event, and encouragement to spectators, notwithstanding also the physical heat that oppressed them, it was evident that there was a lurking chill felt in the breast of many, and it cannot be denied that the very walls were in a cold sweat. Having again reached the Rotherhithe shaft, the procession ascended. Bored and wearied by climbing that of Wapping, everyone fully experienced the declaration of the old Roman poet:

'FACILIS DESCENSUS AVERNI'; but that the 'REVOLURE GRADUM' that 'Sich a getting up stairs' and a getting up sich stairs,
'HOC OPUS, HIC LABOR EST'.

But up they did get at last, puffing and blowing, and, as they emerged from the shaft into the street, uttering in short but expressive ejaculations their delight at once more beholding the light of heaven, and breathing pure air.

... Various papers descriptive of the tunnel met with a ready sale, some exquisite medals commemorative of the event, by Warrington of the Strand, were also sold amongst the visitors. The watermen hoisted a black flag at the tunnel pier to indicate their feelings upon the occasion, considering that, by the tunnel, the 'Redriffe Ferry', and consequently their interests, have been undermined.

... We cannot conclude our notice of this affair without mentioning a disagreeable incident. Just at the close of the proceedings some half-dozen persons who had been listening, according to their own statement, to the conversation which had taken place during the dinner between two gentle-men of the press, and who supposed one of them to be the representative of this journal, acting upon that supposition, assailed him with coarse and men-acing epithets, which he at once resented. They increased their violence until he found it necessary to appeal to some of the leading gentlemen present, and by that means obtained an opportunity of successfully remonstrating against the injustice of the attack made on him. Of course, the great major-ity of the guests did not sympathise with those persons: and to censure the company for their conduct would be to act upon the same unfair principle

Formal procession at the tunnel's opening.

as they did, when they coupled their abuse and threat with 'Down with "The Times"!'. We are bound to acknowledge indeed, that from the secretary and other official persons we received every courtesy and kindness we could expect. The underlings, it is true, were rather uncivil, but underlings generally are so.

In the evening the directors entertained a hundred guests at the *City of London Tavern*. When the time came for toasts, Ben Hawes raised his glass—doubtless filled with the wine laid away 18 years earlier—to his old friend, Brunel. 'The tunnel,' the engineer replied, had been 'the business of his life, and ... he thanked Providence for his success and ... the Duke of Wellington for his powerful and disinterested aid.'

Within 27 hours of the opening, 50,000 people paid their pennies and passed through the Company's turnstiles. Fifteen weeks later the millionth traveller strolled through the spacious archways to which Brunel had dedicated his Great Shield and 18 years' endeavour.

'April the 25th.—still in good health and vigour of body and mind. Thanks be to God!' It was his 74th birthday, and already the handwriting, which the stroke had turned into a child's scrawl, was regaining its customary grace and power. Shortly after the anniversary he took Sophie to Somerset for a long summer holiday.

They stayed at Chilcompton, within easy reach of Bath, where doubtless these happy sightseers found much to please them, but it was to a modern marvel in Bristol that they hurried on 19 July. The launching of a screw-driven Atlantic passenger ship, with a four-cylinder 1,500 I.H.P. triangle-frame engine, and a displacement of 3,600 tons. At noon Prince Albert arrived and named her *Great Britain*, and then, while church bells pealed and bands played, the dry dock gates were opened and the gleaming black ship was towed slowly into the floating harbour under Isambard's watchful eye.

'Many years ago,' wrote Brunel the following day, 'I made the trial of various means of propelling boats, and in order to ascertain the degree of effect, I had a *circular canal* made, in which the various models could be made to operate with great precision. The screw was one of the means.'

When Prince Albert returned to London, filled with the wonder of Isambard's ship, the Queen at once decided that she must see his father's tunnel; and at half past three on 26 July she arrived in the royal barge and followed by her Prince Consort, the Duke of Saxe-Coburg and Gotha, Princess Clementine, and Lord Byron, set foot on the scarlet-carpeted tunnel pier, where Benjamin Hawes, Sir Alexander Crichton and several other directors awaited her.

Escorted by these gentlemen and by Charlier and Page, the Royal Party descended the shaft and walked the length of the archways where the Queen was presented with a gold commemorative medal, on one side of which was 'a correct and beautifully executed likeness of Sir M.I. Brunel, and on the other a view of the interior and a longitudinal section of the tunnel'.

The *Illustrated London News* correspondent captured the atmosphere: 'Though the invited guests contained a number of nobility and elegantly dressed ladies, the company gathered to receive the Royal Party from the tunnel pier was,' he noted, observing a party of river coal porters,

> more numerous than select. ... With faces as black as their coals, they gave the Queen a roaring welcome, one of them shouting 'God bless you, ma'am, I hope you'll come to Wapping again.' The rough manners of this honest fellow, who threw his fantail hat into the air, afforded great amusement to Her Majesty and the Prince.

The *Punch* man was down amongst the stall-holders, who plied their trade below, and saw the gallant costers strew the Queen's path with souvenir handkerchiefs which,

> being three-and-sixpenny goods, when raised from the ground after the transit of Royal feet, may be said to have gone up amazingly, for they were sold during the rest of the day at half-a-guinea each; and there is no doubt that any person requiring one of the 'identical handkerchiefs that the Queen walked over', may be supplied on the same reasonable terms for some considerable period.

As she was leaving the Queen expressed her admiration of the work and her regret at Brunel's absence. 'Had your letter reached me at this place a few hours sooner,' wrote the aggrieved engineer to Charlier from Chilcompton, 'I should certainly have gone up to receive Her Majesty in my own domains.'

Queen Victoria visits the Thames Tunnel.

His disappointment increased when the newspapers reached him.

'July 28th. "The Times" is remarkably liberal, considering the hostility and abuse in former periods from that paper.'

And the following day,

> Considering the favourable impression which has evidently been made on the mind of the Queen and of the Prince Albert, at the view of the tunnel, and the expression of their disappointment at not seeing me, I propose to avail myself at the earliest opportunity of being presented to them. I shall therefore set off on Monday morning for London.

He arrived at Duke Street at three, and learned that three days later the Royal Family would leave by train for Windsor.

> August 3rd ... Went by the Royal Train ... Thirty minutes precisely in going. Dear Isambard, always attentive for my accommodation—excessive rain all the way.
>
> Slough [station]—having approached the Queen's carriage, Prince Albert recognised me, and approached me and the Queen also. She expressed *her regret that she had not seen me at the tunnel*, she hopes, she said, to visit it again—she spoke to nobody else ...

EPILOGUE

———•‣•‣•———

Marc and Sophie came home from Chilcompton soon after the royal visit and moved to a modest house in Park Street, which overlooked St James's Park and was near to Isambard and Mary. From Park Prospect, for this was the house's name, the Court received a steady stream of letters urging action on the Great Descents, and when these fell on stony ground, proposing horse-powered lifts inside the shafts, which would make the tunnel accessible to wheeled traffic and effect 'an easy and expeditious way for the transmission of goods without obstructing the visitors' perambulation'. Brunel opposed the idea of lifts powered by steam engines, because their noise would frighten carriage and dray horses and lead to accidents.

Inexpensive lifts would have been profitable, but the directors did nothing, so Brunel bothered them with plans for forced ventilation, pointing out that the culverts, which doubled as sewers, emitted 'a very offensive effluvia'. It was no good. The directors had had enough. Page was retained as engineer and Brunel was retired, evidently without a pension. His name continued to appear on Company notices, but his work was done.

By day his great tunnel was filled with stall-holders, like an underground street market, and sometimes the foot passengers' homeward journey was enlivened by an exhibition of paintings, or a fancy fair with games of chance, 'Mysterious Ladies' and 'American Wizards'. When darkness cloaked the riverside streets, the connecting arches became the refuge of the temporarily embarrassed and the chronically down-and-out. The tunnel was London's cheapest doss-house. The habitués, mindful of the flaring gaslights, named it Hades Hotel.

'I had just fallen asleep,' wrote one young gentleman, who had given the Company his last penny for the privilege,

> and was dreaming that I was a whale compelled to swallow one of those loathsome lures, when I was awakened by feet scurrying past my covert. I peeped out, and saw a woman's garments whisking from side to side as their owner rushed towards Wapping, whilst from the opposite direction came two pursuers—one with an open bullseye in his hand, which shot out an

249

expending triangle of light, like arms extended to stop the quarry should she double. The heavy boots of the policeman, and of a seafaring man with him, clumped echoing along the corridor—I taking care to keep well within my curtain as they went by me—and in a minute the fugitive was overtaken.

The shrillest shrieks—that had a most infernal sound down there and hysterical protestations that 'she had never so much as seen the fellow's watch—she didn't believe the cowardly fellow had one' startled the stillness of the night; and then she flings herself upon the ground, kicking and screaming like a passionate child, and swearing that 'they shall carry her then'; what time the policeman waits in ruthless stolid patience—a sort of Dutch Erynnys—until she shall be tired. Finding that there is not much chance of this, he loses his patience, shakes her roughly, pulls her from the pavement and, in a gruff voice, bids her 'hold her noise and come along—have had enough of that there nonsense'. The trio re-passed me on their way to the Surrey side in company—the girl alternately striving to propitiate the policeman by appeals to his 'gentlemanliness' and gallantry, and vowing that she will have her accuser's heart out; the sailor, now that he had recovered his property, desirous to release the sobbing and vindictive thief, but prevented from yielding to his cowardice or kindness by the constable, who sternly tells him that he'll be no party to 'crumplymising a fel'ny'.*

The reality was very different from the engineer's dream. The bright-eyed subscribers were disappointed too. Even the Exchequer Loan Commissioners, who had advanced £250,000, were unhappy. In the nine months of 1843 during which the tunnel was open, 1,817,336 people passed through the turnstiles, and remitted £7,572 3s. 10d.—not enough to pay even the Treasury's interest, let alone a dividend to shareholders.

In these circumstances honour counts for little. The watermen did not get the compensation promised by the 1824 Act, and Brunel did not receive the £5,000 which the Company had contracted to pay him 'when the first public toll ... shall have been received for the use of the subscribers'. Instead, Charlier wrote suggesting a payment of £1,500—all that the directors had in hand.† He accepted, but a wry note in the diary reveals his feelings.

> December 8th. Benjamin [Hawes] wrote to him and sent him the following extract from Charlier's, viz. 'I heartily congratulate you on the pleasant settlement of the long-pending question, and I wish the award had been ten times as much as it is; mais que voulez-vous?' What am I to understand from this? He does not state how or when the paltry sum of £1,500 is to be paid.

---

*   The account was published in *Chambers' Journal*, 1860.
† Whether he had earlier received the other £5,000, which was to be paid 'when the body of the tunnel shall be securely effected, and carried sixty feet beyond each embankment of the river', seems doubtful.

Then he filled the end pages of the diary with notes from a biography of Sir Christopher Wren.

A cabal formed by the Commissioners of St Paul for persecuting Wren — thwarting him. He found it necessary to petition Queen Anne.

The petition would do for the Tunnel concern.

The cabal in continuing, Sir Christopher Wren exposed their malicious deeds, to reduce his salary and to pay only when the cathedral is finished.

Most applicable to the Tunnel case.

A new commission was formed, the cabal increased. He was then eighty three years of age and was sadly annoyed.

Suggestions from others!

He says, 'If I glory, it is to the singular mercy of God, who has enabled me to begin and finish my great work'. He was superseded by Benson in the office of the architect to St Paul.

Most applicable to my own case.

Brunel's work was done, but his career flowed on into the broad reaches of his son's life, as L.T.C. Rolt's splendid biography of Isambard has revealed.* There was no interruption to their work, and no change of professional attitude. Problems were subjected to the same scrupulous analysis; visions were imparted with the same bold conviction; details were lit with the same deft artistry; and works were carried forward with the same resolute devotion. It seems miraculous that the most creative engineer of the first quarter of the 19th century should have been succeeded by a son who added lustre to the name. The two in partnership made engineering history in the first half of the 19th century.

Isambard supported his parents during their happy autumn years in Westminster. It was a social time, filled with family meetings, romps with grandchildren, visits to old friends, and railway trips to Devon in the summer.

Another stroke in 1845 permanently paralysed Brunel's right side—but not his spirit—and he learned to write left-handed. Two years later with Sophie he visited Watcombe, where Isambard planned to build his dream house. The site overlooks Babbacombe Bay, and the old engineer was wheeled around it, stopping from time to time to gaze out to sea or to pick his favourite blue convolvulus so that the grandchildren could see the little black insect which inhabits its blooms. 'This little creature, so small as to be hardly visible without a glass, has yet all the functions for life and enjoyment provided for it by a good Creator.'

* *Isambard Kingdom Brunel*, Longmans, 1957.

The years passed and horizons contracted. Old friends died; the grand-children grew and were caught up in the world around them; but the fascination of Isambard's imperial progress remained, and there were memories of distant lands and great adventures. One faithful friend, Mrs Crosland, has left us with a glimpse of the old couple:

> I believe I was a good listener, and assured of my sympathy they poured out their reminiscences freely, or, rather, I should say, Lady Brunel did, for the old man was not voluble, though he often by a nod of the head or some short exclamation confirmed his wife's words. She was a little old lady, with her faculties bright and apparently unimpaired; he with a ponderous head surmounting what might be called a thick-set figure. The old couple usually sat side by side and often the old man would take his wife's withered hand in his, sometimes raising it to his lips with the restrained fervour of a respectful lover.

Brunel died on 12 December 1849, at the age of 80, and was buried in Kensal Green Cemetery, which lies between a gasworks and the Harrow Road. The ground is laid out on the lines of the Necropolis of London, which he had planned with Pugin, and is an oasis of peace.

Sophie moved to Duke Street and spent her widowhood in a room with a balcony overlooking the Park. She filled it with sentimental relies; a cast of his hand clasping hers around which she twined ivy from the grave; the milk jug and the tumbler from the prison at Gravelines, the miniatures he had painted, and each day in summer time a fresh vase of convolvulus from Watcombe. After five lonely years, on 5 January 1855, she was laid at her husband's side and covered by the simple stone he had designed.

Lesser contemporaries, who entered commerce or politics, have their statues and biographies, but memorials to Marc Brunel are more elusive.

There is a simple one by Hacqueville church, which the villagers erected in 1883; there is a little tablet in the wall by the gateway of La Ferme Brunel, and a plaque commemorating Marc and Isambard on the wall of Lindsey House in Chelsea. Less formally, there is the bridge spanning the Avon Gorge at Clifton, which was completed in 1864 to honour the memory of Isambard, who died in 1859. And there is the tunnel.

In 1865 the East London Railway Company bought Brunel's tunnel, extending it northwards to the Great Eastern Railway's terminus at Liverpool Street and southwards to New Cross, to connect with the London, Brighton and South Coast Railway, and also with the South-Eastern Company's metals. A track was laid in each archway, and in 1913, after 48 years of steam, this most easterly of London's cross-river rail links was electrified. Rotherhithe station is a little to the south of the old Cow Court shaft (which has been capped over), but a new entrance on top of the northern shaft marks Wapping

A northbound train arrives at Wapping.

station. The traveller descends in a lift now, but the timber stairways, which so bothered the correspondent *of The Times*, were still intact 60 years ago.

Whisked in a tube train from Whitechapel to New Cross, the traveller will see little of Brunel's handiwork. To view the tunnel, one must walk through in the silent small hours of morning, after the last train has passed. The archways dip surprisingly steeply, but their walls are sound and dry and now not even the beat of a ship's propeller disturbs the silence to proclaim the river overhead and recall one's thoughts to the old engineer and the brave men who greeted him so often with their cheerings.

If the reader cannot walk the tunnel, he could, as he travels through it on the Underground, remember the Great Shield, whose invention made his journey possible. Or he could contemplate his machine-made shoes, or the furniture in his home, or indeed anything that is mass-produced; for these are the workaday memorials to Marc Brunel.

Having been privileged to read the million or more words with which the engineer recorded his later hopes and labours, and having found not one that is spiteful or mean, the writer, like Charles MacFarlane, is 'perfectly charmed with him', and admires most of all 'his thorough simplicity, and unworldliness of character, his indifference to mere lucre, and his genuine absent-mindedness. He lived as if there were no rogues in this nether world.'

Appendix A

PATENT SPECIFICATIONS FILED BY MARC ISAMBARD BRUNEL

———◆·◆◆·◆———

Date Number	Subject of application
11 Apr. 1799 2305	Machine for Writing and Drawing
10 Feb. 1801 2478	Ships' Blocks
25 Nov. 1802 2663	Trimmings and Borders for Muslins, Lawns and Cambric
7 May 1805 2844	Saws and Machinery for Sawing
23 Sept. 1806 2968	Cutting Veneers
14 Mar. 1808 3116	Circular Saws
2 Aug. 1810 3369	Shoes and Boots
28 Jan. 1812 3529	Saw Mills
26 Jan. 1813 3643	Saw Mills
12 Mar. 1814 3791	Rendering Leather Durable
20 Jan. 1818 4204	Forming Drifts and Tunnels
5 Dec. 1818 4301	Manufacture of Tin Foil
25 Jan. 1820 4434	Stereotype Printing Plates
22 Dec. 1820 4522	Copying Presses
26 June 1822 4683	Marine Steam Engines
16 July 1825 5212	Gas Engines

Inventions of Others

1 Oct. 1810 3384	Obtaining Motive Power
14 Mar. 1816 3993	Knitting Machines

THE PORTSMOUTH
BLOCKMAKING MACHINES*

Excluding the circular and frame saws used for converting timber and the special machines used for the manufacture of dead-eyes, large 'made blocks' and the lignum vitae pins for blocks destined for powder magazines, there were three sets of Brunel machines installed in the blockmill.

The first set, for making elm shells, comprised six machines—although three sizes of several of them were installed.

Machines for preparing the shells *No. of machines installed*	Model in Nat. Maritime Museum	Machine in Portsmouth Museum	Machine in Portsmouth Dockyard	Machine in Science Museum
1 Reciprocating saw				
1 Circular saw (pendulum saw)				*
4 Circular saw benches				
1 Large reciprocating saw				
8 Boring machines	*	*		*
3 Mortising Machines	*	*		*
3 Corner saws	*		*	
3 Shaping machines	*	*		*
2 Scoring machines	*		*	*

There were six machines in the second set, which produced the lignum vitae shivers, and again several were made in three sizes.

Machines for preparing the sheaves				
1 Reciprocating saw				
2 Circular saws (lignum vitae saws)			*	*
2 Rounding saws	*			*
2 Coaking machines	*			*
1 Drilling machine				
2 Riveting hammers				
3 Broaching machines				
3 Face-turning lathes	*			
Other machines				
3 Pin-turning lathes				
1 Polishing machine for pins (3 machines in one frame)				
1 Lathe for wooden pins				
2 Machines for making dead-eyes				
1 Machine for boring 'made' blocks				

* This appendix is based on material in the Science Museum Monograph *The Portsmouth Blockmaking Machinery* by K.R. Gilbert. If you wish to see a specific machine, check its location. Museums sometimes exchange exhibits.

Appendix C

THE THAMES TUNNEL
BALANCE SHEET AT 31 DECEMBER, 1844*

Reproduced from Memoir of Sir M.I. Brunel by Richard Beamish.

Receipts

	£	s	d
Amount received on 3,874 shares	179,510	15	0
By subscriptions	1,500	0	0
Exchequer Loan Commissioners	250,500	0	0
Rents and wharfage	5,767	12	5
Old materials	3,450	14	7
Indemnity by loss from fire	40	0	0
Interest on premium on Exchequer Bills	3,083	16	0
Visitors to view the Tunnel, and sale of books to 31 December 1844	24,396	19	4
	£468,249	17	4

Expenditure

	£	s	d
Purchase of property, rent, taxes, Parliamentary and law charges	64,962	15	4
Machinery and labour	338,243	16	1
Salaries to engineers, secretary and clerks	43,986	1	1
Payment to directors	7,618	1	3
	454,810	13	9
To pay interest on Exchequer Bills 31 December, 1844	13,430	3	7
	£468,249	17	4

* The statements show the total receipts and expenditure from the commencement to the completion of the work.

CONSTRUCTION TIMETABLE

2 March 1825	Ceremonial stone laid in the Rotherhithe shaft.
21 November 1825	Rotherhithe shaft completed.
31 January 1826	The shield completed its breakout: archways 14 feet long.
18 May 1827	First irruption: archways 549 feet long.
30 September 1827	Tunnelling recommenced.
12 January 1828	Second irruption: archways 605 feet long.
8 August 1828	Tunnel walled up and work suspended.
5 December 1833	First advance from Treasury received.
25 March 1835	Tunnelling with second shield started.
23 August 1837	Third irruption: archways 736 feet long.
11 September 1837	Work resumed.
3 November 1837	Fourth irruption: archways 742 feet 6 inches long.
21 December 1837	Work resumed.
20 March 1838	Fifth irruption: archways 763 feet long.
10 April 1838	Work resumed.
11 June 1840	Brunel took possession of site for the Wapping shaft.
25 March 1843	The tunnel, 1,200 feet long, opened to foot passengers, 18 years and 23 days after the stone-laying ceremony at Rotherhithe.

INDEX

compiled by Auriol Griffith-Jones
Page numbers in *italic* refer to illustrations

The first three hundred and fifty feet.